Soviet Marxism

Soviet Marxism

A CRITICAL ANALYSIS

By Herbert Marcuse

NEW YORK

COLUMBIA UNIVERSITY PRESS

The transliteration system used in this series is based on the Library of Congress system, with some modifications

COPYRIGHT © 1958 COLUMBIA UNIVERSITY PRESS, NEW YORK

First printing 1958
Fourth printing 1969

Published in Great Britain by Routledge & Kegan Paul Ltd.

Clothbound editions of Columbia University Press books are Smyth-sewn and printed on permanent and durable acid-free paper.

LIBRARY OF CONGRESS CATALOG CARD NUMBER: 57-10943

PRINTED IN THE UNITED STATES OF AMERICA

ISBN 0-231-08379-3   (pbk.)

Contents

Introduction to the 1985 Edition, by
Douglas Kellner, University of Texas, Austin

HERBERT MARCUSE'S *SOVIET MARXISM* is one of the first and best attempts by a "critical Marxist" to present a comprehensive and balanced evaluation of Soviet society and ideology.[1] Most of the Marxian critiques of the Soviet Union had been written by Trotskyists, Social Democrats, or ex-Marxists who turned with a fury against the Soviet Union for betraying Marxism (or their own expectations). Marcuse's study, however, begins an attempt by "Western Marxists" to overcome sectarian discourse about the Soviet Union with critical and analytical discussion. Many previous representatives of Western Marxism tended to defend uncritically the Soviet Union, or to attack it harshly—or, as with Jean-Paul Sartre and Maurice Merleau-Ponty, to swing sharply from one attitude to another.[2] Walter Benjamin, Bertolt Brecht, Ernst Bloch, and

1. On the differences between "critical" and "scientific" Marxism, see Alvin W. Gouldner, *The Two Marxisms* (New York: Seabury, 1982). Marcuse is a paradigm of a "critical Marxist" who uses the Marxian theory as an instrument of critique; he is one of the first to systematically apply Marxism to critique Soviet Marxism.

2. After having defended Communism in *The Communists and the Peace* in 1952 (New York: Braziller, 1968), Jean-Paul Sartre then attacked Stalinism in *The Ghost of Stalin* after the brutal suppression of the uprisings in Hungary, Poland, and East Germany in 1956 (New York: Braziller, 1968). Maurice Merleau-Ponty, having defended Communism in *Humanism and Terror* (Boston: Beacon, 1969), attacked Stalinism in 1957 in his *Adventures of the Dialectic*, which included a polemic against Sartre and other intellectuals who engaged in apologetics for the Soviet Union.

others, whatever their private doubts, refused to criticize the Soviet Union openly. Even Karl Korsch, who had developed one of the first independent Marxist critiques of the Soviet Union in the 1920s, reluctantly concluded in the postwar period that it was reactionary to attack the Soviet Union since the only significant political choice, he believed, was between U.S. capitalism and Soviet Communism.[3]

Marcuse's colleagues in the Institute for Social Research generally maintained a discrete silence on the issue in the 1930s and 1940s, although some of its members, like Wittfogel and Horkheimer, eventually became bitter anti-Communists.[4] Marcuse was the first member of the so-called Frankfurt School to attempt a thoroughgoing analysis of the relationship between classical Marxism and Soviet Marxism, and between Soviet ideology and reality. Thus his book *Soviet Marxism* is important for its contributions to developing a critical Marxian discourse on the Soviet Union that avoids the sectarian polemics of Communist apologists, anti-Communist ideologues, or Marxian sects.

Herbert Marcuse first studied Marxism during World War I, and he published many books and articles that

3. See Karl Korsch, letter to Brecht, in Douglas Kellner, ed., *Karl Korsch: Revolutionary Theory* (Austin: University of Texas Press, 1977), pp. 289ff., and my discussion of Korsch's earlier critique of Soviet Communism, pp. 44–82, passim.

4. On the position of members of the Institute for Social Research toward the Soviet Union in the 1930s and 1940s, see Helmut Dubiel, *Wissenschaftsorganisation und politische Erfahrung* (Frankfurt: Suhrkamp, 1978). On the late Horkheimer's anti-Communism, see my review article "The Frankfurt School Revisited," *New German Critique* (Winter 1975), 4:131–152. On Wittfogel's changing stances toward Communism, see G. L. Ulmen, *The Science of Society: Toward an Understanding of the Life and Work of Karl August Wittfogel* (The Hague: Mouton, 1978).

interrogated and developed the Marxian theory from the 1920s until his death in 1979.[5] He told me in 1978 of the excitement that his generation experienced with the advent of the Russian Revolution of 1917, which they believed presented new emancipatory alternatives to Western civilization. Marcuse was briefly a member of the Social Democratic Party in 1917–18 and although he never joined the Communist Party, he said that he often voted Communist during the Weimar period as a "protest." Fearing persecution from the Nazis, Marcuse fled from Germany and settled in the United States in 1934, where he remained for the rest of his life. His first book in English, *Reason and Revolution* (1941), traces the rise of social theory from the French Revolution to the present and focuses on the relationships between Hegel and Marx.[6] Marcuse's own brand of Marxism was strongly influenced by the Hegelian Marxism of Georg Lukacs, Karl Korsch, and his colleagues in the Institute for Social Research.

Marcuse became a specialist in Communism and the Soviet Union during World War II in his work with the OSS and then the State Department. After World War II he became the chief political analyist for the central European section of the State Department and helped prepare a lengthy classified intelligence report on "The Potentials of World Communism." After his Institute colleagues who had also worked for the U.S. government—Franz Neumann, Otto Kirchheimer, and Leo Low-

5. On Marcuse's life and work, see my book *Herbert Marcuse and the Crisis of Marxism* (London and Berkeley: Macmillan and University of California, 1984).

6. Herbert Marcuse, *Reason and Revolution* (New York: Oxford, 1941; reprinted by Beacon Press, 1960).

enthal—left government service for academic posts, Marcuse was forced to stay in Washington because of his wife Sophie's illness. Marcuse thus witnessed the beginnings of the Cold War and the repression of radicals and liberals in government service during the McCarthy era, although he told me that he was not directly subject to a witch-hunt himself. Rather, he was tired of being a government bureaucrat and was eager to return to writing and teaching. Consequently, at the time of his wife's death in 1951, he left his State Department job and sought an academic position.

Marcuse's first appointments were with the Russian Institute at Columbia University and the Russian Research Center at Harvard. In the acknowledgments in *Soviet Marxism*, he notes that his work on the political tenets of Soviet Marxism, which forms the first half of the book, was carried out in 1952–53 at Columbia, while the second half of the book on the ethical tenets of Soviet Marxism was prepared at Harvard in 1954–55. Although both the Columbia and Harvard research institutes were centers of Cold War anti-Communism, Marcuse openly taught Marxism at Columbia and was known as "Marxist-in-residence" at Harvard. His study of Soviet Marxism reveals that Marcuse was neither an orthodox Communist nor a Cold Warrior. Instead he presents a rather ambivalent reading of both regressive and progressive elements of the Soviet Union which he believes reflects the ambivalence of Soviet Marxism as both a realization and distortion of Marxism.

Marcuse assumed throughout his life that the original

Marxian theory is an "emancipatory" and "progressive" articulation of humanity's aspirations for freedom, happiness, and a better world. He argues that the "fundamental ambivalence" in the attempts to realize Marxism in the Soviet Union consists in the fact that "the means for liberation and humanization operate for preserving domination and submission, and the theory that destroyed all ideology is used for the establishment of a new ideology."[7] Marcuse's writing strategy in *Soviet Marxism* is to confront Soviet "ideology" with "reality" so as to provide an "immanent critique" of both Soviet ideology and society by exposing its distortions of Marxism and its failure to realize Marxian socialist ideals in practice. Marcuse claims that his "immanent critique" "starts from the theoretical premises of Soviet Marxism, develops their ideological and sociological consequences, and reexamines the premises in the light of these consequences. The critique thus employs the conceptual instruments of its object, namely Marxism, in order to clarify the actual function of Marxism in Soviet society and its historical direction."[8]

In his Introduction to *Soviet Marxism*, Marcuse explicitly sets forth a Marxian method of historical analysis which relates ideology to its social reality. He identifies "objective trends" and "tendencies" within Soviet society and conceptualizes Soviet development "in terms of the interaction between Soviet and Western society." Throughout

7. Herbert Marcuse, "Preface to the Vintage Edition, 1961," *Soviet Marxism* (New York: Vintage, 1961), p. xiv.

8. Herbert Marcuse, "Introduction," *Soviet Marxism* (New York: Columbia University Press, 1958; reprinted 1985), p. 1. The Introduction to the 1958 edition was inexplicably left out of the 1961 Vintage Paperback edition.

the book, he shows how trends of international geopolitics
and the capitalist world market influenced Soviet development. Marcuse's study combines Marxian ideology critique of Soviet Marxism with political analysis of the Soviet Union, using as sources documents, speeches, and
party pronouncements as well as the classical texts of
Marxism-Leninism. The interconnection of philosophical
and political factors makes *Soviet Marxism* a complicated
and often difficult presentation of a complex and contro-
versial phenomenon. The book has been widely misun-
derstood and most interpreters, or critics, have failed either
to discern its dialectical analysis of both liberating and
oppressive features, or the complexity of Marcuse's interpretation of possible liberalizing trends in the Soviet Union
in conjunction with continued repression. Consequently,
New Left critics, who assume a predominantly critical
posture toward the Soviet Union, praise the book as a
critique of Stalinism, the Soviet bureaucracy, and the Soviet state, and miss Marcuse's important analysis of liberalizing trends in Soviet society.[9] Anti-Soviet liberals and
conservatives who have discussed the book often claim
that Marcuse provides apologetics for the Soviet Union,
and overlook his frequently sharp critiques.[10] And Communist reviewers who attack *Soviet Marxism* claim that

9. For example, Johann Aranson titles his chapter on *Soviet Marxism* "Marcuses
Kritik des Stalinismus" in *Von Marcuse zu Marx* (Neuwied and Berlin: Luchterhand,
1971), and Jean-Michel Palmier in his *Sur Marcuse* (Paris: 10/18, 1968) describes it
as a "passionate polemic against the Stalinist bureaucracy . . . an analysis without
doubt pessimistic of Soviet Marxism and its cruel contradictions," pp. 24, 34.

10. See, for example, L. Stern, *Dissent* (Winter 1958), 5(1):88–93, and George
Lichtheim's review in *Survey* (January–March 1958) reprinted in *Collective Essays* (New
York: Viking, 1974), pp. 337–347. *Soviet Marxism* received its sharpest critique from
the Left from Marcuse's friend Raya Dunayevskaya, *News and Letters* (June–July and
August–September 1961).

Marcuse's interpretation is wholly negative and argue that he takes the position of a Cold War, anti-Soviet propagandists.[11]

In fact, however, Marcuse's interpretation is not a clear-cut "for" or "against" the Soviet Union but is instead a portrayal of contradictory tendencies within a complex and difficult-to-interpret society. Marcuse breaks with the Cold War anti-Communist discourse that demonizes the Soviet Union yet provides sharp criticism of its departures from what he sees as the emancipatory features of Marxism. The book thus begins a trend within the Left to develop reasoned critiques of the Soviet Union without sectarian rhetoric that both criticizes repressive features of bureaucratic Communism while appreciating potentials for social progress within the Soviet system.

Marcuse's analysis of "liberalizing trends" and "progressive" elements within Soviet society led liberal and left critics to claim that Marcuse was not critical enough of the Soviet Union. This raises the question of the extent to which Marcuse's analysis of the liberalizing trends in the Soviet Union may have been influenced by the "thaw" produced by Khrushchev's denunciation of Stalin produced after the Twentieth Congress of the Communist Party in 1956.[12] Communists and others were animated by the hope that Khrushchev's speech would mark the end

11. See Marcuse's citations of Communist reviews in "Preface," p. v, and the attack by Robert Steigerwald in *Herbert Marcuses 'dritter Weg'*, who titles his chapter, "The book against Soviet Marxism" and claims that Marcuse's interpretation is a form of anti-Soviet Cold War propaganda that serves the interests of Western capitalistic imperialism.

12. For the text of Khrushchev's speech and his recollections concerning its background, see *Khrushchev Remembers* (Boston: Little, Brown, 1970). For responses to Khrushchev's speech, see Columbia University Russian Institute, *The Anti-Stalin Campaign and International Communism* (New York: Columbia University Press, 1956).

of Stalinism and create a new type of Communism. Marcuse told me, however, that he had no "illusions" about Khrushchev and his only references to him in the text of *Soviet Marxism* analyze those features in Khrushchev's Twentieth Congress speech which denote continuity with the objectives of the Stalinist regime, followed by citation of Khrushchev's proclamation that "the continued strengthening of the state and of the party agencies remain on the agenda."[13] Thus, in 1958, Marcuse did not seem to believe that the change in political leadership was a decisive force of de-Stalinization.

Rather, Marcuse derived his analysis of the existence of liberalizing tendencies from study of the socioeconomic situation and other trends in the Soviet Union (see especially pp. 154–175 below). He argues that the "industrial base" has been created to produce a higher form of Communism and that there are structural imperatives in the bureaucracy, ideology, technology, and world political constellation that may drive these tendencies to a higher stage of civilization. Hence Marcuse reveals himself here to be committed to the Marxian method of social analysis, focusing on the base of Soviet society to discern its essential features, rather than being guided in his analysis by the superstructure of the new Soviet leaders.

In the 1961 preface to the Vintage edition of *Soviet Marxism*, Marcuse claims that the "trend towards reform and liberalization within the Soviet Union has continued."[14] He also seems clearly sympathetic toward

13. Marcuse, *Soviet Marxism*, p. 164.
14. Marcuse, "Preface," p. vi.

Khrushchev here, accepting Isaac Deutscher's analysis of the modifications of Soviet policy, internal and external, in the Khrushchev regime. Furthermore, Marcuse seems to accept Khrushchev's doctrine of "peaceful co-existence" and call for disarmament at face value, as well as Khrushchev's claim that the Soviet Union is moving toward the "second phase" of Communism. These remarks suggest that Marcuse continued to believe in liberalizing trends in the Soviet Union in the early 1960s and that the Khrushchev administration was the vehicle of liberalization.

In the 1963 Preface to the French edition of *Soviet Marxism*, however, Marcuse notes that focus on the issue of whether fundamental changes are taking place in the Soviet Union under Khrushchev deflects attention from the question of whether fundamental changes are taking place in U.S. politics, "in particular since the arrival to power of the Kennedy administration." [15] In Marcuse's view, it seemed that U.S. politics was becoming more aggressive and interventionist in the Third World and was forcing the Soviet Union to focus more on competition with the West and the arms race, thus suspending possibilities of liberalization in an intensified Cold War atmosphere. He highlights here his thesis that Soviet Communist parties are more and more the "historical inheritors of the pre-war Social Democratic parties," but indicates that they now face another Communist movement on their Left, namely the Chinese Communists who "reclaim the heri-

15. Herbert Marcuse, "Preface a l'edition francaise," *Le marxisme sovietique* (Paris: Gallimard, 1963), pp. 7ff.

tage of Marxism-Leninism." Consequently, in the early 1960s, Marcuse perceived a shifting, fluid political situation that made it increasingly difficult to perceive liberalizing tendencies in the Soviet Communist countries.

In historical retrospect, it can be argued that the ousting of Khrushchev in 1964 and the subsequent course of Soviet Communism put a brake on the liberalizing tendencies which Marcuse discerned. This suggests that Marcuse may have exaggerated the liberalizing trends and underestimated the continuity with the Stalinist period. Later Marcuse became more critical of the post-Khrushchev regime, especially after the invasion of Czechoslovakia in 1968. Thus his views on the Soviet Union were responses to a changing and fluid historical situation and he modified his analyses and appraisals in response to changing historical circumstances.

Yet he does offer provocative critical perspectives on both the Soviet political system and its ideology. In my view, Marcuse's critique of Soviet ideology is more effective than his critique of the Soviet political system and constitute's *Soviet Marxism*'s lasting achievement. Indeed, since the 1930s, critique of ideology has been Marcuse's forte. In *Soviet Marxism*, he turns the Marxian critique of ideology against Soviet Marxism itself in the last several chapters of Part I and throughout Part II on "The Ethical Tenets of Soviet Marxism." For Marcuse, the most striking and paradoxical feature of Soviet Marxism is that a blatant revisionism masquerades as a relentless orthodoxy in which the function of the dialectic "has undergone a significant change." Marcuse argues that whereas the Marxian dialectic is a tool of critical and revolutionary thought that analyzes the contradictions and antagonisms of a social order, Soviet Marxism surrenders the critical dialectic and uses it to justify the existing regime, by codifying it into a philosophical system which contains categories, laws, and principles that are used to legitimize the rationality of the established Soviet society. Marcuse shows in an illuminating discussion how various texts of Engels, Lenin, and Stalin are used to produce a version of Marxism at odds in significant ways with Marx's own historical materialism.

Soviet Marxism is of interest for Marcuse's own thought because it reveals parallels between his theories and critiques of the Soviet Union and advanced capitalist societies. Although Marcuse claimed in a 1961 Preface to the Vintage edition that he rejected theories of the "convergence" of capitalist and Communist societies and that he choose to stress their differences, he also analyzes similar features of social control and domination operative in both societies.[16] With regard, however, to Marcuse's tendency in *One-Dimensional Man* and other writings to equate different, historically specific trends and institutions under one generic concept of "advanced industrial society," the more historically specific analyses of *Soviet Marxism* serve as an antidote to some of the more generalizing tendencies in some of his other works. Thus *Soviet Marxism* is important within Marcuse's corpus as a critique of Soviet communism that parallels his critique of advanced capitalism and which calls attention to both similarities and differences within these social systems.

In the 1961 Preface of the Vintage Edition, Marcuse

16. Marcuse, "Preface to the Vintage Edition," p. xi.

claims that the contradictory reception of the book suggested "that I have achieved a modicum of success in
freeing myself from Cold War propaganda and in present-
ing a relatively objective analysis based on a reasoned
interpretation of historical developments." [17] Readers
sympathetic to the Soviet Union will no doubt find Marcuse's presentation too critical, while others will no doubt
find it not critical enough. Others may differ with both his
presentation of "fundamental trends" and his interpretations of Soviet politics and ideology. Yet Marcuse's attempt to escape from ideological discourses on Soviet
Marxism and to present a balanced interpretation provide
a model that more biased ideological interpretations should
consider. This approach takes on added relevance during
an era when the President of the United States stigmatizes
the Soviet Union as an "evil empire" and when rampant
anti-Communism threatens to intensify hostilities between
the two superpowers and to lead the world to the brink of
nuclear war. In this context, Marcuse's attempt to provide
a reasoned and balanced assessment of the Soviet political system and ideology provides a welcome relief from
the anti-Soviet diatribes which have pervaded discourses
about the Soviet Union throughout the Cold War and which
have intensified in recent years.

17. *Ibid.*, p. v.

Acknowledgments to the First Edition

THE FIRST PART of this work is the result of my studies as a Senior Fellow at the Russian Institute, Columbia University, during the years 1952–53. The second part was prepared at the Russian Research Center, Harvard University, in 1954–55, under a special grant from the Rockefeller Foundation. I am much indebted to the Russian Research Center, and especially to its Director, William L. Langer, and Associate Director, Marshall D. Shulman, for their kindness in relinquishing to Columbia University Press their publication rights to the second part.

I also wish to express my thanks to George L. Kline, Columbia University, who prepared some of the material used in the second part of this essay; to Alfred E. Senn, for his assistance with Russian references; and to Arkadii R. L. Gurland, who offered valuable help and comments.

My friend, Barrington Moore, Jr., read the manuscript and helped me as usual with his incisive criticism.

The index was prepared by Maud Hazeltine.

HERBERT MARCUSE

Brandeis University
June, 1957

Introduction

THIS STUDY attempts to evaluate some main trends of Soviet
Marxism in terms of an "immanent critique," that is to say,
it starts from the theoretical premises of Soviet Marxism,
develops their ideological and sociological consequences,
and reexamines the premises in the light of these consequences. The critique thus employs the conceptual instruments of its object, namely, Marxism, in order to clarify
the actual function of Marxism in Soviet society and its
historical direction. This approach implies a twofold assumption:

(1) That Soviet Marxism (i.e., Leninism, Stalinism,
and post-Stalin trends) is not merely an ideology promulgated by the Kremlin in order to rationalize and justify its
policies but expresses in various forms the realities of
Soviet developments. If this is the case, then the extreme
poverty and even dishonesty of Soviet theory would not
vitiate the basic importance of Soviet theory but would
itself provide a cue for the factors which engendered the
obvious theoretical deficiencies;

(2) That identifiable objective trends and tendencies
are operative in history which make up the inherent rationality of the historical process. Since this assumption is

easily misrepresented as acceptance of Hegelian metaphysics, a few words may be said in the way of defense and
explanation.

Belief in objective historical "laws" is indeed at the very
core of Hegel's philosophy. To him, these laws are the
manifestation of Reason—a subjective and objective force,
operating in the historical actions of men and in the material and intellectual culture. History is thus at one and
the same time a logical and teleological process, namely,
progress (in spite of relapses and regressions) in the consciousness and the realization of Freedom. The sequence in
the principal stages of civilization is thereby ascent to
higher forms of humanity—quantitative and qualitative
growth. Marx has retained this basic notion while modify-
ing it in a decisive sense: history progresses through the
development of the productive forces, which is progress,
not in the realization of Freedom, but in the creation of the
prerequisites of Freedom; they remain mere prerequisites
in the interest of class society. Thus, for Marx, history is
certainly not the manifestation of Reason but much rather
the opposite; Reason pertains only to the future of classless society as a social organization geared to the free development of human needs and faculties. What is history
to Hegel is still prehistory to Marx.

The assumption of historical laws can be separated from
all teleology. Then it means that the development of a
specific social system, and the changes which lead from one
social system to another, are determined by the structure
which the respective society has given itself, that is to say,
by the basic division and organization of social labor, and

that the political and cultural institutions are generated by and correspond to this basic division and organization. The manifold dimensions and aspects of societal life are not a mere sum-total of facts and forces but constitute a clearly identifiable unit so that long range developments in any one dimension must be comprehended in their relation to the "base." On the ground of such structural unity, consecutive social systems can be distinguished from one another as essentially different forms of society whose general direction of development is in a demonstrable sense "predetermined" by its origins. The very impossibility to fix an exact date (even within a century or more) when the one social system ends and the other begins (for example, feudalism and capitalism) indicates the underlying trend which transforms one system into another. The new society emerges within the framework of the old, through definable changes in its structure—changes which are cumulative until the essentially different structure is there. In the last analysis there are no "extraneous" causes in this chain, for all apparently outside factors and events (such as discoveries, invasions, the impact of far distant forces) will affect the social structure only if the ground is prepared for them, for example, if they "meet" corresponding developments within the respective society or if they meet social wants and needs (as the barbarian influx into the *weakened* Roman empire, or as the influence of international trade and commerce and of the discoveries on the *internally changing* feudal societies from the thirteenth to the sixteenth century).

The basic form of societal reproduction, once institutionalized, determines the direction of development not only within the respective society but also beyond it. In this sense the historical process is rational and irreversible. As an example of the development within: The present stage of Western industrial society, with its increasing private and governmental regulation of the economy (in other words, with its increasing *political* economy and culture) appears as the "logical," i.e., inherent, outcome of the free enterprise and free competition prevalent at the preceding stage. No Marxist categories are necessary in order to elucidate the connection between the concentration of economic power and the corresponding political and cultural changes on the one hand and the capitalistic utilization of growing productivity of labor and technical progress on the other. As an example of the development beyond: The emergence of the feudal system from the basic institutions of the agricultural economy in the late Roman empire under the impact of the barbarian tribal-military organization provides perhaps the clearest example of inherent historical rationality and irreversibility. By the same token, it seems a reasonable anticipation that, whatever the next stage of industrial civilization may be, the basic institutions of large-scale mechanized industry and the explosive growth of the productivity of labor commanded by it will bring about political and cultural institutions irrevocably different from those of the liberalist period—a historical tendency which is likely to supersede some of the present most conspicuous differences between the Western and the Soviet system.

This brief outline of the notion of objective historical

laws may serve to show the ateleological character of the hypothesis. It implies no purpose, no "end" toward which history is moving, no metaphysical or spiritual Reason underlying the process—only its institutional determination. Moreover, it is a historical determination, that is to say, it is not in any sense "automatic." Within the institutional framework which men have given themselves in interaction with the prevailing natural and historical conditions, the development proceeds through the action of men —they are the historical agents, and theirs are the alternatives and decisions.

In applying the hypothesis to the interpretation of Soviet Marxism, one qualification imposes itself from the beginning. It seems that the determining trend cannot be defined merely in terms of the structure of Soviet society, but that it must be defined in terms of the interaction between Soviet and Western society. Even the most cursory survey of Soviet Marxism is confronted with the fact that at almost every turn in the development Soviet theory (and Soviet policy) reacts to a corresponding Western development and vice versa. This seems self-evident and hardly worth mentioning were it not for the fact that it is usually taken too lightly, taken into account merely with respect to diplomacy and propaganda, or understood as arrangements of expediency, short-term adjustments, and so on. However, the interaction seems to go much further and to express an essential link between the two conflicting systems, thus affecting the very structure of Soviet society. In its most visible form, the link is in the technical-economic basis common to both systems, i.e., mechanized (and increasingly mechanized) industry as the mainspring of societal organization in all spheres of life. As against this common technical-economic denominator stands the very different institutional structure—private enterprise here, nationalized enterprise there. Will the common technical-economic basis eventually assert itself over and against the different social institutions, or will the latter continue to widen the difference in the utilization of the productive forces in the two social systems? (According to Marxian theory, the technical-economic basis is in itself "neutral" and susceptible to capitalist as well as socialist utilization, the decision depending on the outcome of the class struggle—a notion which well illustrates the limits of Marxian "determinism.") The question plays a decisive role in evaluating the international dynamic and the prospects of a global "state-capitalism" or socialism; its discussion lies outside the scope of this study, which, however, may provide some preparatory material.

The interaction between Western and Soviet developments, far from being an external factor, pertains to the determining historical trend—to the historical "law" governing Soviet Marxism as well as to the reality reflected in Soviet Marxism. From the beginning, the specific international dynamic released by the transformation of "classical" into organized capitalism (in Marxist terms, monopoly capitalism) defines Soviet Marxism—in Lenin's doctrine of the *avant garde,* in the notion of "socialism in one country," in the triumph of Stalinism over Trotskyism and over the old Bolsheviks, in the sustained priority of heavy industry, in the continuation of a repressive totalitarian centralization. They are in a strict sense responses to the (in Marxian terms, "anomalous") growth and readjustment of Western industrial society and to the decline in the revolutionary potential of the Western world resulting from this readjustment. The degree to which these developments have shaped Soviet Marxism may be illustrated by the function of the term "coexistence." The notion of coexistence has received very different emphases with Soviet Marxism—from a short-term tactical need to a long-range political objective. However, the very distinction between "short term" and "long range" is meaningless without identifiable standards of measurement, which in turn presuppose a demonstrable theoretical evaluation of the historical direction of Soviet developments. In Soviet Marxist language everything is short term if compared with the final event of world communism. Outside the realm of this language it is nonsensical to call "short term" policies which may last decades and which are imposed not by the political fluctuations but by the structure of the international situation. Viewed in this context, coexistence is perhaps the most singular feature of the contemporary era, namely, the meeting of two antagonistic forms of industrial civilization, challenging each other in the same international arena, neither one strong enough to replace the other. This relative weakness of both systems is characteristic of their respective structures and therefore a long-range factor; the end of one system's effectiveness would be tantamount to the end of the system. In Western industrial society, the weakness derives from the constant danger of overproduction in a narrowing world market and grave

social and economic dislocations, a danger necessitating
constant political countermeasures, which in turn limit the
economic and cultural growth of the system. On the other
side, the Soviet system still suffers from the plague of un-
derproduction, perpetuated by its military and political
commitments against the advanced Western world. The
implications of this dynamic will be traced in the following
chapters.

The development from Leninism to Stalinism and beyond will be discussed as the result, in its main stages and
features, of the "anomalous" constellation in which a socialist [1] society was to be built coexistent rather than subsequent to capitalist society, as the competitor rather than the
heir of the latter. This does not mean that the policies (such
as the Stalinist industrialization) which decided the fundamental trend of Soviet society were an inexorable necessity. There were alternatives, but they were in an emphatic
sense historical alternatives—"choices" presented to the
classes which fought the great social struggles of the inter-
war period rather than choices at the discretion of the
Soviet leadership. The outcome was decided in this struggle; it was decided in Europe by about 1923; and the
Soviet leadership did not make this decision though it con-
tributed to it (at that time probably to a lesser degree than
is usually assumed).

If these propositions can be corroborated, the question
as to whether or not the Soviet leadership is guided by

[1] Use of the term "socialist" for Soviet society in this study nowhere implies that this society is socialist in the sense envisaged by Marx and Engels.
However, it is assumed that the initial intention and objective of the Bolshevik Revolution was to build a socialist society.

Marxist principles is without relevance; once incorporated into the foundational institutions and objectives of the new society, Marxism becomes subject to a historical dynamic which surpasses the intentions of the leadership and to which the manipulators themselves succumb. An immanent discussion of Soviet Marxism may help to identify this historical dynamic to which the leadership itself is subjected —no matter how autonomous and totalitarian it may be. Thus, in examining Soviet Marxism and the (theoretical) situation from which it originated, we are not concerned with abstract-dogmatic validity but with concrete political and economic trends, which may also provide a key for anticipating prospective developments.

A few words must be said in justification of such an approach. Marxian theory purports to be an essentially new philosophy, substantially different from the main tradition of Western philosophy. Marxism claims to fulfill this tradition by passing from ideology to reality, from philosophical interpretation to political action. For this purpose, Marxism redefines not only the main categories and modes of thought, but also the dimension of their verification; their validity is to be determined by the historical situation and the action of the proletariat. There is theoretical continuity from the early Marxian notion of the Proletariat as the objectified truth of capitalist society to the Soviet Marxist concept *partinost* (partisanship).

Under these circumstances, a critique which merely applies the traditional criteria of philosophical truth to Soviet Marxism does not, in a strict sense, reach its objective. Such a critique, no matter how strong and well founded it may be, is easily blunted by the argument that its conceptual foundations have been undermined by the Marxist transition into a different area of historical and theoretical verification. The Marxist dimension itself thus seems to remain intact because it remains *outside* the argument. But if the critique enters that very dimension, by examining the development and use of the Marxist categories in terms of their own claim and content, it may be able to penetrate the real content beneath the ideological and political form in which it appears.

A critique of Soviet Marxism "from without" must either discard its theoretical efforts as "propaganda" or take them at their face value, namely, as philosophy or sociology in the traditional sense of these disciplines. The first alternative seems to beg the question as to what is meant seriously in Soviet Marxism and on what grounds the distinction is made.[2] The second alternative would engage in philosophical and sociological controversies outside the context in which the Soviet Marxist theories are presented and which is essential to their meaning. Treated in this manner, as items in the history of philosophical or sociological thought, the articles of the *Concise Philosophical Dictionary*, for example, or the logic discussion of 1950–51, are totally irrelevant—their philosophical faults are obvious to any scholar; their function is not the academic formulation of generally valid categories and techniques of thought but the definition of their relation to the political reality.[3] In contrast, an immanent critique, far from taking these theories at their surface value, could

---

[2] See pp. 39 f. below.   [3] See Chapter 5.

reveal the political intention which is their real content. The approach suggested here shifts the emphasis of the critique from the spectacular public controversies, such as the Aleksandrov debate or the logic and linguistic discussion, to basic trends in Soviet Marxism and uses the former only by way of illustration of the latter.

The immanent critique proceeds under the assumption that Marxian theory plays a decisive part in the formulation and execution of Soviet policy, and that from the Soviet use of Marxian theory inferences may be drawn for the national and international development of the Soviet state. The fact is that the Bolshevik Party and the Bolshevik Revolution were, to a considerable degree, developed according to Marxist principles, and that the Stalinist reconstruction of Soviet society based itself on Leninism, which was a specific interpretation of Marxian theory and practice. The ideology thus becomes a decisive part of reality even if it was used only as an instrument of domination and propaganda. For this reason, a recurrent comparison between Soviet Marxism and pre-Soviet Marxian theory will be necessary. The problem of Soviet "revisions" of Marxian theory will not be treated as a problem of Marxian dogmatics; the relation between the different forms and stages of Marxism will rather be used as an indication of the way in which the Soviet leadership interprets and evaluates the changing historical situation as the framework for its policy decisions.

Soviet Marxism has assumed the character of a "behavioral science." Most of its theoretical pronouncements have a pragmatic, instrumentalist intent; they serve to ex-

plain, justify, promote, and direct certain actions and attitudes which are actual "data" for these pronouncements.
These actions and attitudes (for example, accelerated collectivization of agriculture; Stakhanovism; integral anti-
Western ideology; insistence on the objective determinism of basic economic laws under socialism) are rationalized and justified in terms of the inherited body of
"Marxism-Leninism" which the Soviet leadership applies
to the changing historical situation. But it is precisely the
pragmatic, behaviorist character of Soviet Marxism which
makes it an indispensable tool for the understanding of
Soviet developments. The theoretical pronouncements of
Soviet Marxism, in their pragmatic function, define the
trend of Soviet developments.

Distinction must therefore be made between overt formulation and actual meaning of Soviet Marxist statements.
This distinction is not conveyed by the convenient term
"Aesopian language," which conceals rather than points up
the real distinction. To be sure, in Soviet usage the meaning of "democracy," "peace," "freedom," etc., is very different from that understood in the Western world—but so
is the meaning of "revolution" and "dictatorship of the
proletariat." The Soviet usage also redefines the meaning
of the specifically Marxian concepts. The latter themselves
are transformed in so far as Soviet Marxism claims to be
Marxism in and for a new historical situation; they form
the Marxist answer to the fundamental economic and political changes during the first half of the century.

From this point of view, Soviet Marxism appears as the
attempt to reconcile the inherited body of Marxian theory

with a historical situation which seemed to vitiate the central conception of this theory itself, namely, the Marxian conception of the transition from capitalism to socialism. Preparatory to the discussion of Soviet Marxism, we must, therefore, circumscribe the historical as well as the theoretical situation from which Soviet Marxism derived. We must try to identify the point at which the historical development seemed to explode the Marxian analysis. This is the crucial point for the understanding of Soviet Marxism.

Part I of this study aims at analyzing the basic conceptions by virtue of which Soviet Marxism appears as a unified theory of contemporary history and society. We take these concepts in their dogmatic statement only in order to develop them in the context of the social and political processes which they interpret and which alone makes them meaningful. Emphasis is throughout on the tendencies which Soviet Marxism seems to reflect and anticipate. Whereas Part I is thus focused on the objective factors underlying Soviet Marxism, Part II deals with the subjective factor, that is, with the "human material" which is supposed to follow the lead and to attain the goals set by Soviet Marxism. The material for this part is taken from Soviet ethical philosophy.

PART I: POLITICAL TENETS

1. *The Marxian Concept of the*
Transition to Socialism

THE ORIGINAL CONCEPTION

The dialectic-historical structure of Marxian theory implies that its concepts change with a change in the basic class relationships at which they aim—however, in such a way that the new content is obtained by unfolding the elements inherent in the original concept, thus preserving the theoretical consistency and even the identity of the concept. This also pertains to the notion in which the Marxian theory of the transition to socialism culminates—the notion of the objective historical coincidence between progress of civilization and the revolutionary action of the industrial proletariat. The latter is, in Marxian theory, the only social force that can accomplish the transition to a higher stage of civilization. Marx derives this coincidence from the intrinsic laws of capitalist development and thus gives it a definite place in the historical process, that is to say, the coincidence itself "passes." According to Marx, there is only one form of its passing: the proletarian revolution abolishes, with the liquidation of all classes, the proletariat as a class and thereby creates a new agent of progress— the community of free men who organize their society in accordance with the possibilities of a humane existence for all its members. But the actual development of capitalism suggested still another way of surpassing the historical coincidence, namely, through a fundamental change in the relations between the two conflicting classes whereby the proletariat fails to act as the revolutionary class. The emergence of this alternative is perhaps the most decisive factor in the development of Soviet Marxism.

The failure of the proletariat to act as the revolutionary class and the defeat of a proletarian revolution are anticipated in Marxian theory; per se, they do not constitute events which must refute the theory. In Marxian theory, they are generally explained by objective and subjective "immaturity" and considered as a temporary regression, after which the revolutionary trend will be resumed with a subsequent growth in the class consciousness of the organized proletariat. But the situation is quite different if, with or without a defeated revolution, the development of mature capitalism shows a long-range trend toward class collaboration rather than class struggle, toward national and international division rather than solidarity of the proletariat in the advanced industrial countries. In Marxian theory, capital and (wage) labor define each other, or, more specifically, the growth of the revolutionary proletariat in the long run *defines* the irreversible direction of capitalist development. Consequently, if the trend is reversed on the side of the proletariat, the capitalist development reaches a new stage to which the traditional Marxian categories no longer apply. A new historical period begins, characterized by a change in the basic class relations. Then, Marxism is faced with the task of redefining the conception of the transition to socialism and of the strategy in this period.

How did the Marxian dialectic comprehend the relation between two qualitatively different stages of the historical process—in this case, between capitalism and socialism? According to Marx, the new stage of the historical process is the "determinate negation" of the preceding stage—that is, the new stage is determined by the social structure which prevailed at the preceding stage. For example, the transition from capitalism to socialism is preconditioned by the following features of capitalist society:

(1) A high level of technological and industrial productivity which is not used to capacity for creating a humane life for all, because such use would conflict with the interest in profitable private utilization

(2) The growth of productivity beyond the limits of private control, which expresses itself in certain changes in the social institutions of capitalist enterprise (concentration of economic power coalescing with political power, decline of free competition and of the managerial function of the individual entrepreneur) and the consequent trend toward public control and appropriation

(3) The growth of the political organization of the laboring classes, who, acting as a class-conscious force, pursue their "real interest," not in, but *against* the capitalist system

These quantitative changes gain momentum until, in the proletarian revolution, they explode the prevailing structure and replace it by a qualitatively different one. Thus, the new historical level is not reached in just one leap;

the transition rather consists of various phases and completes itself only through these phases. The leap matures in the highest phase of the attained stage, but the first phase of the new stage still retains the birthmarks of its origin in the preceding stage. Marx's distinction of two "phases" of socialism in the *Critique of the Gotha Program* (1875), far from being an incidental correction, follows from the very principle of the dialectical method. In their historical continuity, capitalism and socialism are joined by far stronger links than those necessitated by a period of "adjustment." During the first phase of socialism, the specific socialist principle of the free development and satisfaction of individual needs remains subordinated to the new development of the productive forces, especially of the productivity of labor. The societal wealth (material and intellectual) must be abundant enough to make possible a distribution of the social product according to individual needs regardless of the individual contribution to socially necessary labor. In economic-technological terms, this means "rationalization"; for the laborer, it means continued toil and continued delay in the free satisfaction of individual needs. The first phase of socialism still chains the worker to his specialized function, still preserves the "enslaving subordination of individuals under the division of labor," [1] and thereby the antagonism between rationality and freedom; the rational way of developing *society* conflicts with the self-realization of the *individual*. The interest of the whole still demands the sacrifice of freedom, and justice for all still involves injustice. This antagonism dis-

[1] Marx, "Critique of the Gotha Program," in Marx and Engels, *Selected Works* (2 vols.; Moscow, Foreign Languages Publishing House, 1949–50), II, 23.

solves into the establishment of a genuine *res publica* only to the degree to which the socialized production creates the material and intellectual prerequisites of free and universal satisfaction of needs.

The fact that progress prior to the socialist revolution has occurred within the framework of class society and that material and intellectual productivity has been arrested by the interest of private appropriation causes in any case a time lag between the means and the end of liberation. The higher the level of material and intellectual productivity attained at the presocialist stage, the shorter the time lag, the briefer the first phase. Marx and Engels did not speculate on its duration, nor was such speculation relevant to them, for their conception of socialism implied that the qualitative change from capitalism to socialism, the "negation of the negation," takes place with the beginning of the *first* phase itself as the change from domination to self-determination. No matter how long the first phase would last, and no matter how much repression it would involve, this repression would be self-imposed by the "immediate producers," by the proletariat constituted as a state. The social distribution of labor time among the various branches of production, and thus the satisfaction of the individual needs and faculties, would be determined by collective decision of the producers of the societal wealth. Whatever coercion would have to be applied would be applied by the coerced themselves. There would be no coercive state organs separate from and above the associated laborers, for they *are* the socialist state. Wherever Marx and Engels contrast the socialist state with its preceding forms, they do so in terms of the actual *subjects* who *constitute* the state, not in terms of specific institutions. The socialist state is nothing but the "revolutionary dictatorship of the proletariat"; [2] socialist society is an "association of free men"; [3] the productive forces are "in the hands of producers working in association"; [4] production is organized on the basis of "a free and equal association of the producers." [5]

The qualitative change that, in the Marxian conception, characterizes the entire first phase presupposes the activity of a class-conscious proletariat. The proletariat that is to constitute itself as the socialist state has been, up to the very moment of the revolution, the object of capitalist domination and, as such, part of the capitalist system. If this system has entered the period of the "final crisis," if destruction and impoverishment are prevalent, then, in the Marxian expectation, the proletariat will organize itself as the revolutionary class, follow its objective historical mission, and function within the capitalist system only as its "gravedigger." But if capitalism continues as a "going concern," even increasing the standard of living of its working classes, they may become part of the capitalist system in quite a different, positive sense. As early as 1858 Engels noted the *Verbürgerlichung* of the proletariat in England, [6]

[2] *Ibid.*, p. 577.   [3] Marx, *Capital*, I, Chap. I, Sect. 4.

[4] Engels, "Anti-Dühring," in *A Handbook of Marxism*, ed. by E. Burns (New York, International Publishers, 1935), p. 294.

[5] Engels, *Origin of the Family, Private Property, and the State* (New York, International Publishers, 1942), p. 158. The problem of the "withering away" of the state will be discussed below, pp. 102 f.

[6] Letter to Marx, October 7, 1858, in Marx and Engels, *Correspondence, 1846–1895; A Selection with Commentary and Notes* (New York, International Publishers, 1935), pp. 115–16; see also his letter to Kautsky, September 12, 1882, in *ibid.*, pp. 399–400.

and in 1884 he formulated the consequence: As long as the proletariat is not yet ripe for its self-liberation, so long will the majority of the proletariat see in the established social order the only possible one and will constitute politically the "tail of the capitalist class, its extreme left wing." [7] Only a virtually constant crisis could keep the class struggle acute and the proletariat class-conscious against the capitalist system, as its "absolute negation." Under such conditions, the proletariat would fulfill its "historical mission," that is, the abolition of the capitalist system. But in periods of stability and prosperity the proletariat itself is bound to come under the sway of "capitalist ideas," and its immediate (economic) interests supersede its real (historical) interest. This relation can be reversed only in the class struggle itself, that is to say, if the proletariat becomes again a *political* force and as such operates as a catalyst in the capitalist economy.

The Marxian distinction between real and immediate interest is of the greatest importance for understanding the relationship between theory and practice, between strategy and tactics in Marxism. The distinction implies a historical conflict between theory and practice, the origin and solution of which lie in the development of capitalism. The conflict thus appears as an *objective* factor. If the societal relationships determine consciousness, they do so also with respect to the proletariat. And if the societal relationships are class relationships, they also introduce the discrepancy

[7] *Origin of the Family*, p. 158. For the later reinterpretation of this idea in the Leninist doctrine of the growing "labor aristocracy," see below, pp. 41 ff. See E. H. Carr, *The Bolshevik Revolution, 1917–1923* (3 vols.; London, Macmillan, 1953), III, 182.

between the form in which reality *appears* to men and the "essence" of reality. The discrepancy between essence and phenomena is a cornerstone of the Marxian method, but the metaphysical categories have become sociological ones. In the analysis of capitalism Marx describes the discrepancy in terms of the "veil of commodity production" (reification); he derives it from the separation of physical from intellectual work and from the "enslavement of man by the means of his labor." As applied to the proletariat, although it is "in reality" the negation of the capitalist system, this objective reality will not immediately appear in the proletarian consciousness—the "class in itself" is not necessarily "class for itself." Since, to Marx, the "essence" of the proletariat is a historical force which the theoretical analysis only defines and demonstrates, the "real interest" of the proletariat as defined by this analysis is not an abstract and arbitrary construct but a theoretical expression of what the proletariat itself *is*—although it may not or not yet be conscious of what it really is.

In point of fact, when Marx wrote, his concepts did not correspond to those of the proletariat and were probably less like them than they would be today. Marxian theory and its political goals were alien to the existence and interest of the contemporary proletariat, at least to its majority. Marx and Engels were fully aware of the gulf between essence and phenomena and correspondingly between theory and practice. They considered it as expressive of the historical "immaturity" of the proletariat and believed that it would be overcome by the ultimate political radicalization of the working classes—itself the concomitant of the aggravating contradictions of capitalism. Indeed, there seemed to be a demonstrable link between the real and the immediate interest of the proletariat in spite of the obvious discrepancy, namely, the dehumanization and impoverishment of the laborer, which appeared as an objective barrier against the "sway of capitalist ideas," against the dissolution of the revolutionary class.

To Marx and Engels, precisely because the transition from capitalism to socialism was the historical function of the proletariat as a revolutionary class, the specific political *forms* of this transition appeared as variables which could not be fixed and established by theory. Once the proletariat had constituted itself as revolutionary class, conscious of its mission and ready to carry it out, the ways and means for accomplishing its task were to be derived from the then prevailing political and economic situation. Violence was at least not inherent in the action of the proletariat; class consciousness neither necessarily depended upon nor expressed itself in open civil warfare; violence belonged neither to the objective nor to the subjective conditions of the revolution (although it was Marx's and Engels's conviction that the ruling classes could and would not dispense with violence). It was thus more than "politics" when Marx and Engels drew attention to the possibilities of a legal and democratic transition to socialism [8]—especially

---

[8] We refer to the following statements: Marx's speech at Amsterdam, 1872, quoted in Iu. M. Steklov, *History of the First International* (New York, International Publishers, 1928), p. 240; Marx, "Konspekt der Debatten über das Sozialistengesetz" (written in 1878), in Marx and Engels, *Briefe an A. Bebel, W. Lieblknecht, K. Kautsky, und Andere* (Moscow, Verlagsgenossenschaft Ausländischer Arbeiter in der USSR, 1933), p. 516; Engels, "Introduction to Marx's *Class Struggles in France*," in Marx and Engels,

at a time when the numerical and political strength of labor was growing continuously and when the labor parties were professing strongly revolutionary aims.

But while the concrete forms of the transition were variable, its class basis was not. The revolution was to be the direct organized action of the *proletariat as a class*—or it was not at all. Marx and Engels did not recognize any other agent of the revolution nor any "substitute" for it, for substitution would signify the immaturity of the class as such.[9] The "greatest productive force is the revolutionary class itself."[10] The "conquest of political power" can only be the result of the political movement of the working class which *as a class* opposes the ruling classes.[11] The class organizes itself into a "party," but this party develops *naturwüchsig* out of the "soil of modern society itself";[12] it is the *self-organization* of the proletariat.

The Marxian conception thus maintains the identity of

Selected Works, I, 109–27; Engels, *Critique of the Social Democratic Draft Program*, 1891, Sect. II.

[9] The Marxian notion of socialism implies some form of "representation," because the proletariat cannot act *as a class* without organization and division of functions. However, Marx and Engels considered only representation which was constituted by the class itself, that is to say, directly delegated by and directly responsible to the "immediate producers." If the "consciousness" of the class was "immature" or corrupted, the leadership representing the class could help it mature, but could never lead it into action. In such circumstances, the leadership would be, in a strict sense, a *theoretical* one.

[10] Marx, *The Poverty of Philosophy* (New York, International Publishers), p. 146.

[11] Marx, Letter to F. Bolte, November 23, 1871, in Marx and Engels, *Selected Works*, II, 423; and in *Briefe und Auszüge aus Briefen von Joh. Phil. Becker, Jos. Dietzgen, Friedrich Engels, Karl Marx u. A. an F. A. Sorge und Andere*, ed. by F. A. Sorge (Stuttgart, Dietz, 1906), p. 42.

[12] Marx, Letter to Freiligrath, in F. Mehring, *Freiligrath und Marx in ihrem Briefwechsel* (Ergänzungshefte zur Neuen Zeit, No. 12; Stuttgart, Dietz, 1912), p. 43.

the historical agent prior to and after the revolution, and the political instruments of the class struggle, especially the proletarian party, remain expressive of this identity. The conception recognizes changes within the proletariat, in the degree of class consciousness, in the size and weight of the "labor aristocracy," etc., but these changes do not destroy the identity of the class as the sole carrier of the revolution. If this class does not exist, that is, act as a class, then the socialist revolution does not exist.

SUBSEQUENT MODIFICATIONS

Marx derived the afore-mentioned conclusions from a "theoretical model" of capitalism which omits all features (such as foreign trade, government intervention, "third persons") that do not pertain to the basic economic process which constitutes the capitalist system. As the analysis proceeds, in the second and third volumes of *Capital*, these omitted features are reintroduced and theory makes its way from the essence to the concrete historical reality of capitalism; the theoretical model is recast in its essential relation to the historical reality. Now, according to Marx, in its historical reality capitalism develops "countertrends" against its inherent contradictions, for example, capital export (economic and political), monopolies, government intervention. Moreover, one sector of capitalist society which had found little attention in Marx's theoretical analysis proved of decisive significance in reality, namely, the large class of peasants. The countertrends and the "neglected factor" became the focal points in the development of post-Marxian theory.

The discussion of "countertrends" moves into the center

of Marxian theory with the doctrines of "finance capital" and "imperialism." These doctrines, comprising a variety of interpretations from the "revisionist" to the "orthodox" Leninist version, attempted to bring Marxist theory into line with the continued vitality of the established society and especially with the rising standard of living for the working classes in the advanced industrial countries—facts which seemed strikingly to contradict the Marxian notion of the impending final crisis of capitalism and of the impoverishment of the proletariat. In spite of the wide differences in interpretation, the doctrines of imperialism agreed that, around the turn of the century, capitalism had entered a new stage. The main features of the stage were said to be the transformation of free into regimented competition, dominated by national and international cartels, trusts, and monopolies, the amalgamation between banking and industrial capital, government and business, and an expansionist economic policy toward "noncapitalist" and weaker capitalist areas (e.g., intensified exploitation of colonial and dependent countries). However, in the evaluation of this development, the theories of imperialism were irreconcilably divided into the "reformist" and "orthodox" camp. The theory of the former, emerging in Eduard Bernstein's writings of 1900–1901 [13] and culminating in the doctrine of economic democracy (*Wirtschaftsdemokratie*),[14] maintained that, within the framework of "organ-

[13] See Eduard Bernstein, *Evolutionary Socialism: A Criticism and Affirmation*, trans. by Edith C. Harvey (New York, Huebsch, 1909).
[14] Formulated by Rudolf Hilferding at the conference of the German Social Democratic Party at Kiel, 1927, and in Fritz Naphtali, *Wirtschaftsdemokratie*, published by the German Trade Union Federation, Berlin 1928.

ized capitalism," the proletariat could continue to improve its economic as well as its political position and ultimately establish socialism by legal and democratic means through the increasing economic and political influence of organized labor. In sharp contrast, the orthodox interpretation, in its extreme represented by Lenin, saw in the growth of capitalism a tenuous and temporary stabilization bound to explode in armed conflicts among the imperialist powers and in sharpening economic crises. Lenin explained the reformist tendencies among the proletariat in terms of the rise of a small "labor aristocracy," "corrupted" by high wages paid out of monopolistic surplus profits, with a vested interest in the established system.

We are here concerned only with the Leninist interpretation. The emergence of Leninism as a new form of Marxism is determined by two main factors: (1) the attempt to draw the peasantry into the orbit of Marxian theory and strategy, and (2) the attempt to redefine the prospects of capitalist and revolutionary development in the imperialist era. The two main currents of Leninist thought are closely interrelated; the viability of advanced capitalism (unexpected from the traditional Marxist point of view) and, consequently, the continued strength of reformism among the proletariat in the advanced capitalist countries called almost inevitably for a shift in Marxist emphasis to the backward countries, which were predominantly agricultural and where the weakness of the capitalist sector seemed to offer better chances for a revolution. True, the notion that the capitalist chain must be broken at its "weakest link"—a notion stressed by Stalin after the revolution

—was originally Trotsky's rather than Lenin's, but the whole trend of Leninist thought from the beginning is in this direction. When the "workers' and peasants' revolution," rather than the workers' revolution, becomes the center of Soviet Marxism, it is not only because the revolution happened to be successful in Russia but because the revolutionary potential of the industrial working class seemed to recede throughout the advanced capitalist world. It was this fact that, in the long run, decided the development of Soviet Marxism. We therefore take as a starting point Lenin's analysis of the situation of the proletariat at the imperialist stage.

Significant in this interpretation is the underestimation of the economic and political potentialities of capitalism, and of the change in the position of the proletariat. In fact, the refusal to draw the theoretical consequences from the new situation characterizes the entire development of Leninism and is one of the chief reasons for the gap between theory and practice in Soviet Marxism. For, while Lenin from the beginning of his activity reoriented the revolutionary strategy of his party in accordance with the new situation, his theoretical conception did not follow suit. Lenin's retention of the classical notion of the revolutionary proletariat, sustained with the help of the theory of the labor aristocracy and the avant garde, revealed its inadequacy from the beginning. Even prior to the First World War it became clear that the "collaborationist" part of the proletariat was quantitatively and qualitatively different from a small upper stratum that had been corrupted by monopoly capital, and that the Social Democratic Party

and trade union bureaucracy were more than "traitors"—
rather that their policy reflected pretty exactly the economic and social condition of the majority of the organized
working classes in the advanced industrial countries. And indeed, Lenin's strategy of the revolutionary avant garde
pointed to a conception of the proletariat which went far beyond a mere reformulation of the classical Marxian concept;
his struggle against "economism" and the doctrine of spontaneous mass action, his dictum that class consciousness
has to be brought upon the proletariat "from without" anticipate the later factual transformation of the proletariat
from the subject to an object of the revolutionary process.
True, Lenin's *What Is to Be Done?* [15] where these ideas
found their classical formulation, was written for the struggle of the Russian Marxists for leadership over a backward
proletariat, but their implications go far beyond this context. The ultimate target is stated at the beginning of Lenin's pamphlet: it is the rising reformist camp in "international social democracy," represented for Lenin by Bernstein and Millerand, who demanded a "decided change
from revolutionary social democracy to bourgeois reformism." Moreover, the phrase "class consciousness from without" did not originate from the Russian situation but was
coined by Karl Kautsky in his polemics against the draft
of the new program of the Austrian Social Democratic
Party.[16] Lenin aimed beyond the exigencies of the specific
Russian situation, at a general international development
in Marxism, which in turn reflected the trend of large sec-

[15] Lenin, *Chto delat'?* (What Is to Be Done?) appeared first in 1902.
[16] See *What Is to Be Done?* (New York, International Publishers, 1929),
p. 40.

tions of organized labor toward "class cooperation." As
this trend increased, it threatened to vitiate the notion of
the proletariat as the revolutionary subject on which the
whole Marxist strategy depended. Lenin's formulations intended to save Marxian orthodoxy from the reformist on-
slaught, but they soon became part of a conception that no
longer assumed the historical coincidence between the proletariat and progress which the notion of the "labor aristocracy" still retained. The groundwork was laid for the
development of the Leninist party where the true interest
and the true consciousness of the proletariat were lodged in
a group different from the majority of the proletariat. The
centralistic organization, which was first justified by and
applied to the "immaturity" of backward conditions, was
to become the general principle of strategy on an international scale.

The construction of the Leninist party (or party leadership) as the real representative of the proletariat could not
bridge the gap between the new strategy and the old theoretical conception. Lenin's strategy of the avant garde acknowledged in fact what it denied in theory, namely, that
a fundamental change had occurred in the objective and
subjective conditions for the revolution.

In his *Finanzkapital*,[17] published in 1910, Rudolf Hilferding interpreted this change in terms of Marxian theory.

[17] *Das Finanzkapital; Eine Studie über die jüngste Entwicklung des
Kapitalismus* (Marx-Studien III; Vienna, Wiener Volksbuchhandlung, 1910).
Hilferding's term designates not merely a specific form of capital, but a
specific form of capitalist organization. He identifies its two essential elements
as (a) the "abolition" (*Aufhebung*) of free competition by the formation of
cartels and trusts, and (b) the ever closer amalgamation between "banking
capital" and "industrial capital."

He pointed out that, under the leadership of finance capital, the entire national economy would be mobilized for expansion, and that this expansion, through the collusion of giant monopolistic and semimonopolistic enterprises, would tend toward large-scale international integration, economic as well as political. On this new intercontinental market, production and distribution would be to a great extent controlled and regimented by a cartel of the most powerful capitalist interests. In the huge dominion of such a "general cartel," the contradictions of the capitalist system could be greatly controlled, profits for the ruling groups secured, and a high level of wages for labor within the dominion sustained—at the expense of the intensified exploitation of markets and populations outside the dominion. Hilferding thought that such international capitalist planning would require the abolition of democratic liberalism in the economy as well as in the political and ideological sphere; individualism and humanism would be replaced by an aggressive militarist nationalism and authoritarianism. Similar ideas were subsequently (1914) advanced by Karl Kautsky in his concept of "ultra-imperialism." [18]

These developments were presented only as tendencies the realization of which for any length of time was doubted by Hilferding as well as Kautsky. Nor did these writers draw the full conclusions concerning the changing class situation of the proletariat. But the economic and political conditions had been outlined under which the capitalist

[18] Kautsky, "Der Imperialismus," *Die Neue Zeit*, XXXII, 2, No. 21 (September 11, 1914), 921.

world could be stabilized and hierarchically integrated—
conditions which in Marxian theory appeared as utopian
unless the actual forces which would supersede the contradictions and conflicts among the imperialist powers developed. Once they materialized, an economic basis for integration could indeed emerge. It did emerge, very gradually
and with many regressions and breaks, under the impact of
two World Wars, atomic productivity, and the growth of
Communist power. These events altered the structure of
capitalism as defined by Marx and created the basis of a
new economic and political organization of the Western
world.[19] This basis came to be utilized effectively only after
the Second World War. From then on, the conflicting competitive interests among the Western nations were gradually integrated and superseded by the fundamental East-
West conflict, and an intercontinental political economy
took shape—in extent much smaller than the former free
world market, but susceptible to a planned regulation of
that blind "anarchy" in which Marxism saw the root of
capitalist contradictions. At the same time, the laboring
classes were split on an international scale into (to use
Toynbee's terms) an *internal* and *external* proletariat, the
latter consisting of those (urban and rural) proletarian and
semiproletarian classes, outside and inside the area of ef-

[19] Soviet Marxism maintains—and indeed must maintain if the Marxian
conception is to be preserved—that these events are intrinsically related: the
"permanent war economy," as the sole outlet for the imperialist contradictions, leads to atomic productivity, and the latter enforces economic as well
as political integration of the Western powers. According to this conception,
the events which bring about the transformation of the Western world
are not extraneous but rather internal to the dynamic of the capitalist
system, and the same forces that make for war make for progress in
productivity and for "temporary stabilization."

fective reconstruction, which did not benefit from it by higher wages, better living conditions, or greater political influence.

The external proletariat (including, as its largest part, the peasantry), which came to provide the Soviet leadership with a mass basis for the struggle against capitalism after the First World War, emerged as a historical "subject" seemingly by virtue of (from the Marxian viewpoint) an exogenous event, namely, by virtue of the fact that the revolution succeeded in backward Russia, failed to materialize in the advanced industrial countries, and subsequently spread from Russia into preindustrial areas, while the advanced industrial countries continued to remain immune. But this event was not quite as exogenous as it seems. The gradual "immunization" of decisive areas of Western society had already begun to show its effectiveness prior to the First World War; the nationalist attitude of the Social Democratic parties in 1914—at that time the unchallenged Marxist organization of labor—was only its most conspicuous manifestation. The immunization then proved its power in the Central European revolutions from 1918 to 1923, where the majority of organized labor defeated the Communist assault in alliance with the bourgeoisie and the army. In England, the predominance of the reformist Labor Party had never been seriously disturbed. In France and Italy, Communist strength continued to trail far behind that of Social Democracy; and in Germany, the only country where it came to a powerful resurgence after the defeat, Social Democratic as well as Communist labor succumbed quickly to the Fascist regime. The sustained weakness of

the revolutionary potential in the advanced industrial countries confined the revolution to that area where the proletariat had not been thus affected and where the regime had
shown political disintegration together with economic backwardness.

Marxian theory explained the rising standard of living,
which lay at the economic roots of the immunization process, in terms of the growing productivity of labor, the effective organization of the industrial workers, which counteracted the pressure on the wage level, and in terms of
monopolistic surplus profits in the most advanced capitalist areas. According to Marxism, none of these factors
could neutralize for any length of time the inherent contradictions of the capitalist mode of production. The benefits
for the working class were expected to be wiped out period-
ically by wars and crises since there was no basis for long-
range international capitalist consolidation. This interpretation did not provide for the possibility (soon to become a
fact) that such an international basis would materialize.
On it, Western industrial society created its new economic
and political institutions. The catastrophic violence, the unprecedented extent of physical and cultural destruction,
and also the equally unprecedented growth of technical
productivity which characterized the period after 1918,
corresponded to the scope of the task. It was the very structure of the established civilization that was challenged and
that had to be reaffirmed against a competing civilization.
The technological and political potential developed in this
struggle made it soon appear that minor adjustments would
not suffice to meet the challenge. The need for the total mo-

bilization of all material and mental forces necessitated the abolition of laissez-faire in economic and cultural life, the methodical control of the political process, and national regrouping under the actual hierarchy of economic power —at the expense of cherished traditional sovereignties. The overriding interest of Western society as a whole modified national and class interests: the national parties aligned themselves with the international economic and political forces. Labor was no exception and, at the end, Social Democracy became part of the Western, and Communism part of the Eastern, orbit. For Marxism, the capitalist world had never come closer to the dreaded specter of a "general cartel" which would replace the anarchy of capitalist production and distribution by ultraimperialist planning. And it was the very progress of the Soviet system which had promoted the realization of this dreaded possibility.

2. Soviet Marxism: The Basic Self-Interpretation

THE LENINIST HERITAGE

A comparison between the above analysis of the historical presuppositions of Soviet Marxism with the official Soviet pronouncements shows that the latter do not explicitly acknowledge these presuppositions. Leninist as well as Stalinist theory has recurrently and emphatically denied the possibility of a long-range international integration of the Western world. The readjustments of the post-Stalinist period, while explicitly rejecting the "theory of absolute stagnation of capitalism" and Stalin's theses on the shrinkage of the capitalist system, still retain the notion of the "intensification of the capitalist contradictions" in the present era.[1] Soviet Marxism has equally emphatically denied the concomitant changes in the structure of the laboring class in the Western countries; the classical Marxist notion of the revolutionary proletariat having been a mainstay of Soviet theory. However, all the decisive policies

---

[1] See Mikoyan's speech, February 16, 1956, at the Twentieth Congress of the Communist Party of the Soviet Union, in *XX S"ezd Kommunisticheskoi Partii Sovetskogo Soiuza: Stenograficheskii otchet* (The Twentieth Congress of the Communist Party of the Soviet Union: Stenographic Account) (2 vols.; Moscow, Gospolitizdat, 1956), I, 319–21; Khrushchev's speech of February 14, in *ibid.*, I, 14–20; also New York *Times*, February 19, 1956; and Khrushchev's speech of November 6, 1957, (as broadcast by Moscow Home Service, p. A-47).

of constructing socialism in the Soviet orbit are based on the structural changes which characterize the contemporary period, and on the decline of the revolutionary proletariat in the Western world. This dichotomy raises the problem of the objective sincerity of Soviet Marxist theoretical pronouncements—part of the larger problem of the relationship between Soviet theory and practice.

We have already mentioned that "Aesopian language" is systematically employed *within* the Soviet Marxist camp itself and for Marxist audiences and communications. Soviet Marxism continues to use the "orthodox" Marxian notions to designate situations and policies which obviously contradict these notions. Under these circumstances it would seem to be appropriate to dismiss Soviet Marxism as mere "propaganda." This is a deceptive solution, because the distinction between "propaganda" and "truth" presupposes a demonstrable "truth" with which propaganda can be contrasted. If it is maintained that the truth expresses itself only in the practice and not in the theory of Soviet Marxism, that the theory serves only as an ideological prop for mass manipulation, then this contention has to be proved. It is by no means self-evident in the face of the difficulties which the regime creates for itself by constantly teaching and publicizing Marxian ideas that can be reconciled with reality only by great expenditure of physical and intellectual force. The fact is that, regardless of its "level," the exposition of Marxist theory continues to be one of the main efforts of the regime, and the tension between theory and practice continues to exist.

But if it seems inappropriate to dismiss the whole of theory as propaganda, it seems equally inappropriate to

retain parts of it as the truth and classify others as "subter-
fuge." There are no criteria for such a selection—unless
we can detect certain Marxist notions that remain constant
through the various changes in Soviet theory and strategy.
Then it might be possible to arrive at an identification of the
"basic elements," and to derive the "revisions" and "rejec-
tions" from these elements, thus obtaining a body of theoretical principles in relationship to practice. It is this approach which guides the subsequent discussion.

The formation of Soviet Marxist theory proceeds on the
basis of Lenin's interpretation of Marxism, without going
back to original Marxian theory. A brief summary of the
essential links between Leninism and subsequent Soviet
Marxism will suffice to clarify the starting point.

We suggested above that the characteristic features of
emerging Leninism, i.e., the shift in the revolutionary agent
from the class-conscious proletariat to the centralized party
as the avant garde of the proletariat and the emphasis on
the role of the peasantry as ally of the proletariat, developed under the impact of the sustained strength of capitalism at the "imperialist stage." The conception which was
initially aimed at the "immaturity" of the Russian proletariat became a principle of international strategy in the
face of the continued reformist attitude of the "mature"
proletariat in the advanced industrial countries. To counteract the integration of a large sector of organized labor
into the capitalist system, the "subjective factor" of revolutionary strategy is monopolized by the Party, which assumes the character of a professional revolutionary organization directing the proletariat.

The Leninist conception may be presented as a development of the Marxian distinction between the "immediate" and the "real" interest (and consciousness) of the proletariat. Here are the principal stages: (*a*) Societal being determines consciousness: the individual proletarian, in capitalist relationships of production, desires to improve his individual conditions immediately and continually within the capitalist system. (*b*) The "economistic" policy of the trade unions, in achieving such improvement, sustains the proletariat as an exploited class and thereby sustains capitalist society; but at the same time it modifies the social structure in so far as it provides a basis for "class peace." (*c*) This change in the social structure "deflects" the proletariat from its objective historical position as the revolutionary class which can liberate itself only by abolishing the capitalist system. (*d*) The objective historical position can be "rescued" only by subordinating the immediate subjective interest to the real interest of the class, by transforming the economic into a political struggle. This task is the function of the Leninist party. Since, according to Marxian theory, the economic struggle by itself can never achieve more than a brief improvement, the capitalist process, through recurrent depressions and crises, will redress the balance and lead to the radicalization of the proletariat, thus reestablishing the coincidence of its immediate and real interests.

But what happens when the process (*c*) affects the bulk of the proletariat in the advanced capitalist countries? Has not Marxian theory then lost the mass basis required for its realization? And is not the connection between theory and

reality also lost, unless the former redefines itself by redefining the latter? These questions seem to have driven
Leninist theory toward a reevaluation of contemporary capitalist development, which has become the theoretical foundation for the doctrine of "socialism in one country."

This doctrine, which predates the Bolshevik Revolution,
revealed itself from the beginning as defined and determined by the new stage of industrial society. Lenin's "law
of the uneven development of capitalism" was at first only
the expression of an actual state of affairs, but the inferences drawn from it form the very core of Soviet Marxism.
Lenin noted that "uneven economic and political development is an absolute law of capitalism" and immediately
added, therefore, "the victory of socialism is, at the beginning, possible in a few capitalist countries," or even in a
single capitalist country.[2] The conclusion clearly implies
here that socialism may be victorious first in a few or even
in one single *advanced* capitalist country, while the more
backward countries will lag behind. One year later, Lenin
wrote that socialism will achieve victory first in one or several countries while the others will remain bourgeois or
"pre-bourgeois" for some time.[3]

Lenin retained the Marxian conclusion that the socialist

[2] "The United States of Europe Slogan" (written in 1915), in *The
Strategy and Tactics of World Communism*, House Document No. 619,
Supplement I (Washington, D.C., U.S. Government Printing Office, 1948),
p. 29; Lenin, *Selected Works* (12 vols.; New York, International Publishers, 1937–38), V, 141.

[3] "Voennaia programma proletarskoi revoliutsii" (The War Program of the
Proletarian Revolution), in *Sochineniia* (Works) (3d ed., 30 vols.; Moscow,
Institut Lenina, 1928–37), XIX, 325. See also *History of the Communist
Party of the Soviet Union* (New York, International Publishers, 1939), p.
169.

revolution will be the result of the exploding contradictions
in a *fully matured* capitalist country—and not even the triumph of the Bolshevik Revolution made him abandon this
conviction. His hesitation to acknowledge the socialist character of the revolution is well known—a hesitation in spite
of his thesis that the "bourgeois-democratic revolution"
had to be surpassed by a workers' and peasants' revolution
which would replace the parliamentary republic by a
Soviet republic. As late as March, 1919, he called the October Revolution a "bourgeois revolution in so far as the
class struggle on the countryside had not yet developed." [4]
And he added that only in the summer of 1918 did the real
proletarian revolution on the countryside begin. He clung
to the notion that the Russian Revolution must be rescued
by the German revolution.

But it is precisely Lenin's belief in the tentative and preliminary character of the Russian Revolution which leads
him to formulations clearly foreshadowing the Stalinist
policy. Socialism presupposes capitalism—or at least the
achievements of capitalism, namely, a high degree of industrialization, a high productivity of labor, and a highly
developed, skilled, and disciplined labor force. Stages in
this sequence may perhaps be "jumped" (Lenin was hesi-
tant also with respect to this problem [5]), but without the
achievements of a fully industrialized and rationalized

[4] His speech on rural policy to the Eighth Congress of the Russian Communist Party, March 23, 1918, in *Sochineniia* (Works), XXIV, 162.
[5] See for example the contradictory statements in "Two Tactics of Social
Democracy" (written in 1905), in *Selected Works*, III, 75; and in the
report of the Commission on the National and Colonial Question to the
Second World Congress of the Comintern, 1920, in *Selected Works*, X,
239–44.

economy there can be no socialism, no distribution of the
social product according to individual needs and faculties.
In a backward country, industrialization has priority over
socialization, that is, over production and distribution according to individual needs. At the meeting of the All-
Russian Central Executive Committee in April, 1918, in
his polemic against the "left Communists" who foresaw the
"road to state capitalism," Lenin declared:

In reality, state capitalism would be a step forward for us. If we
were capable of attaining state capitalism in Russia within a short
time, this would be a victory. . . . I said that state capitalism
would be our savior. If we would have it in Russia, then the
transition to full socialism would be easy and certain. For state
capitalism is a system of centralization, integration, control, and
socialization. And this is precisely what we lack.[6]

And one month later he quoted a statement of September,
1917, to the effect that "state-monopolistic capitalism is the
complete material preparation for socialism," the "anteroom" of socialism, the historical stage immediately preceding socialism, and he added, "Is it not clear, that, in the
material, economic sense, in terms of production, we are
not yet in the 'anteroom' of socialism? And that we cannot
reach the door to socialism by any other way than through
this 'anteroom'?"[7]

The implications of these statements remain obscured
by the fact that the German revolution of 1918 seemed to

[6] *Sochineniia* (Works), XXII, 482.
[7] "O 'levom' rebiachestve i mel'koburzhuaznosti" (On "Leftist" In-
fantilism and Petty-Bourgeois Attitudes), *Pravda*, May 9–11, 1918.

unleash that chain of revolutions in mature countries which would restore the "orthodox" way of international revolution. The Soviet state would not only be "protected" by the proletarian state of a highly developed industrial country but would also share in its technical and material wealth, and the transition to socialism would thus be secured and accelerated. The almost desperate orientation toward Germany is contained in the record of the meetings of the Comintern and its executive committee and of Lenin's speeches during the first years of the revolution. But from about 1921 on, Soviet policy drew the consequences from the defeat of the German revolution. In view of the central role which the relationship between mature capitalism and the transition to socialism plays in Marxian theory, the failure of the German revolution—coupled with the growing leadership of the United States in the reconstruction of the Western world—seemed to necessitate a reevaluation of the international development. If the capitalist potential should, for a long time to come, prove stronger than the revolutionary potential, if not even the First World War and its effect on the economy could break the hold of reformism over the "mature proletariat," then the historical agent of the revolution had changed not only in a geographical but also in a social sense. If there was real "capitalist stabilization," then not only would the Soviet state, for a long time to come, "coexist" with the far more powerful capitalist world, but it would also have to look toward the developing revolutionary movement in the colonial and semicolonial countries as more than a mere "reserve" for

the revolutionary army. Not only the international strategy, but also the construction of socialism in Soviet society,
would have to be redefined.

Lenin's *Pravda* article, "Better Fewer, But Better,"
(March, 1923), combines the traditional and the new evaluation of the international development in a few telescoped
propositions. They center on the statement that the Western
European capitalist countries are not accomplishing their
way to socialism "in the way we formerly expected." [8]
Lenin continued: They "are not accomplishing it by the
even ripening of socialism, but by the exploitation of some
countries by others . . . combined with the exploitation
of the whole of the East." How does imperialist exploitation of vanquished capitalist countries (in Lenin's context,
Germany specifically) alter the "expected" accomplishment of socialism? Lenin's text suggests several answers:
(*a*) by shifting the capitalist center from Central Europe to
the West, ultimately to the United States; [9] (*b*) by rapidly
drawing "the East, India, China, etc.," into the capitalist
world system; (*c*) by, at the same time, accelerating nationalist and revolutionary movements in the East (and in
the vanquished capitalist countries?). Lenin's propositions
imply, on the one hand, capitalist growth (through the
"new exploitation of the defeated countries and of the
East") and, on the other, growth of the revolutionary potential "in the East" ("we have the advantage in that the

---

[8] In *Selected Works*, IX, 399.

[9] In 1915, in his article "The United States of Europe Slogan," Lenin
wrote: "In comparison with the *United States of America*, Europe as a
whole signifies economic stagnation. . . . The times when the cause of democracy and Socialism was associated with Europe alone have gone forever."
Selected Works, V, 140–41. Italics added.

whole world is now passing into a movement that must give rise to world socialist revolution").

The difficulties presented by these formulations are augmented by Lenin's statement that "we are laboring under the disadvantage that the imperialists have succeeded in splitting the world into two camps." [10] The "disadvantage" can only be explained in terms of the new strength accruing to capitalism through exploitation of the vanquished countries, "combined" with the exploitation of the whole East, and through the collaboration of the working classes of the imperialist victor countries. Lenin stressed the fact that "a number of the oldest states in the West are in a position to utilize their victory for the purpose of making a number of insignificant concessions to their oppressed classes which, insignificant as they are, nevertheless retard the revolutionary movement in these countries and create something which has the appearance of *class peace*." [11]

This comes close to Hilferding's conception of the establishment of an effective national interest uniting labor and capital in advanced imperialist countries. However, in contrast, Lenin's analysis led to a "guidance" for Soviet policy which was based on the expectation of interimperialist *conflicts* and which has become "obligatory" for Soviet Marxism. Here again, the ambiguities of Lenin's statements are striking. He raised the question of how to "save ourselves from the impending conflict with these imperialist coun-

[10] *Selected Works*, IX, 399. In Stalinist theory, in view of the greatly increased strength of the Communist camp, this "split" appears as an *advantage*, and as a success, not of the "imperialists," but of the Communists.

[11] *Ibid.*, IX, 398. Italics added.

tries," thereby implying the typical Stalinist contraposition
of the Soviet and the imperialist camp. But he immediately
answered with the "hope that the internal antagonisms and
conflicts between the thriving imperialist countries of the
West and the thriving imperialist countries of the East will
give us a second respite," [12] without discussing the obvious
possibility that the former conflict (between the imperialist
countries and the Soviet Union) may "neutralize" or "suspend" the conflict within the imperialist camp. In any case,
he declared, the "final outcome" of the struggle between
socialism and imperialism, namely, the victory of socialism,
is "absolutely assured" by the fact that the population of
"Russia, India, China, etc.," constitutes the overwhelming
majority of the earth's population, and is rapidly being
"drawn into the struggle for its emancipation." What was
"interesting" to Lenin was not the final outcome, but the
Soviet policy of "preventing the West European counter-
revolutionary states from crushing us." And he held that
the Soviet policy of "ensuring our existence" until this
conflict erupted, must aim at making the East "more civilized." And this in turn made it necessary "to develop
electrification, hydro-peat, to construct Volkhovstroy, etc."
"In this and in this alone lies our hope." [13]

Without reconciling them, Lenin's analysis contains the
old and the new elements of the situation: the "internal
antagonisms and conflicts within the imperialist camp"

[12] *Ibid.*, IX, 399. The conception of the respite or "breathing space"
began to play a decisive role in Soviet foreign and domestic policy in 1920.
See E. H. Carr, *The Bolshevik Revolution, 1917–1923* (3 vols.; London,
Macmillan, 1953), III, 318 ff.

[13] *Selected Works*, IX, 400–401.

stand side by side with the "impending conflict" between this camp and the Soviet state. The policy conclusions which Lenin derived from this analysis take equal account of both sets of contradictions.

The interimperialist contradictions. The survival of the Soviet state depends ultimately on them. The Soviet state must obtain and preserve a long "respite" by utilizing the conflicts among the imperialist powers. Thus Lenin had already formulated the substance of Soviet foreign policy at the Eighth All-Russian Congress of Soviets in December, 1920: "Our existence depends, first, on the existence of a radical split in the camp of the imperialist Powers." [14]

The contradictions between the capitalist world and the Soviet state. Temporary stabilization and "class peace" in the victorious capitalist countries shifts the revolutionary potential from these countries to the "revolutionary and nationalist East." The shift is more than a geographical change—it signifies the emergence of a new agent of the historical process. Lenin designated this agent only as the population of "Russia, India, China, etc." The vagueness of this designation is characteristic: Lenin did not introduce a new theoretical concept which would alter the structure of Marxian doctrine, nor did he elaborate the notion of the new international character of the class struggle. But his policy guidance is clear: the interimperialist contradictions are the decisive ones; they must be utilized for the accomplishment of the main task—Soviet industrialization.

[14] *Sochineniia* (Works), XXVI, 14–15. For translation see Carr, *The Bolshevik Revolution*, III, 331.

Soviet Marxism has followed Lenin's twofold guidance: its main theoretical effort has been to correlate the two sets of contradictions as a basis for policy, and to determine their relative weight. We cannot discuss here the various turns and variants of the Soviet Marxist analysis of the international situation from the Fifth Congress of the Comintern in 1924 to the Twentieth Party Congress in 1956, but we shall try to demonstrate that the basic Soviet conception of capitalist development has not fundamentally changed throughout the entire period. To be sure, the zigzag of right and left turns has continued in Communist tactics, but since the Sixth World Congress at the latest, they appear as short-lived tactical trials in contradistinction—and often in conflict—to the underlying conception and strategy. In order to clarify this distinction between tactical devices and the basic conception, we shall begin by trying to identify the Soviet Marxist categories which have remained constant throughout the various turns during the Stalinist period.

THE ANALYSIS OF CONTEMPORARY CAPITALISM

Soviet Marxism sees the entire capitalist development since the First World War as comprising *one* period: the subdivisions of this period appear to represent only stages in the growth of one and the same basic trend. Its main features [15] as interpreted by Soviet Marxism are as follows:

[15] They are taken from: (a) the program, theses, and resolutions of the Comintern; (b) the theoretical statements of Soviet leaders that have been "canonized" as obligatory; (c) the principal discussions and papers of Soviet economists, especially the discussions of 1947 (the Varga controversy), 1949, and 1950, and the analyses of the contemporary capitalist situation in *Voprosy Ekonomiki* (Problems of Economics) after the Nineteenth Party Congress. Specific references will be given below.

1. The triumph of monopoly capitalism over the surviving elements of "free" capitalism

2. The organization of monopoly capitalism on an international scale on the basis of a permanent (potential or actual) war economy, with growing "state capitalist tendencies"

3. Economic and political subjugation of the weaker capitalist powers by the stronger, and of the stronger by the strongest capitalist power (the United States); thereby creation of large intercontinental areas of "exploitation"

4. Total mobilization of all human, material, and technical resources for the struggle against communism

5. Restriction or outright abolition of the democratic process, of civil and political liberties, and of liberal and humanitarian ideologies

6. Containment, by force and by "corruption," of the revolutionary potential within the capitalist system

7. Global sociopolitical division into the "imperialist" and "socialist" camp

Before explaining this interpretation, three questions must be answered: (1) How does Soviet Marxism justify the assumption of one basic trend for the entire period after the First World War in view of the obvious difficulty of placing fascism and the Western democracies, the "grand alliance" and the "cold war" on one common denominator? (2) How is the notion of the successful containment of the revolutionary forces within the capitalist system reconcilable with the recurrent "left turns" and aggressive ventures of Communist strategy, and (3) with the spectacular growth of the French and Italian Communist parties after the Second World War?

As to the first question, Soviet Marxism sees fascism as a specific phase in the national and international class struggle, namely, as the open, terroristic "dictatorship of the most reactionary, most chauvinistic and most imperialist elements of finance capital." [16] This dictatorship is the attempt to "solve" the capitalist crisis by intensified exploitation of the working classes and of the colonies, by the "enslavement of the weak nations," and by preparing or actually waging war against the Soviet Union. This formulation contains all the chief characteristics subsequently applied to "Anglo-American or American imperialism." Such transfer is implied in Point 3 of the Soviet Marxist analysis: the hierarchical international organization of contemporary capitalism under the supremacy of the strongest economic power, necessitating the sacrifice of traditional sovereignties and democratic liberties. The economic basis for German Fascist supremacy was too narrow. This "anomaly" was corrected by the Second World War, which redressed the international balance and redivided the spheres of influence in accordance with actual economic strength, that is, with the emergence of the United States as the strongest capitalist power. Fascism and the defeat of fascism thus appear as "logical" steps in the international reorganization of monopoly capitalism.

But if the struggle against the Soviet Union is one of the essential elements of this reorganization (Point 4), how

[16] Thirteenth *Plenum of the Executive Committee of the Comintern: Theses and Decisions* (New York, Workers Library Publishers, 1934), pp. 3 f.; Dimitrov's report to the Seventh World Congress of the Comintern, 1935, in *United Front Against Fascism* (New York, New Century Publishers, 1935), pp. 5–7.

can one explain the alliance between the capitalist West
and the USSR during the Second World War? Soviet Marxism has two answers: (*a*) the Western powers needed the
aid of the USSR to defeat German Fascism, and (*b*) even
during the alliance, the Western struggle against the USSR
continued (cited as examples are the delay in opening the
second front, Churchill's Balkan strategy, and the Western
powers' alleged efforts to obtain a separate peace with
Germany).

As to the second and third questions, before the Second
World War, Soviet Marxism subdivided the contemporary
capitalist development into three periods. The acute revolutionary situation after the First World War (the "first
period") was followed by a period of "relative stabilization" (the "second period"). In his first Political Report
to the Central Committee, delivered at the Fourteenth Party
Congress in 1925, Stalin analyzed the international situation in terms of a "stabilization of capitalism." He called
it a temporary and "partial" stabilization,[17] and three
years later, at the Sixth World Congress of the Comintern,
the coming of a "third period" was announced. The Communist parties were directed toward leftist radicalism.
Mass demonstrations in the face of resolute armed resistance, the disastrous struggle against "social fascist" labor
parties and trade unions, alliances with the extreme right,
the proclamation of a new "revolutionary tide" in China—
these were the manifestations of the left turn, which seemed
to find its economic justification in the great depression of

---

[17] *Political Report of the Central Committee* (Moscow, Foreign Languages
Publishing House, 1950), pp. 10 f.

1929. In 1932, the Twelfth Plenum of the Executive Committee of the Comintern again announced the "end of capitalist stabilization" and the beginning of a new cycle of wars and revolutions. The "third period" was said to be characterized by a "growing revolutionary upsurge" in the capitalist countries and by a "sharpening of the economic crisis." [18] This is perhaps the most extreme "left turn" the Comintern made after the failure of the Central European revolution, and in his report to the Plenum on the international situation Kuusinen stated that every effort should be made to "prepare the proletariat and the rest of the working population for the struggle for power in the new period." [19] But the strategy directions seem to presuppose quite a different evaluation of the capitalist situation. The Thesis on Kuusinen's report adopted by the Twelfth Plenum has, in contrast to the report itself, a predominantly defensive tone. Although retaining the phrase, "the growing revolutionary upsurge," the Thesis calls for the struggle against the "capitalist offensive" [20] rather than for the seizure of power, for waging the class struggle "on the basis of the united front from below," [21] for a mass political strike when the "proper condition for it exists," [22] and ends with the usual exhortation to the Communist parties to direct the movement "along the channel of the World Socialist Revolution."

[18] *Capitalist Stabilization Has Ended; Thesis and Resolutions of the Twelfth Plenum of the Executive Committee of the Communist International* (New York, Workers Library Publishers, 1932), p. 7.

[19] O. Kuusinen, *Prepare for Power* (New York, Workers Library Publishers 1932) p. 40.

[20] *Capitalist Stabilization Has Ended* p. 16.   [21] *Ibid.* p. 22.

[22] *Ibid.* p. 17.

Thus even the most "leftist" Comintern program does not contradict our assumption that Stalinist strategy implied effective containment of the revolutionary potential in the Western world after the failure of the Central European revolutions. The strategy of the "united front against fascism," which followed in 1935, went one step further in acknowledging the decline of the revolutionary potential in the West, by committing the Communist parties to a "minimum program" within the framework of the "bourgeois-democratic" state.

The situation at the end of the Second World War may serve as another illustration of the degree to which Stalinist policy, in spite of declarations to the contrary, operated under the assumption of a "capitalist stabilization." At that time, in France and Italy, the popular strength of the Communist parties was greater than ever before, and, for the first time, their armed strength seemed adequate for an attempt at seizing power. However, after a few scattered and uncoordinated local putsches, the Communists pursued a policy of cooperation, surrendered their military units, and adhered to a "minimum program" which, even during the subsequent period of the great political strikes, never aimed at revolution as the immediate objective. This strategy may be explained by the weakness of its "mass basis." The national Communist parties were confronted with a situation which defied the traditional concepts of Marxian revolutionary strategy; it soon became apparent that they fought in an entirely different arena. The Allied armies which, together with the legitimate national contingents, confronted the Communists in France, Italy, and Western

Germany, unmistakably symbolized the new situation
which continued to prevail even after their withdrawal:
the "class enemy" could no longer be defeated "on the bar-
ricades" in Paris or Lyon or Toulouse, in Milan or Turin
or Bologna. Its central positions now were in Washington
and New York, in the Allied headquarters and commis-
sions. The civil war had become a matter of international,
intercontinental policy in a far more objective sense than
that of a dictatorship of the USSR over foreign Communist
parties. And in the international constellation at the end of
the war, all the odds were in the hands of the Western
Allies, specifically, of the United States. To be sure, after
the quick Western demobilization, the Soviet armies could
have overrun the Continent. But if Marxism played any
role at all in Soviet policy decisions, then it influenced
Stalin to the extent that he could not envisage the defeat
of the capitalist world through a blitzkrieg in Europe,
waged by an exhausted and largely destroyed Russia
against the practically unimpaired forces of the econom-
ically most powerful nation in the world. And Stalin, whose
theory still stuck to the traditional notion of the aggravating interimperialist contradictions, may well have been
surprised at the rapidity with which the "united capitalist
front" against Communism reasserted itself after the war
(Churchill's speech at Fulton, Missouri, 1946; the "Tru-
man Doctrine" and the Marshall Plan, 1947; Anglo-
American negotiations on the Ruhr, 1947).

The Stalinist answer was the doctrine of the "two camps"
and the aggressive strategy of 1947–1948 usually associated with Zhdanov. The doctrine comes closest to the open

recognition of international capitalist unification [23] and thus closest to discarding the traditional notion of the inner imperialist contradictions—though it actually does neither. For the "two-camp" doctrine includes the Western proletariat in the "anti-imperialist camp" and reiterates the idea of the inevitability of internal and external wars. At about the same time, Varga's cautious recognition of the stabilizing and "productive" function of the capitalist state at this stage was violently rejected. Stalinist foreign policy followed the notion underlying the "two-camp" doctrine that the contradictions between the imperialist and the Communist camp had, for the time being, superseded those between the imperialist powers: Communist rule was tightened and expanded; loopholes were being closed (establishment of Cominform, 1947; coup in Czechoslovakia, Soviet walkout from the Allied Control Council in Germany, Berlin blockade, and break with Tito, 1948). But as early as 1948–1949, the intransigent Communist strategy in the West was petering out (failure and abandonment of the political strikes in France and Italy) and was being replaced by a new "united-front" policy, which has been retained and stepped up ever since. In the East, the course was different: the Indian party adhered to an extreme left strategy until 1950; military operations in Indo-China were increased; and the war in Korea began at a time when the Western parties were on the defensive. During the en-

[23] See Zhdanov's report to the Cominform conference, September 1947, in *The Strategy and Tactics of World Communism*, House Document No. 619, Supplement I, p. 216. "A new alignment of political forces has arisen." Zhdanov continued by stating that the Western as well as the Far and Middle Eastern countries in the "imperialist camp" follow the leadership of the United States in all main questions.

tire Stalinist period, Western and Eastern policy were
never effectively correlated; from the time of the dismal
consequences of Stalinist "guidances" in the first phases
of the Chinese revolution, Stalinism seemed to follow
rather than direct the momentum of the "colonial revolutions." There, the new historical agent of the revolution
seemed to ripen "naturally," and the peasant masses,
which Lenin had incorporated into revolutionary strategy,
seemed to fulfill their function. The West, the capitalist
world, remained the determining problem for Soviet Marxism.

The Soviet Marxist interpretation of capitalism centers
on the notion of the "general crisis" of the capitalist system. The crisis itself is seen as expressive of the monopolistic stage of capitalist development—a stage at which the
fundamental conflict between the social character of the
productive forces and their private capitalist utilization
has reached its peak, the last stage before the turning point
to socialism. The foreign policy of the Western nations and
the internal economic and political changes within these
nations are explained in terms of this conflict.[24]

The "general crisis," which comprises a whole historical
period, is subdivided into two main phases.[25] The second

[24] For what follows see: M. Rubinshtein, "Osnovnoi ekonomicheskii zakon
sovremennogo kapitalizma" (The Basic Economic Law of Contemporary
Capitalism), *Voprosy Ekonomiki* (Problems of Economics), 1952, No. 10,
pp. 38–55; I. Lemin, "Obostrenie protivorechii i neizbezhnost' voin mezhdu
kapitalisticheskimi stranami" (The Sharpening of Contradictions and the
Unavoidability of Wars Between Capitalist Countries), *Voprosy Ekonomiki*
(Problems of Economics), 1952, No. 12, pp. 34–53; and I. Trakhtenberg,
"Osobennosti vosproizvodstva i krizisov v sovremennom kapitalizme" (Char-
acteristics of Production and Crises in Contemporary Capitalism), *Voprosy
Ekonomiki* (Problems of Economics), 1952, No. 10, pp. 69–85.

[25] For example, G. V. Kozlov, "Obshchii krizis kapitalisma i ego obostrenie

phase, which began with the Second World War, is the sharpening of the crisis. The crisis itself was unleashed by the emergence of the Soviet state and was intensified by its subsequent growth. The specific features of the crisis are the tremendous shrinking of the capitalist world market and the establishment of two parallel but opposed world markets: the capitalist and the "socialist." While the former decreases, the latter increases without depression and dislocation—steadily. Much of the colonial and semicolonial and almost the whole Eastern European market has "broken away" from the capitalist orbit. Moreover, capitalism has not only been cut off from a large part of its former sales market but also from access to many of its former resources of raw materials and cheap labor. The consequence: capitalist production proceeds on an ever-narrowing basis; the difficulties in the extraction and realization of surplus value and, therefore, of profit (already greatly intensified by the "higher organic composition" of capital, that is—in terms of total capital—the growing proportion of constant capital and the decreasing proportion of wages) increase, and force the most powerful capitalist groups into a brutal struggle for their share in the greatly reduced market. This in turn aggravates the competitive conflicts among the capitalist powers. The struggle for markets assumes, at the late imperialistic stage, the form of the subjugation of the weaker by the stronger capitalist powers, culminating in the supremacy

---

na sovremennom etape" (The General Crisis of Capitalism and Its Sharpening at the Present Stage), *Voprosy Ekonomiki* (Problems of Economics), 1952, No. 4, pp. 68 ff.

of American imperialism. According to Soviet Marxism, the trend indicated by Lenin in 1915 has reached its apex. The militarization of the economy, the "classical" feature of imperialism, becomes the "normal" state of affairs. The war economy, while yielding monopolistic surplus profits to the top capitalists, depresses the level of consumption even in the richest capitalist countries, channels the bulk of capitalist investments into direct and indirect war industries, and thus increases the disproportionality between the two main divisions of capitalist production. The crisis affects the very reproduction of the system.

According to this interpretation, the rise of the Soviet state has set in motion a chain reaction which, by intensifying the inherent capitalist contradictions, has aggravated the conflicts between the capitalist powers.[26] This was the theoretical conclusion at the time of the Sixteenth Party Congress (1930) and again at the time of the Twentieth Congress (1956). The contradictions which, in the Marxian conception, are inherent in the structure of capitalist production, reassert themselves as the determining ones— contrary to all appearances. Soviet Marxism consistently denies that the international integration of capitalism into one camp against the common enemy can "neutralize" these contradictions. The doctrines of "ultraimperialism"

---

[26] I. Lemin, "Obostrenie protivorechii i neizbezhnost' voin mezhdu kapitalisticheskimi stranami" (The Sharpening of Contradictions and the Unavoidability of Wars between Capitalist Countries), *Voprosy Ekonomiki* (Problems of Economics), 1952, No. 12, p. 44. This gives the reasons for the violent reaction against Varga's book, *Izmeneniia v ekonomike kapitalizma v itoge vtoroi mirovoi voiny* (Changes in the Economy of Capitalism Resulting from the Second World War) (Moscow, Gospolitizdat, 1946). See p. 66 below.

and "organized capitalism" are again emphatically rejected [27]—as they were forty years ago. The efforts of the American monopolists to establish an American "world trust" have failed. The competitive conflicts within the capitalist orbit sharpen in spite of all integration; the "subjugated" nations balk and strive for reconquering their former position in the world market; Western Germany and Japan reemerge as the most dangerous competitors.[28] The operation of the fundamental economic laws which in Marxian theory determine the course of events thus leads to the growth and explosion of the imperialist contradictions, to military conflicts within the imperialist camp, to the "further deepening of the general crisis of the capitalist system and the approach of its final breakdown." [29]

There are the customary warnings against interpreting the situation in terms of an impending collapse of the capitalist system. Thus, Trakhtenberg states that the increasing difficulty in finding a "way out" of the economic crisis does not mean the "absolute impossibility" of a way out, nor of a prolongation of the crisis. He points to the inflationary boom of the armament economy prevailing in the capitalist orbit at present, but concludes by reiterating that under the surface of a capitalist "revival" the disintegrating forces of the economic crisis continue to grow.[30]

It is hard to see how the thesis on the sharpening capital-

[27] I. Lemin, "Obostrenie protivorechii i neizbezhnost' voin mezhdu kapitalisticheskimi stranami" (The Sharpening of Contradictions and the Unavoidability of Wars between Capitalist Countries), *Voprosy Ekonomiki* (Problems of Economics), 1952, No. 12, p. 45.
[28] *Ibid.*, p. 40.　　　　[29] *Ibid.*, p. 53.
[30] I. Trakhtenberg, "Osobennosti vosproizvodstva i krizisov v sovremennom kapitalizme" (Characteristics of Reproduction and Crises in Contemporary

ist crisis can provide the pivotal orientation for Soviet Marxism. Repeated for over thirty years in apparent contradiction to the facts, it seems so paradoxical that it is easily dismissed as propaganda. In reality, however, it is a policy-making concept.

In Marxist terminology, the "general crisis" of capitalism (as distinguished from cyclical "depressions") is characterized by the fact that capitalism is no longer capable of functioning in its "classical," "normal" way. The reproduction of capitalist society can no longer be left to (relatively) free enterprise and (relatively) free competition, with the economic laws asserting themselves freely, i.e., in a blind and anarchic manner. The advent of "imperialism" terminates the "classical" period of capitalism and initiates its general crisis; the system can continue to function only through expanding state controls with monopolistic regimentation and domination, wars or preparation for wars, and "intensified exploitation." The "general crisis" does not mean impending collapse and a revolutionary situation, but rather a whole stage of historical development. Thus it means at the same time the continued existence of the capitalist system, and far from excluding "stabilizations," it implies them as its very essence. To Soviet Marxism, the determining factor in the world situation is that the development of socialism *coexists* with and parallels the general crisis of capitalism (instead of *following* it, as envisaged by Marxian theory).

Capitalism), *Voprosy Ekonomiki* (Problems of Economics), 1952, No. 10, p. 85.

The theses on the tasks of the Comintern and the Communist Party of the Soviet Union (CPSU) in 1925, as adopted by the Fourteenth Conference of the CPSU, speak of "two stabilizations": "Side by side with the partial stabilization of capitalism in bourgeois Europe occurs the indubitable growth of state industry and the strengthening of the socialist elements of the national economy in the USSR." [31] The "partial stabilization of capitalism" to which these theses referred has, according to Soviet theory, since been surpassed by other (and even more lasting) forms of partial stabilization (permanent war economy and the formation of one "imperialist camp"), but the parallelism has remained, and with it the "anomaly" of the development toward socialism. As long as it prevails, it is likely to be the basic factor in the orientation of Soviet policy. In this respect, too, "coexistence" is not merely a statement of fact but also a statement of theory. As such it appeared in Lenin's last political guidance, in the Resolutions of the Fourteenth Party Congress,[32] and it has not been discarded since. Even at the time of the foundation of the Cominform and the corresponding intransigent and "hard" foreign policy, Zhdanov declared that "Soviet foreign policy proceeds from the fact of the coexistence for a long period of the two systems—capitalism and socialism. From this it follows that cooperation between the

[31] *Vsesoiuznaia Kommunisticheskaia Partiia (B) v rezoliutsiiakh i resheniiakh s"ezdov konferentsii, i plenumov TsK* (The All-Unon Communist Party [Bolsheviks] in the Resolutions and Decisions of Congresses, Conferences, and Plenums of the Central Committee) (2 vols.; Moscow, Gospolitizdat, 1936), II, 27.
[32] *Ibid.,* II, 48.

USSR and countries with other systems is possible, provided that the principle of reciprocity is observed and that
obligations once assumed are honoured." [33] Coexistence
makes the avoidance of a military conflict with the major
"imperialist" powers (in Soviet language, a "policy of
peace") the objective that must stand in the center of the
entire foreign policy of the government and must "determine all its basic steps" [34]—not because of any innate
peacefulness of the Soviet leaders, but because such a
conflict would "suspend" the capitalist contradictions and
break the "respite" which Lenin declared the prerequisite
for the survival of the Soviet state. Just as the "general
crisis" of capitalism marks a whole period of historical development, so does the "respite": it comprises nothing less
than the time required for bringing the civilization of the
backward East up to the level of the advanced industrial
countries. If and when this objective has been attained,
another turning point in the development of Soviet society *and* capitalist society will have been reached: the
commencing of the "second phase" of socialism would
also initiate the reactivation of the revolutionary potential
in the Western world.

Within the framework of this analysis (extremely crude
and superficial if compared with the theoretical work of
Hilferding, Rosa Luxemburg, Lenin, and Bucharin), modifications and corrections have been introduced since the

[33] Report at the Cominform conference, September, 1947, in *The Strategy
and Tactics of World Communism*, House Document No. 619, Supplement
I, p. 219.
[34] *Vsesoiuznaia Kommunisticheskaia Partiia (B)* (The All-Union Communist Party [Bolsheviks]), II, 48.

time of the Nineteenth Congress of the CPSU. They appear first as mere changes in emphasis, trifling enough and not altering the underlying conception. However, they assume greater significance in the context of Soviet developments during the last period of Stalin's life and after his death, as anticipating the possibility of a long term shift in Soviet policy. In this function, they will be discussed in the chapter on "The Transition from Socialism to Communism"; here only a preliminary statement will be given.

The first of these modifications concerns the interimperialist contradictions and those between the Western world and the Soviet camp. Stalinist policy was in its general tendency oriented toward the actual predominance of the East-West conflict over the interimperialist contradictions. Then, at the time of the Nineteenth Congress, a shift became noticeable. It was first announced by Stalin's dictum on a theoretical controversy: he enjoined the party and its spokesmen that the interimperialist contradictions must be considered as the determining ones.[35] "Theoretically," the conflict between the capitalist and socialist camp is greater than the interimperialist conflicts—"in actuality," however, the latter supersede the former. The derogatory contrast between theory and actuality here served as a warning to bring both into line. And indeed, Stalin's statement was followed by a reexamination of the international situation and by a change in domestic and foreign policy which has become ever more conspicuous since his death. The statement suggested the increasing reliance on the "nor-

[35] "Economic Problems of Socialism in the USSR," in *Current Soviet Policies*, ed. by Leo Gruliow (New York, F. A. Praeger, 1953), pp. 7 ff.

mal" workings of the international political economy, on
the inherent difficulties of the capitalist system rather than
on an assault on its positions from without.[36]

The second modification pertains to the evaluation of
contemporary monopoly capitalism, more specifically, to
that of the growing economic and political function of
the state in the present era. The question whether or not
Soviet Marxism could admit the emergence of "state capitalism" had played a considerable role in the postwar discussion. Varga's book, published in 1946, had been rejected because of its emphasis on state capitalism, particularly as manifested in the United States. His notion of the
integrating and organizing role of the capitalist state
seemed to vitiate the Marxian thesis of the class character
of the state and of the impossibility of coping with the
"anarchic" character of capitalism through centralized
planning. For Soviet Marxism this was not only an ideological offense; it threatened to undermine the theoretical
ground of a revolutionary strategy which denied the long
range effectiveness of capitalist stabilization. In defense
of his thesis on the strengthening of the capitalist state and
its changing role in the capitalist "war economy," Varga
had cited Lenin's proposition on the "transformation of
monopoly capitalism into state-monopoly capitalism" [37]
as suggesting the advent of a new stage of imperialist development which can no longer be interpreted in the sacrosanct terms of the previous stage. But, in spite of the fact

[36] For the modification of the thesis on the "inevitability of war" see pp.
161 f. below.

[37] In the Preface to the first edition of *State and Revolution* (New York,
International Publishers, 1932), p. 5.

that in the subsequent discussion of Varga's book such transformation was recognized,[38] his position was rejected. Only "state-capitalist *tendencies*" were acknowledged, but no new stage characterized by "state capitalism." [39] Recent articles,[40] however, speak without reservation of "state-monopolistic capitalism" and lay great stress on the positive economic function of the capitalist state—much in the sense used in Varga's previously condemned book. Again, the change in emphasis seems quite insignificant, especially since the same articles stress, in traditional Soviet Marxist terms, the progressing "decay" of monopoly capitalism and the aggravated tensions in its economy, internal as well as international. The possibility of any "ultraimperialist" integration of the capitalist world is just as strongly ridiculed as it was before, and capitalist unity is pictured as permeated with intense competitive conflicts on a reduced world market. However, these well-known clichés of Stalinist doctrine now appear within a programmatic reevaluation of capitalism. The flat rejection of one of the most intensively publicized theses in Stalin's

[38] English translation of this discussion in *Soviet Views on the Post-War World Economy* (Washington, D.C., Public Affairs Press, 1948) ; see especially p. 9.

[39] E. Varga, "The Decline of British Imperialism," in *Current Digest of the Soviet Press*, II, No. 32 (September 23, 1950), pp. 3 ff. (condensed from *Voprosy Ekonomiki* [Problems of Economics], 1950, No. 4, pp. 48–71).

[40] V. Cheprakov, "Burshuaznye ekonomisty i gosudarstvenno-monopoliticheskii kapitalizm" (Bourgeois Economists and State-Monopoly Capitalism), *Voprosy Ekonomiki* (Problems of Economics), 1955, No. 9, pp. 134–47; and V. Cheprakov, "Leninskaia teoriia neravnomernosti razvitiia kapitalizma i obostrenie mezhimperialisticheskikh protivorechii v poslevoennyi period" (The Leninist Theory of the Unequal Development of Capitalism and the Sharpening of the Imperialistic Contradictions in the Post-War Period), *Voprosy Ekonomiki* (Problems of Economics), 1956, No. 4, pp. 30–47.

last article (namely, the shrinking of production in the
United States, Britain, and France),[41] the warning against
taking a "simplified view of Lenin's theses on the decay of
imperialism," [42] the admission that since "the time of
Lenin the world situation has fundamentally changed" [43]
—all these in the context of the discussion of the international situation—point to a reformulation of some of the
sacrosanct tenets of the Stalinist era. The former refusal
to recognize a "new stage" of capitalist development is at
least implicitly invalidated when it is acknowledged that
the improving conditions of the workers and the "growth
of production in capitalist countries" (though they did
not take place "on a sound economic foundation") are
due to "basic factors." They are said to be chiefly the
following: [44] (1) the "militarization of the economy" with
its influence on the general level of output; (2) the expansion of the capitalist market, which was rendered possible
by the defeat of Germany and Japan and by the introduction of the Marshall Plan; (3) the long overdue renewal
of fixed capital and modernization of equipment; (4) intensified "exploitation of the working class," mainly
through rationalization and the ensuing higher productivity of labor. These factors are, of course, operating predominantly in the United States, and the fact that they are
now so heavily emphasized in the most authoritative Soviet

[41] Mikoyan, at the Twentieth Party Congress, in *XX S"ezd Kommunisticheskoi Partii Sovetskogo Soiuza* (The Twentieth Congress of the Communist Party of the Soviet Union), I, 323. Although Stalin's name was mentioned specifically in the broadcast of Mikoyan's address, it was omitted in
the official report of the Congress.

[42] Khrushchev, in *ibid.*, I, 15.   [43] Mikoyan, in *ibid.*, I, 323.

[44] Khrushchev, in *ibid.*, I, 15–16, and Khrushchev's speech of November 6,
1957 (as broadcast by Moscow Home Service, p. A-47).

Marxist statements is tantamount to a revaluation of the strength of American capitalism. The draft resolution of the American Communist Party adds another decisive factor of strength: "The ruling class was not so hard pressed as to be unable to continue its established method of governmental rule." [45] In Marxian theory, these economic and political factors are indeed "basic" enough to render the "repeated estimates of impending economic crisis" "harmful" and "unrealistic." [46]

However, it is important to note again the "positive" aspects of this revaluation for the Soviet state. Quite apart from the "unsound foundation" of the stabilized capitalist system, the latter would live up to Engels's [47] and Lenin's [48] notion of the "last stage" of capitalism. Fully developed "state-monopolistic capitalism" [49] would better than mere state-capitalist "tendencies" qualify for the historical level at which capitalism reaches its unsurpassable "limits."

THE "GENERAL CRISIS" AND THE WESTERN PROLETARIAT

The extent to which the Soviet Marxist argument applies the traditional Marxian categories to the analysis of West-

[45] New York *Times*, September 23, 1956.   [46] *Ibid.*
[47] "Anti-Dühring," in *A Handbook of Marxism*, ed. by E. Burns (New York, International Publishers, 1935), pp. 292 ff.
[48] *Imperialism: The Highest Stage of Capitalism* (New York, International Publishers, 1933), pp. 7, 14, 15.
[49] Its main features are summarized in Cheprakov, "Leninskaia teoriia neravnomernosti razvitiia kapitalizma i obostrenie mezhimperialisticheskikh protivorechii v poslevoennyi period" (The Leninist Theory of the Unequal Development of Capitalism and the Sharpening of the Imperialistic Contradictions in the Post-War Period), *Voprosy Ekonomiki* (Problems of Economics), 1956, No. 4, pp. 30–47.

ern society becomes especially clear in the evaluation of
the Western proletariat. During the Stalinist period, Soviet
Marxism denied the existence of an economic basis for any
long-range stabilization of capitalism; the post-Stalinist
modifications come close to recognizing such a basis (although they regard it as "unsound"). In both cases, however, Soviet *theory* denies any fundamental change in the
class situation. The Western proletariat continues to be
considered as the revolutionary class (though not in a
"revolutionary situation"), and, by the same token, as the
final disruptive force in the general crisis. The very same
Resolution of the Fourteenth Party Congress which proclaimed a policy of "peaceful coexistence" as the center
of Soviet foreign policy demanded a strengthening by all
means of the "union between the proletariat of the USSR,
as basis for the world revolution, and the Western European
proletariat and the subjugated peoples." [50] In his conclud-
ing remarks to the Nineteenth Congress, Stalin harked back
to this union by recalling the role of the Soviet proletariat
as the "shock brigade" of the "world revolutionary and
workers' movement." [51] The Twentieth Congress reiterated
the thesis that the laboring masses in the capitalist countries were the strongest force in the struggle against imperialist aggression. The reconciliation of large sections
of labor with the capitalist system and the increase in their
standard of living are explained in terms of "relative impoverishment." Lenin's notion of the "corruption" of the
"labor aristocracy" is retained with slight modifications:

[50] *Vsesoiuznaia Kommunisticheskaia Partiia (B)* (All-Union Communist
Party [Bolsheviks]), II, 48.
[51] *Current Soviet Policies*, p. 235.

the challenge of Soviet socialism, the growth of world communism, and the power of organized labor in the capitalist countries compel the monopoly capitalists to "make a series of social concessions, whose extent and duration depend on the level of the struggle of the working class in the capitalist countries." [52]

But while Soviet theory continues to be concerned with the sharpening class struggle in the capitalist countries, Soviet policy has adjusted itself to the factual situation and has put the Western proletariat "on ice" until the turning point is reached at which it will be reactivated as a revolutionary force. The lumping together of the proletariat with other "peace-loving" social groups indicates recognition of the underlying historical tendency. The "revolutionary class" assumes the features of democratic reformism. Soviet Marxism makes use of a well-known theoretical concept in order to explain and justify this tendency.

According to Soviet Marxism, the failure of the Central European revolutions and the subjugation of formerly independent capitalist countries under American hegemony threw the revolutionary development in Western Europe back to a stage prior to the "bourgeois-democratic revolution." Monopoly-capitalist domination undermines national sovereignties, democratic rights, and liberal ideologies; the great progressive achievements of the ascending bourgeoisie have been betrayed by the monopolistic bourgeoisie. Under these circumstances, it becomes the task of

[52] V. Cheprakov, "Nekotorye voprosy sovremennogo kapitalizma" (Some Questions on Contemporary Capitalism), *Kommunist* (Communist), 1956, No. 1 (January). See also Khrushchev's speech of November 6, 1957 (as broadcast by Moscow Home Service, p. A-47).

the proletariat and the Communist parties in the subjugated countries to lift and carry the "banner of bourgeois democratic freedoms," of "national independence and national sovereignty" [53]—in other words, to take over, or rather to resume, at a higher stage, the historical role of the progressive against the reactionary bourgeoisie. The "minimum program" of the Western Communist parties thus conforms to the Soviet evaluation of the international constellation and must be considered a long-range feature rather than a brief expediency. As such the "minimum program" is incorporated into the ritual formulas of Soviet Marxism: "Defense of national sovereignty and the struggle against the threat of foreign enslavement have become vitally important for the working class and the working people of all countries in the present epoch." [54] Not "proletarian solidarity" but the sponsorship of the "bourgeois-democratic" program provides the tenuous link between the Soviet state and the masses that follow the national Communist parties (a good index for the change in the historical "subject") and this program is used as a lever for activating the interimperialist contradictions.

The "united-front" policy [55] belongs to the same conception. It is dictated by the objective conditions of "organized capitalism" which has made large sections of the laboring classes into beneficiaries of the new prosperity and thereby has seemed to provide a late justification for reformist and antirevolutionary attitudes. If, as Marxism

[53] Stalin, in *Current Soviet Policies*, p. 236.

[54] P. Fedoseev, "Socialism and Patriotism," in *Current Digest of the Soviet Press*, V, No. 28 (August 22, 1953), 4 (condensed from *Kommunist* [Communist], No. 9 [June, 1953], pp. 12–28).

[55] The "united front" is discussed here only in its function in the West, not in the Communist orbit, where it has a very different significance.

has never ceased to claim, the effectiveness of the revolution depends on winning over the majority, not only of the proletariat but of the people, then Communist strategy has to be adjusted to the conditions under which the majority is not revolutionary. And in so far as the nonrevolutionary conditions pertain to a whole stage of the capitalist development, the united-front policy is a fundamental stratagem which cannot be discarded at the discretion of the leadership. Indeed, the united front has been an objective of Soviet policy at least ever since 1934, although the emphasis and scope of the effort have changed several times. What is decisive for the evaluation is not whether the united front aims at the rank and file, or also at the leadership of the socialist parties and trade unions, not whether it aims beyond these groups at some or all of the "bourgeois parties," but whether the policy is likely to alter the very character of the Communist parties. Even the problem of the success of the policy is of minor importance. Since the response of the would-be noncommunist allies is determined by the degree of the functioning of Western society, the united front is bound to remain abortive and "localized" as long as this society remains a going concern. If this should no longer be the case, the united-front policy would be all but superfluous. However, the mere sustained *effort* to achieve a united front may make the Communist parties in important aspects the political heirs of the Social Democratic parties.[56] As the latter tend to lose the working-class character and approach that of the middle-class parties, a vacuum may arise in which the

---

[56] See p. 242 below. See also the Joint Communiqué of Communist and Workers' Parties, New York *Times*, November 22, 1957.

Communists may appear as the sole representatives of working-class interests—interests which in turn would call for nonrevolutionary representation. A tendency in this direction is noticeable in France and in Italy, and the declarations, at the Twentieth Congress of the CPSU, on the possibility of a parliamentary way to socialism [57] recall substantially Engels's preface to Marx's *Class Struggles in France,* which was for a long time taken as guidance for Social Democratic strategy. We may venture the suggestion that this tendency would be much stronger were it not for the identification of the interests of the national Communist parties with that of the USSR and for the political countermeasures against the Communist parties.

In view of the constancy of the main elements of Soviet Marxism, the question must be asked whether there is a "break" between Leninism and Stalinism. The differences between the first years of the Bolshevik Revolution and the fully developed Stalinist state are obvious; they readily appear as the steady growth of totalitarianism and authoritarian centralization, as the growth of the dictatorship not of but over the proletariat and the peasantry. But if the dialectical law of the turn from quantity into quality was ever applicable, it was in the transition from Leninism (after the October Revolution) to Stalinism. The "retardation" of the revolution in the West and the stabilization of capitalism made for qualitative changes in the structure of Soviet society. Lenin tried to counter the isolation of the revolution in a backward country by establishing the pri-

---

[57] Khrushchev, at the Twentieth Party Congress, in *XX S" ezd Kommunisticheskoi Partii Sovetskogo Soiuza* (The Twentieth Congress of the Communist Party of the Soviet Union, I, 38 ff.; Mikoyan, in *ibid.,* pp. 312 ff.

ority of industrialization over socialist liberation (it is epitomized in his definition of socialism as electrification plus Soviet power)—the priority of the Soviet state over Soviet workers.[58] Lenin died before the ascent of fascism in Germany; from then on, the "respite" for which he had striven seemed to be of an ever shorter duration. Thus, Stalin accelerated the program of "civilization" which Lenin had made the prerequisite for the preservation of the Soviet system. The height of the Stalinist terror coincided with the consolidation of the Hitler regime. At the outbreak of the Second World War, Soviet civilization had progressed far enough to withstand the most powerful war machine of an advanced industrial country. Postwar reconstruction was amazingly fast in view of the unprecedented destruction—but so was the reconstruction in the other camp. Soviet policy at the end of the war, with its series of occupations and "revolutions from above," regardless of the constellation of the indigenous social forces in the respective countries, indicates that Stalin did not believe that a revolutionary system was maturing in Europe, or that the Soviet state could depend for its long-range preservation on the colonial revolutions. Lenin's prescription was still valid, and set the overriding objective of the Soviet state during the "first phase" of socialism. It has been ritualized in the formula, *"to outstrip the economic level of the chief capitalist countries."* [59] Soviet society

[58] For the most striking examples of this attitude (then fully endorsed by Trotsky), see Carr, *The Bolshevik Revolution*, II, *passim*, especially pp. 93 f., 188 f., 213–16.

[59] Stalin at the Eighteenth Party Congress in 1939, in *Leninism* (New York, International Publishers, 1942), p. 448; and again after the war in his speech of February 9, 1946, in *Pravda*, February 10, 1946. The formula

continued to grow; the development of socialist production continued to increase the material and technical potential while repressing the human potential.

But the very success of Stalinist civilization leads to an
impasse, which is clearly defined in the Marxist-Leninist
theory of imperialism. According to this theory, the war
economy provides an outlet for the aggravating inherent
contradictions of capitalism, although the capitalist consolidation thus created is precarious and short-lived and
bound to explode in wars between the competing imperialist countries. However, if and when there is a "common
enemy" *outside* the capitalist world, whose growing power
and expansion requires the maintenance of a "permanent"
war or preparedness economy in which the imperialist
powers unite, while at the same time technological progress
enables capitalism to maintain this economy without no-
ticeably reducing the standard of living (perhaps even increasing it!), then a situation prevails where the very
growth of the Soviet orbit seems to sustain the unity and
stability of the "imperialist" orbit. The former cannot
break this impasse without fundamentally altering its policy—and this in turn is conditional upon a corresponding
advance of Soviet society. Such a change in policy—aiming at the dissolution of the "war economy" on which the
capitalist stabilization is held to rest—presupposes that
the Soviet state has attained a level of competitive strength
which enables it to "relax" its intransigent and aggressive

---

also concludes N. Voznesenskii's *Voennaia Ekonomika SSSR v Period Oteche-
stvennoi Voiny* (The Military Economy of the USSR in the Period of the
Fatherland War) (Moscow, Gospolitizdat, 1947); it was not because of
this conclusion that the book was repudiated.

strategy. Only such a relaxation, sustained systematically and for a long time, could possibly shatter the international capitalist stabilization and revert the capitalist system to that "normality" in which the internal contradictions are supposed to ripen and ultimately to explode. The ideological and political changes, which began at the time of the Nineteenth Congress and gained momentum during 1955–1956 indicated an impending shift in policy. Its timing was not a matter of discretion by the Soviet leadership, nor was Stalin's death the decisive factor. The latter must rather be seen in the fulfillment of the fundamental prerequisite for restoring the "normal" capitalist-socialist dynamic, namely, the attainment of the level of advanced industrial civilization for Soviet society. If, as we propose, the recent policy changes suggest that, in the Soviet Marxist evaluation, this prerequisite has now been established, then these changes would usher in an essentially new stage in international Communist developments.

The following chapters will survey the main features of Soviet Marxism during the Stalinist period and try to connect them with the underlying trend in the construction of Soviet society.

3. *The New Rationality*

WE SHALL BEGIN with the attempt to define, in a preliminary way, the rationale of the civilization of "socialism in one country," that is to say, the principles which govern its construction and its inner dynamic. In doing so, we accept as guidance neither the term "socialism," nor its simple negation, nor "totalitarianism" and its synonyms—not socialism because the validation of the concept depends on agreement on definition and can even then only be the result of the examination; not totalitarianism because the notion is applicable to a wide variety of social systems with different and antagonistic structures. We shall rather try to arrive at the identification of these principles by assembling those features of the construction of Soviet society which have remained generally constant throughout all stages, regressions, and modifications. They may be restated, in summary form, as follows:

1. Total industrialization, on the basis of nationalized production, with priority of "main division I" (production of the means of production)

2. Progressive collectivization of agriculture aiming at the ultimate transformation of collective into state property

3. General mechanization of labor, extension of "poly-

technic" training, leading to "equalization" between urban and rural occupations

4. Gradual rise in the general standard of living conditional on the maintenance of the goals set in Points 1–3

5. Building up of a universal work morale, competitive efficiency, elimination of all transcendent psychological and ideological elements ("Soviet realism")

6. Preservation and strengthening of the state, military, managerial, and party machinery as the vehicle for these processes (1–5)

7. Transition to the distribution of the social product according to individual needs after attainment of the goals set in Points 1–5

The goals are conditional upon the attainment of the productivity level of the advanced industrial countries; this is the termination point for the presently prevailing trends. Beyond this point, new and qualitatively different trends are stipulated; they will be indicated in Chapter 8, in an attempt to evaluate the prospects of the "transition to communism."

The following principles refer to the Soviet Marxist interpretation of this transition:

1. The development of Soviet society from socialism to communism takes place as the dialectical process of unfolding internal and external contradictions.

2. The internal contradictions can be solved rationally, without "explosion," on the basis of the socialist economy under the control and direction of the Soviet state.

3. The fundamental internal contradiction, which provides the motor power for the transition to communism, is

that between the constantly growing productive forces and the lagging relations of production. Its rational and controlled development makes for a gradual and administrative transition to communism.

4. The gradual transition to communism occurs under conditions of capitalist encirclement (environment). The external contradictions involved in this situation can be finally solved only at the international level—through a socialist revolution in some of the advanced capitalist countries.

5. This solution is itself a long-range process, covering a whole period of capitalist and socialist development. The weakness of the revolutionary potential in the capitalist world and the still prevailing backwardness of the Soviet orbit necessitate a new extended "respite" and "coexistence" of the two systems.

6. The Soviet Union must preserve this respite by utilizing conflicts among the imperialist powers,[1] avoiding a war with them, and discouraging revolutionary experiments ("seizure of power") in the advanced capitalist countries.

7. The solution of the external contradictions will ripen through (*a*) the inherent capitalist and intercapitalist contradictions, which will make the proletariat again the his-

---

[1] The last two points summarize Lenin's conception for the "third historic phase of the Russian Revolution" (beginning with the victory of the October Revolution and lasting into the present), as paraphrased by Stalin. See Stalin, *Sochineniia* (Works), (13 vols.; Moscow, Gospolitizdat, 1946-51), VI, 153; also L. F. Shorichev, *Voprosy strategii i taktiki v trudakh I. V. Stalina perioda 1921–1925 godov* (Problems of Strategy and Tactics in the Writings of J. V. Stalin, 1921-1925) (Moscow, Pravda, 1950).

torical agent of the revolution; (*b*) the growing economic, political, and strategic power of the USSR.

8. The "main reserves" supporting these basic revolutionary forces are the semiproletarian and petty peasant masses in the developed countries, and the liberation movements in the colonies and dependent countries.

The social process guided by these principles is more than the industrialization of the backward areas of the East on the basis of nationalization under totalitarian administration. What is happening here extends beyond the borders of the Communist orbit. Communist industrialization proceeds through "skipping" and telescoping whole historical periods. The fundamental difference between Western and Soviet society is paralleled by a strong trend toward assimilation. Both systems show the common features of late industrial civilization—centralization and regimentation supersede individual enterprise and autonomy; competition is organized and "rationalized"; there is joint rule of economic and political bureaucracies; the people are coordinated through the "mass media" of communication, entertainment industry, education. If these devices prove to be effective, democratic rights and institutions might be granted by the constitution and maintained without the danger of their abuse in opposition to the system. Nationalization, the abolition of private property in the means of production, does not, by itself, constitute an essential distinction as long as production is centralized and controlled over and above the population. Without initiative and control "from below" by the "immediate producers," nationalization is but a technological-political device for increasing the productivity of labor, for accelerating the development of the productive forces and for their control from above (central planning)—a change in the mode of domination, streamlining of domination, rather than prerequisite for its abolition. By abrogating the individual as the autonomous economic and political subject, certain "obsolete" brakes on the development of the productive forces are eliminated. Individual units of production (material and intellectual) are no longer adequate instrumentalities for integrating society; technological progress and mass production shatter the individualistic forms in which progress operated during the liberalist era.

But, at the same time, technical progress and growing productivity threaten to counteract this trend. Increasing social capacity and wealth militate against the repressive organization and division of labor. Awareness of these countertrends manifests itself in the recent policy changes and in the increased Soviet Marxist emphasis on the necessary transition to the "second phase of socialism," which will be discussed below.[2]

The Soviet system seems to be another example of a late-comer "skipping" several developmental stages after a long period of protracted backwardness, joining and running ruthlessly ahead of a general trend in late industrial society. The skipped stages are those of enlightened absolutism and liberalism, of free competitive enterprise, of matured middle-class culture with its individualistic and

[2] See Chapter 8.

humanitarian ideologies. The effort to catch up, in record
time and from a state of backwardness, with the level of
the advanced industrial countries led to the construction
and utilization of a huge productive apparatus within a
system of domination and regimentation incompatible with
individualistic rationality and liberalism. Here lie the
roots of the relentless struggle of Soviet Marxism against
the liberal and idealist elements of "bourgeois ideologies"; the struggle reflects the societal organization of the
productive forces as instruments of control rather than
liberation.

The idea of Reason which was representative of modern
Western civilization centered on the autonomy of the *Ego
Cogitans,* whose independent thinking discovered and implemented the laws of the rational organization of nature
and society. The Ego was itself subject to the objective laws
of nature—but subjective and objective Reason were to coincide in a society that had mastered nature and transformed it into a practically inexhaustible material for the
development of human needs and faculties. Attainment of
this goal called for the emancipation of the individual as
long as the state, the established authorities, were an im-
pediment to technical and economic progress. The latter
was expected to result from the reasonably free functioning of a multitude of individual enterprises (economic,
political, cultural), and the rationality of the whole was
to assert itself through the competitive process of these individual units. This process required a high degree of individual autonomy, foresight, calculability, perspicacity
—qualities that had to be acquired not only in the actual

business of living but also in the preparation for it: in the
family, in school, in the privacy of thinking and feeling.
Social progress thus depended to a large extent on the autonomy of the individual, that is, on the distinction and
tension between subjective and objective Reason, and on
a solution of this tension in such a way that objective Reason (the social need and the social interest) preserved and
developed subjective Reason (the individual need and the
individual interest).

Technological progress and the development of large
industry contained two (antagonistic) tendencies which
had a decisive impact on this process: (1) mechanization
and rationalization of labor could free an ever greater
quantum of individual energy (and time) from the material work process and allow the expenditure of this
energy and time for the free play of human faculties beyond the realm of material production; and (2) the same
mechanization and rationalization generated attitudes of
standardized conformity and precise submission to the
machine which required adjustment and reaction rather
than autonomy and spontaneity.[3] If nationalization and
centralization of the industrial apparatus goes hand in
hand with counteracting the first of these tendencies, i.e.,
with the subjugation and enforcement of labor as a full-
time occupation, progress in industrialization is tantamount to progress in domination: attendance to the machine, the scientific work process, becomes totalitarian,
affecting all spheres of life. The technological perfection

[3] Thorstein Veblen, *The Instinct of Workmanship* (New York, B. W.
Huebsch, 1922), pp. 306 ff.

of the productive apparatus dominates the rulers and the ruled while sustaining the distinction between them. Autonomy and spontaneity are confined to the level of efficiency and performance within the established pattern. Intellectual effort becomes the business of engineers, specialists, agents. Privacy and leisure are handled as relaxation from and preparation for labor in conformity with the apparatus. Dissent is not only a political crime but also technical stupidity, sabotage, mistreatment of the machine. Reason is nothing but the rationality of the whole: the uninterrupted functioning and growth of the apparatus. The experience of the harmony between the individual and the general interest, between the human and the social need, remains a mere promise.

The Soviet Marxist self-interpretation of this rationality may serve to elucidate its function. According to this interpretation, the October Revolution has created a "conformity" between production relations and the "character of the productive forces" which eliminates the conflict between the individual and society, between the particular and the common interest. Consequently, Reason ceases to be split into its subjective and objective manifestations; it is no longer antagonistic to and beyond reality, a mere "idea"—but is realized in the society itself. This society, defined as socialist in terms of Marxian theory, becomes the sole standard of truth and falsehood; there can be no transcendence in thought and action, no individual autonomy because the Nomos of the whole is the true Nomos. To transcend that which is, to set subjective reason against state reason, to appeal to higher norms and values, belongs to the prerogatives of class society, where the Nomos of society is not the Nomos of its individuals. In contrast, Soviet society institutionalizes the real interests of the individuals—by this token, it contains all standards of true and false, right and wrong. "Soviet realism" is not a mere matter of philosophy and aesthetics; it is the general pattern of intellectual and practical behavior demanded by the structure of Soviet society.

To be sure, outside the validity of Soviet Marxism, where the equation of the Soviet state with a free and rational society is not accepted, this notion of the "realization of Reason" is itself an ideology. Since in actuality the individual interest is still antagonistic to the interest of the whole, since nationalization is not socialization, the rationality of Soviet realism appears as utterly irrational, as terroristic conformity. However, to stop the evaluation of the new Soviet rationality at this point would be to overlook its decisive function. For what is irrational if measured from without the system is rational within the system. The key propositions of Soviet Marxism have the function of announcing and commanding a definite practice, apt to create the facts which the propositions stipulate. They claim no truth-value of their own but proclaim a preestablished truth which is to be realized through a certain attitude and behavior. They are pragmatic directives for action. For example, Soviet Marxism is built around a small number of constantly recurring and rigidly canonized statements to the effect that Soviet society is a socialist society without exploitation, a full democracy in which the constitutional rights of all citizens are guaranteed and enforced; or, on the other side, that present-day capitalism exists in a state of sharpening class struggle, depressed living standards, unemployment, and so forth. Thus formulated and taken by themselves, these statements are obviously false—according to Marxian as well as non-Marxian criteria. But within the context in which they appear, their falsity does not invalidate them, for, to Soviet Marxism, their verification is not in the given facts, but in "tendencies," in a historical process in which the commanded political practice will *bring about* the desired facts.

The value of these statements is pragmatic rather than logical, as is clearly suggested by their syntactical structure. They are unqualified, inflexible formulas calling for an unqualified, inflexible response. In endless repetition, the same noun is always accompanied by the same adjectives and participles; the noun "governs" them immediately and directly so that whenever it occurs they follow "automatically" in their proper place. The same verb always "moves" the proposition in the same direction, and those addressed by the proposition are supposed to move the same way. These statements do not attribute a predicate to a subject (in the sense of formal or of dialectical logic); they do not develop the subject in its specific relations— all these cognitive processes lie outside the propositional context, i.e., in the "classics" of Marxism, and the routine statements only recall what is preestablished. They are to be "spelled," learned mechanically, monotonously, and literally; they are to be performed like a ritual which accompanies the realizing action. They are to recall and sustain the required practice. Taken by themselves they are no more committed to the truth than are orders or advertisements: their "truth" is in their effect. Soviet Marxism here shares in the decline of language and communication in the age of mass societies. It is senseless to treat the propositions of the official ideology at the cognitive level: they are a matter of practical, not of theoretical reason. If propositions lose their cognitive value to their capacity of bringing about a desired effect, that is to say, if they are to be understood as directives for a specific behavior, then *magical* elements gain ascendancy over comprehending thought and action. The difference between illusion and reality becomes just as obliterated as that between truth and falsehood if illusions guide a behavior that shapes and changes reality. With respect to its actual effect on primitive societies, magic has been described as a "body of purely practical acts, performed as means to an end." [4] The description may well be applied to formally theoretical propositions. The official language itself assumes magical character.

However, the contemporary reactivation of magical features in communication is far from primitive. The irrational elements of magic enter into the system of scientifically planned and practiced administration—they become part of the scientific management of society. Moreover, the magical features of Soviet theory are turned into an instrument for rescuing the truth. While the ritual formulas, severed from their original cognitive

[4] Bronislaw Malinowski, *Magic, Science and Religion* (Anchor Books; New York, Doubleday, 1954), p. 70.

context, thus serve to provide unquestioned directives for unquestioned mass behavior, they retain, in a hypostatized form, their historical substance. The rigidity with which they are celebrated is to preserve the purity of this substance in the face of an apparently contradicting reality and to enforce verification in the face of apparently contradicting facts which make the pre-established truth into a paradox. It defies reason; it seems absurd. But the absurdity of Soviet Marxism has an objective ground: it reflects the absurdity of a historical situation in which the realization of the Marxian promises appeared—only to be delayed again—and in which the new productive forces are again used as instruments for productive repression. The ritualized language preserves the original content of Marxian theory as a truth that must be believed and enacted against all evidence to the contrary: the people must do and feel and think as if their state were the reality of that reason, freedom, and justice which the ideology proclaims, and the ritual is to assure such behavior. The practice guided by it indeed moves large underprivileged masses on an international scale. In this process, the original promises of Marxian theory play a decisive part. The new form of Marxian theory corresponds to its new historical agent—a backward population which is to become what it "really" is: a revolutionary force which changes the world. The ritualization of this theory has kept it alive against the power of factual refutation and communicated it, in ideological form, to a backward and suppressed population which is to be whipped into political action, contesting and challenging advanced industrial civilization. In its magical use, Marxian theory assumes a new rationality.

The paradoxical character of Soviet rationality is not confined to its own orbit; it also pertains to statements referring to the capitalist orbit. To be sure, straight falsehood may often be attributed to mere propaganda requirements. But here too, the recurrent pattern of falsehood beyond plausibility suggests the intent of defiance: the concerted struggle with facts which, measured against the world historical "truth," are accidental and to be negated. If, for example, *Pravda*'s special New York correspondent reports [5] that in the card catalogue of the New York Public Library he did not find a single book "about Stalingrad or the Soviet army in general," the fact that the New York Public Library's catalogue contains about "two dozen cards bearing directly on the Battle of Stalingrad" and "about 500 cards under 'Army, Russia' " is, for the Soviet reporter, "negated" by the essential context of systematic American hostility to the Soviet Union. Or, if William Z. Foster's *History of the Communist Party of the United States*, published in 1952—at a time when the party was practically without any popular support, its leadership in jail, its membership a negligible quantity—ends with a chapter headed "The Party of the Working Class and the Nation," and with a section headed "The Progress of the Communist Party," then the shattering unreality of these statements is itself part of their function: to refuse submission to the facts, to uphold and accomplish the true nature of the party as the "Leninist mass party" against its inadequate factual existence.

[5] New York *Times*, February 2, 1953.

Hypostatized into a ritual pattern, Marxian theory becomes ideology. But its content and function distinguish
it from the "classical" forms of ideology: it is not "false
consciousness," [6] but rather consciousness of falsehood, a
falsehood which is "corrected" in the context of the "higher
truth" represented by the objective historical interest. This
tends to cancel the ideological freedom of consciousness
and to assimilate ideology with the basis as part of consciously directed social action. As the contrast between
ideology and reality sharpens with the growing contrast
between the productive potential of society and its repressive use, the previously free elements of the ideology
are subjected to administrative control and direction. The
weakening of the relative independence of ideologies from
established social needs, the ossification of their content,
is characteristic of the present stage of civilization. In its
ossified form, emptied of its meaning which was critical
of and antagonistic to the established society, the ideology
becomes a tool of domination. If ideas like human liberty
and reason or individual autonomy of thought are no
longer comprehended in their still unfulfilled claim but
are items in the routine equipment of newspapers, states-
men, entertainers, and advertisers who betray them daily
in their business of perpetuating the status quo, then the
progressive notions of the ideology are deprived of their
transcendent function and made into clichés of desired behavior.

The decline of independent thought vastly increases the
power of words—their magical power, with whose destruc-

[6] Engels, Letter to Franz Mehring, July 14, 1893, in Marx and Engels,
Selected Works (2 vols.; Moscow, Foreign Languages Publishing House,
1949–50), II, 451.

tion the process of civilization had once begun. Protected against the intellectual effort which traces the way back from the words to the ideas they once expressed, the words become weapons in the hand of an administration against which the individual is completely powerless. Through the means of mass communication, they transmit the objectives of the administration, and the underlying population responds with the expected behavior.

The rationality which had accompanied the progress of Western civilization had developed in the tension between thought and its object: truth and falsehood were sought in the relation between the comprehending subject and its world, and logic was the comprehensible development of this relation, expressed in propositions. Just as the object of thought was taken as something by and in itself (no matter how inseparable from thought), so the subject was held to be something "for itself"—free to discover the truth about its object—and especially the still hidden truth: its unrealized potentialities. Cognitive freedom was held to be an essential part of practical freedom, of the ability to act in accordance with the truth, to realize the subjective and objective potentialities. Where this relation between subject and object no longer prevails, traditional logic has lost its ground. Truth and falsehood then are no longer qualities of cognitive propositions but of a preestablished and predefined state of affairs to which thought and action are to be geared. Logic then is measured by the adequacy of such thought and action to attain the predetermined goal.

4. *Socialism in One Country?*

THE NEW rationality, which the preceding chapter tried to identify, characterizes the atmosphere in which the construction of Soviet society takes place. More specifically, this rationality pertains to the paradoxical nature of Soviet society, where the most methodical system of domination is to prepare the ground for freedom, where the policy of suppression is justified as the policy of liberation. We did not accept the assumption that Soviet Marxism is simply a superimposed ideology, serving as a prop for the regime; nor did we accept the opposite assumption that Soviet society is a socialist society in the Marxian sense. Therefore we cannot explain the paradox merely as the plain contrast between ideology and reality. The paradox rather seems to reflect the construction of Soviet society under the "anomalous" conditions of coexistence.

We have stressed that as long as control over the means of production and over the distribution of the product is not vested in the "immediate producers" themselves, that is, as long as there is no control and initiative "from below," nationalization is a mere instrument of more effective domination as well as industrialization, of increasing and manipulating the productivity of labor within the framework of mass societies. In this respect, Soviet society follows the general trend of late industrial civilization. However, the question must be asked whether, in spite of this fact, Soviet nationalization, under the historical condition of its progress, does not possess an inner dynamic which may counteract the repressive tendencies and transform the structure of Soviet society—regardless of the real or alleged policies and objectives of the leadership. Within the scope of this study, the dynamic will be traced only in so far as it is reflected in the development of Soviet Marxism, and the discussion will be confined to some selected conceptions which seem to be particularly illuminating. We shall take the conception of "socialism in one country," the dialectic of the Soviet state governed by this policy conception, certain changes in the ideology, and finally the "transition from socialism to communism," in which this dynamic culminates.

The doctrine of "socialism in one country," which provided the general framework for Soviet Marxism during the Stalinist period,[1] also serves to provide a world-historical justification for the repressive functions of the Soviet state. The doctrine has retained throughout its dependence on the international development: the initial isolation of the Bolshevik Revolution, the confinement of socialism to backward areas, and the reconsolidation of capitalism on an intercontinental scale are held responsible for the internal as well as external contradictions which plague Soviet society. Stalinist doctrine holds that the former can

[1] M. M. Rozental, *Marksistskii dialekticheskii metod* (Marxist Dialectical Method) (Moscow, Gospolitizdat, 1951), pp. 57, 108, and *passim*.

be solved by and within the Soviet Union, through the "directing" role of the state, while the latter can be ultimately removed only through the international process [2]—through revolution within the capitalist world. In reality, however, the external contradictions perpetuate the internal ones and vice versa, so that the distinction loses its finality; by its own development, "socialism in one country" dissolves into a larger conception which reestablishes the essential links between the construction of Soviet society and the capitalist development.

The Soviet Marxist designation of the internal contradictions varies with the various stages of the development. Chiefly they are defined in terms of the contradiction between the proletariat and the peasantry,[3] between the socialist state and "our own bourgeoisie," [4] between kulaks and poor peasants, mental and physical labor, "old consciousness" and socialist mentality.[5] Their basis is identified as the contradiction between the growth of the productive forces and the lagging level of consumption. The external contradictions are interpreted in terms of a shift in the class struggle to the international arena:

While one end of the class struggle is being conducted within the boundaries of the USSR, its other end stretches out to the territories

[2] The first "authentic" formulation in Stalin's "Results of the Work of the Fourteenth Party Conference" (written in 1925). See *Sochineniia* (Works) (13 vols.; Moscow, Gospolitizdat, 1946–51), VII, 90–132.

[3] Stalin, "Results of the Work of the Fourteenth Party Conference," quoted in his *Problems of Leninism* (New York, International Publishers, 1934), p. 63.

[4] Stalin, "Letter to Ivanov," in *The Strategy and Tactics of World Communism*, House Document No. 619, Supplement I (Washington, D.C., U.S. Government Printing Office, 1948), p. 151.

[5] Rozental, *Marksistskii dialekticheskii metod* (Marxist Dialectical Method), pp. 293 ff.

of the bourgeois states surrounding us. . . . The more acute aspect
of class struggle affecting the USSR has now been transferred to
the international arena.[6]

According to Marx, the class struggle is international
by its very nature; it would be meaningless to talk about a
"shift" to the international arena. The Soviet Marxist notion has a different connotation: it tries to adjust the Marxian theory of the class struggle to the historical fact of its
"neutralization" in the advanced industrial countries. The
notion is linked to the "two-camp" doctrine; the "democratic socialist" camp, led by the Soviet Union, represents
the fight for the "real" class interests of the international
proletariat. Since the Western proletariat is geographically
"enclosed" in the "imperialist camp" (although "in reality" belonging to the socialist camp), it cannot effectively
assert its "real" interest—this function rather devolves
upon the group of nations joined in the Soviet camp. The
conflict between the real and the immediate interests of the
proletariat, contained from the beginning in Marxian theory, now becomes the conflict between two international
groupings: the "external" proletariat of the backward
countries is supposed to fight for the real interest, assuming
the historical task of the proletariat as a whole. With this
change in protagonist, the content and strategy of the class
struggle also change. The class struggle becomes a fight for
space and populations, and the social issues become a function of political issues. The class interests of the Western

[6] Stalin in 1937, quoted in a lecture on the "Marxist-Leninist Theory of
Classes and Class Struggle," Soviet Home Service, Moscow Radio, March 5,
1951. See also Rozental, *Marksistskii dialekticheskii metod* (Marxist Dialectical Method), p. 302.

proletariat (and for that matter of the entire proletariat) are sustained in Soviet policy only to the degree to which they do not conflict with the political interests of the USSR. Thus, the class struggle is not transferred to the international level, but rather transubstantiated into an international political struggle.

The transubstantiation of the class struggle vitiates all attempts to solve the internal contradictions of Soviet society without changing its very structure. Marxism depends, for the attainment of its goals, on the solution of the conflict between the productive forces and their repressive organization and utilization. According to Marx, the abolition of capitalism is not an end in itself but the means for solving this conflict, thereby terminating the enslavement of man by his labor and the domination of men by men. And in so far as such enslavement is institutionalized in the process of production, it can be abolished only in the process of production, and the individuals can be free only if they themselves control production. There may be several stages on this way to freedom—even stages of repression (Marx has sketched them in his *Critique of the Gotha Program*)—but unless this way is traveled by the laboring class itself, as the sole historical agent of liberation, the socialist revolution has no *raison d'être*. And if the revolution does not from the beginning reverse the relationship between the laborer and the means of his labor, that is to say, transfer control over them to him, it does not have a *raison d'être* essentially different from that of capitalist society. Abolition of private property in the means of production is thus substantially linked with transfer of control to the laborers themselves. As long as such transfer is not accomplished, the revolution is bound to reproduce the very antagonisms which it strives to overcome. They appear in manifold forms: as the repressive utilization of the nationalized means of production, as the contrast between the level of productivity and the level of consumption, as the conflict between social and individual needs, between state and private and semiprivate property; or in the international arena, between the interests of the USSR and those of the foreign Communist parties, between the objectives of national Soviet security and those of socialist policy. They persist even if "socialism in one country" becomes so to speak "socialism in one orbit," for, in the last analysis, they are due to the very factors which brought about and sustained the coexistence of the two systems. If Soviet Marxism justifies the perpetuation of the repressive state machine by the continued prevalence of the "capitalist threat," it admits that the structure of Soviet society still is antagonistic; and that the solution of these antagonisms depends on a fundamental change in the international constellation. In 1938, Stalin implied that the internal contradictions had been solved by the successful building of socialism in the USSR;[7] in 1952, he emphasized again the internal contradictions, which now reappear on a different level.[8]

The historical situation thus overrides the Stalinist con-

[7] "Letter to Ivanov," in *The Strategy and Tactics of World Communism*, House Document 619, Supplement I, p. 150.

[8] "Economic Problems of Socialism," in *Current Soviet Policies*, ed. by Leo Gruliow (New York, F. A. Praeger, 1953), pp. 5, 11, 14. See below, pp. 166 f.

ception of "socialism in one country," according to which the internal contradictions could be solved by the Soviet state while the external contradictions continued to prevail. The external contradictions perpetuate the internal contradictions. According to Soviet Marxism, the "capitalist environment" enforces the continued strengthening of the repressive political and military establishment and prevents the free utilization of the productive forces for the satisfaction of individual needs. But the continued strengthening of the Soviet political and military establishment in turn perpetuates the "capitalist environment" and even promotes its intercontinental unification. Ever since Lenin, Soviet Marxism has held that the USSR will ultimately not be able to survive unless it succeeds in breaking the deadlock in its own favor. The break is expected to come about through the reactivation of the "inherent capitalist contradictions" in the "imperialist camp." They are frozen in the Western defense economy; the dissolution of this integrated political economy is, therefore, the indispensable first objective.

But the Soviet leadership can hope to attain this objective only if the USSR is no longer a military and political threat to the West, that is, if the productive power of the Soviet state is redirected to serve the needs and faculties of its citizens. This would mean that production and the production relations are reorganized in such a way that the rise of the level of material and intellectual culture is not the mere by-product but the goal of the social effort. To Soviet Marxism, such a transformation of Soviet society appears as a historical necessity, as a requirement of international politics in the era of coexistence. Soviet Marxism is forced to recognize the interdependence of the two sets of contradictions which makes the social issues determine the political issues. The vital aim of breaking the deadlock can be achieved only by a transformation of Soviet society which is to establish the economic and cultural superiority of socialism over capitalism, to spread socialism "by contagion," and thus to provide the basis for unfreezing the class struggle in the capitalist world.

In order to evaluate the prospects of this transformation, we shall have to discuss the social structure of the Soviet state, which, according to Soviet theory, is to remain the "directing agent" of social change.

5. *The Dialectic of the Soviet State*

A BRIEF SUMMARY suffices to recall the chief elements in Stalin's theory of the retention and growth of the socialist state. In contrast to Engels's formula of the "withering away" of the state, which is valid for the victory of socialism in all or in a majority of countries, the socialist state must assume new decisive functions under the conditions of "socialism in one country" and "capitalist encirclement." These functions change in accordance with the internal development and the international situation. In the first phase of the development (from the October revolution to the "elimination of the exploiting classes"), the functions of the state were: (*a*) "to suppress the overthrown classes inside the country," (*b*) "to defend the country from foreign attack," and (*c*) "economic organization and cultural education." In the second phase (from the "elimination of the capitalist elements in town and country" to the "complete victory of the socialist system and the adoption of the new constitution") function (*a*) ceased and was supplanted by that of "protecting socialist property"; functions (*b*) and (*c*) "fully remained." Moreover, the state is to continue also in the period of communism "unless the capitalist encirclement" is liquidated, and "unless the danger of foreign military attack has disappeared"—only then will it "atrophy." [1] As early as 1930, Stalin had condensed the dialectic of the socialist state to the formula: "The highest possible development of the power of the State with the object of preparing the conditions for the dying away of the State—that is the Marxist formula." [2] Later on, emphasis was placed on the strengthening of the state power prior to and during the transition to communism. [3]

The continuation of the state in the first period of socialism is implied in the original Marxian conception. Marx assumed that the "enslaving subordination of the individuals to the devision of labor" would continue during the First Phase of socialism. [4] Consequently, the state would continue; its "withering away would be gradual and preceded by a period of transformation" of the political institutions. Thus was the development outlined by Engels as early as 1847, [5] and it was again emphasized in the eighties in his polemic against the anarchists:

The anarchists . . . declare that the proletarian revolution must begin with the abolition of the political organization of the state. But the only organization which the proletariat finds available

[1] Stalin, "Report on the Work of the Central Committee to the Eighteenth Party Congress," in *Leninism* (New York, International Publishers, 1942), p. 474.

[2] Stalin, *Political Report to the Sixteenth Party Congress* (New York, Workers Library Publishers, 1930), p. 171.

[3] Stalin, *Marksizm i voprosy iazykoznaniia* (Marxism and Linguistic Problems) (Moscow, Gospolitizdat, 1950). See also M. M. Rozental, *Marksistskii dialekticheskii metod* (Marxist Dialectical Method) (Moscow, Gospolitizdat, 1951), p. 109.

[4] "Critique of the Gotha Program," in Marx and Engels, *Selected Works* (2 vols.; Moscow, Foreign Languages Publishing House, 1949–50), II, 23; see above, p. 20.

[5] *Principles of Communism*, Questions 17 and 18.

(*fertig*) after its victory is the state. This state may have to undergo considerable changes before it can fulfil its new functions. But to destroy it in one moment would mean to destroy the only organization with which the victorious proletariat would exercise the power which it has just conquered—to subdue its capitalist enemies and to carry through that economic revolution of society without which the victory would of necessity end in a new defeat.[6]

The Marx quotations around which Lenin built his refutation of Kautsky in *State and Revolution* do not contradict this conception.[7] The "state machinery" which is to be shattered, the "bureaucratic and military machinery" which cannot be transferred from one hand to the other but must be "broken up," is the machinery of the bourgeois class state. To be sure, according to Marx, all historical forms of the state were forms of the class state—but in so far as the first phase of socialism still is "affected" with its capitalist heritage, so is its state. However, while the socialist state continues to exercise coercive functions, its substance has undergone a fundamental change: the socialist state *is* the proletariat, constituted as the ruling class.[8] Consequently, in terms of class position and class interests, the subject

[6] Letter to Ph. van Patten, April 18, 1883, in Marx and Engels, *Briefe an A. Bebel, W. Liebknecht, K. Kautsky und Andere* (Moscow, Verlagsgenossenschaft Ausländischer Arbeiter in der USSR, 1933), I, 296. Engels's statement in "Anti-Dühring," written only five years earlier, seems to contradict this notion. There he says that the "first act in which the state appears really as the representative of the whole society—the appropriation of the means of production in the name of the society—is at the same time its last independent act as a state." However, the qualifying terms ("really," "the whole of society," "independent") would make it possible to locate this "act" at the end rather than the beginning of the first phase.

[7] *State and Revolution* (New York, International Publishers, 1932), pp. 25, 33.

[8] "Communist Manifesto," in *The Strategy and Tactics of World Communism*, House Document No. 619, Supplement I (Washington, D.C., U.S. Government Printing Office, 1948), p. 19.

and the object of coercion are identical.[9] In this sense, the state of the first phase is a "non-state," the state "broken up" and "shattered." [10] Since political power is, "properly" speaking, "merely the organized power of one class for oppressing another," [11] the class identity between the subject and object of the state now tends to transform coercion into rational administration. Marx and Engels summarized the changes in the function of the state as this very transformation: "The public functions will lose their political character and be transformed into the simple administrative function of watching over the true interest of society." [12]

In contrast to this conception, the Soviet state exercises throughout political and governmental functions against the proletariat itself; domination remains a specialized function in the division of labor and is as such the monopoly of a political, economic, and military bureaucracy. This function is perpetuated by the centralized authoritarian organization of the productive process, directed by groups which determine the needs of society (the social

[9] Except, of course, where the state power is directed against the "capitalist enemies" within and without. But in the Marxian conception, this function does not change the basic structure of the socialist state; military and police actions against the class enemy are seen as a *levée en masse*, as actions of the armed people themselves.

[10] Marx, Letter to Kugelmann, April 12, 1871, in Marx and Engels, *Selected Works*, II, 420. See Lenin, *State and Revolution*, p. 33.

[11] "Communist Manifesto," in *The Strategy and Tactics of World Communism*, House Document No. 619, Supplement I, p. 19.

[12] Engels, "On Authority," in Marx and Engels, *Selected Works*, I, 577. See also Engels's famous formulation in "Anti-Dühring": "The functions of government transform themselves into simple functions of administration." See Marx and Engels, *Die Allianz der sozialistischen Demokratie und die Internationale Arbeiterassoziation*, ed. by Wilhelm Blos under the title *Marx oder Bakunin?* (Stuttgart, Volksverlag für Wirtschaft und Verkehr, 1920), p. 14.

product and its distribution) independent of the collective control of the ruled population. Whether or not these groups constitute a "class" in the Marxian sense is a problem of Marxist exegesis.[13] The fact is that Soviet Marxism itself stresses the "directing" function of the state as distinguished from the underlying institutions, and that this state retains the separation of the "immediate producers" from collective control over the process of production. Soviet Marxism justifies this "anomaly" by the anomalous circumstances of socialism in a "capitalist environment." These circumstances are supposed to require the continuation and even the growth of the state as a system of *political* institutions, and the exercise by the state of oppressive economic, military, police, and educational functions over and against society. The Soviet state thus takes shape exactly as that structure which Engels described as characteristic of class society: the "common societal functions" become a "new branch of the division of labor" and thereby constitute *particular* interests separate from those of the population.[14] The state is again a reified, hypostatized power.

As such a power, the state, according to Soviet Marxism,

[13] Clearly, if "class" is defined in terms of the relation to the basic means of production, and the latter in terms of ownership, the Soviet bureaucracy is *not* a class. If *control* over the means of production is made the criterion, the question whether or not such control is delegated and in turn effectively controlled by the "immediate producers" would be decisive. We use "class" here as designating a group which exercises governmental (including managerial) functions as a "separate" function in the social division of labor—with or without special privileges. Thus, if the bureaucracy would be open to ascent "from below," it would still be a class as long as the separateness of its function makes it independent from the people whom it manages and administers.

[14] Engels, Letter to Conrad Schmidt, October 27, 1890, in *Über Historischen Materialismus*, ed. by Hermann Duncker (Berlin, Internationaler Arbeiterverlag, 1930), II, 140.

becomes the Archimedean point from which the world is
moved into socialism, the "basic instrument" for the establishment of socialism and communism. Soviet Marxism
links the perpetuated hypostatization of the state to the very
progress of socialist construction.[15] The argument runs as
follows: With the overthrow of capitalism and the nationalization of the economy, the Bolshevik Revolution laid the
foundation for a state which represents the interests of the
urban and rural proletariat. The state is their state, and,
consequently, the further development of the revolution
takes place "from above" rather than "from below." The
liquidation of the "old bourgeois economic order in rural
areas" and the creation of a "socialist collective farm
order" was such a revolution from above, "on the initiative
of the existing regime with the support of the basic masses
of the peasantry." [16] The firm institutionalization of the
state in the revolution from above took shape under the first
Five-Year Plan, which revolutionized the economic order
of the country not only over and above and against the "immediate interests" of workers and peasants, but also by
subjecting them to the bureaucratic-authoritarian organization of production. According to Stalinism, transition to the
subsequent stages of socialism will likewise be made by
strengthening the institutionalized state rather than by dis-
solving it.[17] But the hypostatization of the regime implied

[15] Ts. A. Stepanian, "Usloviia i puti perekhoda ot sotsializma k kommunizmu" (The Conditions and the Paths of the Transition from Socialism
to Communism), in *O sovetskom sotsialisticheskom obshchestve* (On Soviet
Socialist Society), ed. by F. Konstantinov (Moscow, Gospolitizdat, 1948),
p. 544.

[16] Stalin, *Marksizm i voprosy iazykoznaniia* (Marxism and Linguistic
Problems) (Moscow, Gospolitizdat, 1950).

[17] See below, p. 167.

in these formulations might boomerang against alterations in the political structure necessitated by international and internal developments. The power of the state has its objective limits. In the later period of Stalinism, Soviet Marxism emphasized that the state itself is subject to general socioeconomic laws, that its forms "are changing and will continue to change in line with the development of our country and with the changes in the international situation." [18] In Soviet Marxist evaluation, such internal and international developments were asserting themselves on the ground of the achievements of Stalinism and were calling for a corresponding change in Soviet theory and strategy.

Before outlining the trend in the development of the state envisaged by Soviet Marxism, the question must be asked: Who or what is that Soviet state? Neither the rise of the Soviet intelligentsia as a new ruling group, nor its composition and its privileges are any longer disputed facts— least so in the USSR. The recruitment and training of highly qualified specialists, technicians, managers, etc., is continually emphasized and their privileges are advertised. [19] Moreover the uninterrupted growth of this group is considered one of the essential preconditions for the transition to communism. [20] Decisive in the problem of the

---

[18] Stalin, "Report on the Work of the Central Committee to the Eighteenth Party Congress," in *Leninism* (New York, International Publishers, 1942), p. 473.

[19] At least since 1935. See Stalin's speech to the graduates of the Red Army Academy in *Leninism*, pp. 363 f.

[20] For example see Stepanian, "Usloviia i puti perekhoda ot sotsializma k kommunizmu" (The Conditions and the Paths of the Transition from Socialism to Communism), in *O sovetskom sotsialisticheskom obshchestve* (On Soviet Socialist Society), pp. 516 f. and 520.

development of the state are not merely the privileges of the governmental bureaucracy, its numerical strength, and its caste character, but the basis and scope of its power. Obviously the bureaucracy has a vital interest in maintaining and enhancing its privileged position. Obviously, there are conflicts among various groups within the bureaucracy. In order to evaluate their significance for the tendential development of Soviet society, an attempt must be made to determine whether or not there is a political and economic basis for using the special position of the bureaucracy (or special positions within the bureaucracy) for exploding and changing the structure of Soviet society. The following paragraphs suggest only some of the general aspects pertaining to such an attempt.

We have emphasized that Soviet Marxism admits the existence of contradictory interests in Soviet society [21] and derives them from the existence of different forms of Socialist property and labor. As specific sources of contradictions are mentioned: the coexistence of state, collective, and private property in the means of production; the difference between mental and physical labor; the stratification into intelligentsia, workers, and peasants; the uneven

---

[21] "Socialism in our country has been built upon the basis of the solution of internal contradictions by our own forces." *Bol'shaia Sovetskaia Entsiklopediia* (Large Soviet Encyclopedia) (65 vols.; Moscow, OGIZ RSFSR, 1926–47), XLVII, col. 378. For the enumeration of specific contradictions, see, for example, Stalin's speech to the Stakhanovites, 1935, in *Leninism*, p. 368, and his "Economic Problems of Socialism in the USSR," in *Current Soviet Policies*, ed. by Leo Gruliow (New York, F. A. Praeger, 1953), *passim*; Rozental, *Marksistskii dialekticheskii metod* (Marxist Dialectical Method), pp. 283–88; Stepanian, "Usloviia i puti perekhoda ot sotsializma k kommunizmu" (The Conditions and the Paths of the Transition from Socialism to Communism), in *O sovetskom sotsialisticheskom obshchestve* (On Soviet Socialist Society), pp. 528–31; and *Pravda*, August 20, 1947.

development of the two main divisions of social production. As long as the bureaucracy is a special branch in the
division of labor, engendering a special position in society,
it has a separate, special interest. According to Soviet
Marxism, these "internal" contradictions, and with them
the separate position of the bureaucracy, will "flatten out"
with the gradual equalization of mental and physical labor,
which in turn will result from the gradual elimination of
the lag of production relations behind the growth of the
productive forces. The elimination of the class position of
the bureaucracy (but not of the bureaucracy itself) thus
will appear as a "by-product" of the transition from socialism to communism. At that stage, the bureaucracy would
still exercise special functions but no longer within an
institutionalized, hierarchical division of functions; the
bureaucracy would be "open" and lose its "political" content to the degree to which, with the wealth of the material
and intellectual productive forces, the general societal
functions would become exchangeable among the individuals. Is the Soviet Marxist assumption of such a trend even
theoretically consistent with the actual structure of the Soviet state?

Bureaucracy by itself, no matter how huge it is, does not
generate self-perpetuating power unless it has an economic
base of its own from which its position is derived, or unless
it is allied with other social groups which possess such a
power base. Naturally, the traditional sources of economic
power are not available to the Soviet bureaucracy; it does
not own the nationalized means of production. But obviously "the people," who constitutionally own the means

of production, do not control them. Control, therefore, and not ownership must be the decisive factor. But unless further defined, "control" is an insufficient index for the real locus of power. Is it exercised simply by particular interests independent enough to assert themselves against others, or are these interests themselves subject to overriding laws and forces? With respect to the Soviet system and its organization of production, distinction must be made between technical-administrative and social control. The two levels of control would coincide if those which manage the industrial and agricultural key establishments determine by and for themselves and as a special group entrepreneurial and labor policies, thereby wielding decisive influence over the social need and its satisfaction. Such a coincidence cannot be taken for granted. In Soviet doctrine, it is the Party which exercises the social control overriding all technical-administrative control, and since the Party is fused with the state, social control assumes the form of centralized and planned political control. But the same question as to the ultimate superseding control must be asked with respect to the Party—even its top leadership comprises various groups and interests, including managerial ones. Obviously, the "people" can be excluded: there is no effective social control "from below." Thus, two possibilities are left: either (1) a specific group within the bureaucracy exercises control over all the rest of the bureaucracy (in which case this group would be the autonomous subject of social control); or (2) the bureaucracy as a "class" is truly sovereign, i.e., the ruling group (in which case social and technical-administrative controls would co-incide). This alternative will be discussed presently.

Personal power, even if effectively institutionalized, does not define social control. Stalin's dictatorship may well have overridden all divergent interests by virtue of his factual power. However, this personal power was itself subject to the requirements of the social system on whose continued functioning it depended, and over and above the subsistence minimum, these requirements were codeter-mined by the interests controlling the industrial and agri-cultural basis, and by those of the police and the army. The same holds true, to a much greater extent, for the post-Stalinist leadership. The search for the locus of social con-trol thus leads back from personal dictatorship to the alter-native formulated above. But there seems to be no separate homogeneous group to which social control could be mean-ingfully attributed. The top ruling group is itself changing and comprises "representatives" of various bureaucracies and branches of the bureaucracies, economic as well as political: management, army, party. Each of them has a special interest and aspires for social control. But the mo-nopolization of power is counteracted by two forces: on the one side, the Central Plan, in spite of its vagaries, loop-holes, and corrections, ultimately supersedes and integrates the special interests; on the other side, the entire bureauc-racy, up to the highest level, is subject to the competitive terror, or, after the relaxation of the terror, to the highly incalculable application of political or punitive measures, leading to the loss of power. To be sure, the Central Plan

is itself the work of the bureaucracy in the main branches
of the system: government, party, armed forces, management; but it is the result of their combined and adjusted
interests and negotiations, ensuing in a sort of general interest which in turn depends on the internal growth of
Soviet society. This relation also played an important role in
the development of the terror.

Terror is the centralized, methodical application of
incalculable violence (incalculable for the objects of the
terror, and also for the top groups and even the practition-
ers of the terror)—not only in an emergency situation, but
in a normal state of affairs. As long as the Soviet state relied on such incalculable application, it relied on terroristic force—although the terror would approximate a normal competitive social system to the degree to which the
punitive measures (such as removal from office, demotion)
would be nonviolent. In its historical function, terror may
be progressive or regressive,[22] depending upon whether it
actually promotes, through the destruction of repressive
institutions, the growth of liberal ones, and the rational
utilization of the productive forces. In the Soviet state, the
terror is of a twofold nature: technological and political.
Inefficiency and poor performance at the technical and business level are punished; so is any kind of nonconformity:
politically and dangerously suspect attitudes, opinions, behavior. The two forms are interconnected, and efficiency is
certainly often judged on political grounds. However, with
the elimination of all organized opposition, and with the

[22] See Franz Neumann, "Notes on the Theory of Dictatorship," in *The
Democratic and the Authoritarian State* (Glencoe, Ill., Free Press, 1957),
pp. 233–56.

continued success of the totalitarian administration, the terror tends to become predominantly technological, and, in
the USSR itself, strictly political terror seems to be the
exception rather than the rule. The completely standardized clichés of the political charges, which no longer even
pretend to be rational, plausible, and consistent, may well
serve to conceal the real reason for the indictment: differences in the timing and implementation of administrative
measures on whose substance the conflicting parties agree.

The technological terror is omnipresent—but this very
omnipresence implies a high degree of indifference toward
special privilege and position. An action started on a low
level may involve the highest level if the circumstances are
"favorable." The chiefs themselves are not immune—they
are not the absolute masters of oppression. The circumstances which set the machine in motion against a specific
target seem to be the end-constellation of numerous cross
currents in the areas of the respective bureaucracies. The
ultimate decision in prominent cases is also likely to be the
result of negotiations and compromises among the top
groups—each representing its own "apparatus," but each
apparatus again subject to competitive controls within the
framework of the Central Plan and the then prevailing
principles of foreign and domestic policy. This framework
leaves much room for personal and clique influences and
interests, corruption, and profiteering; it also permits one
group (and one individual of the group) to come out on
top—but it also sets the limits beyond which the monop-
olization of power cannot go without upsetting the structure
on which Soviet power rests.

These limits are circumscribed by the exigencies of the planned growth and correlation of the economic, political, and military establishments. The rate and mode of growth, and the priorities of and within the main establishments are apparently determined through struggles and compromises between competing vested interests. Sooner or later, however, the outcome must conform to the basic trend of the construction of Soviet society and to the principles which have governed this trend since the first Five-Year Plan. Once institutionalized, they have their own momentum and their own objective requirements; the vested interests themselves depend on the observance of these requirements. The principles are altered and adjusted in accordance with the changing domestic and international situation, but a long-range general trend emerges into which the modifications are integrated. When Stepanian stated that the development of Marxism presupposes "the unchangeability of its principles and foundations," [23] this was more than propaganda: identical principles (Marxist or not) have indeed governed the controls in all basic spheres of the Soviet system. They are likely to reassert themselves in the conflict of competing powers and vested interests because they pertain to the very structure of the society in which these powers and interests prevail. For example, the efforts to reduce the investments in heavy industry in favor of light industry and an increase in consumers' goods, which came into the open after Stalin's death, assumed the form of a struggle for power among certain

[23] "Usloviia i puti perekhoda ot sotsializma k kommunizmu" (The Conditions and the Paths of Transition from Socialism to Communism), in *O sovetskom sotsialisticheskom obshchestve* (On Soviet Socialist Society), p. 482.

groups of the top leadership. However, the long-range trend of Soviet industrialization and the political setup defined by it seem to have predetermined the decision to a great extent. The Stalinist construction of Soviet society rested on the sustained priority of heavy industry; a fundamental shift in the balance would mean a fundamental shift in the structure itself—in the economic as well as political system. Such a shift was not precluded by the Stalinist program—on the contrary: we emphasized the "tentative" character of this program and its orientation on a "second phase." However, this change is not within the discretion and power of any particular group or individual: it depends on the international constellation and on the economic and political level of the productive forces of Soviet society. More specifically, it depends on the attainment of the capacity level of the advanced industrial countries and the corresponding relative weakening of the capitalist world. Whether or not this level has been attained, and whether or not the international situation is feasible for the change, is a political decision, to be fought out among the leadership of the top bureaucracies—but the decision will be cancelled if it is not corroborated and "verified" by the objective factors of the international and domestic situation, that is, in the last analysis, by the international effectiveness of Soviet policy.

Another example for the perseverance of basic objectives and principles overriding the bureaucratic "struggle for power" may be provided by the agricultural policy: it aims, through all turns, regressions, leaps, and corrections and through consecutive stages of collectivization, at the establishment of complete socialist property on the land, total mechanization, and assimilation of urban and rural life and labor. In foreign policy, through "hard" and "soft" periods, through local wars and "peace offensives," Lenin's guidance stands supreme: to preserve the "respite" for the building of socialism and communism in coexistence with the capitalist world. Here, too, the interpretation of the governing principles, and the decision on the timing and scope of the measures which they stipulate, remain ultimately the monopoly of a top group of leaders. But no matter how its composition and number may change, nor how the extent of consultation and compromise with the lower strata of the bureaucracy may vary, the governing principles seem to be rigid enough to define the limits of special powers and to preclude their institutionalization within a system governed by these principles.

The Soviet bureaucracy thus does not seem to possess a basis for the effective perpetuation of special interests against the overriding general requirements of the social system on which it lives. The bureaucracy constitutes a separate class which controls the underlying population through control of the economic, political, and military establishments, and exercise of this control engenders a variety of special interests which assert themselves in the control; however, they must compromise and ultimately succumb to the general policy which none of the special interests can change by virtue of its special power. Does this mean that the bureaucracy represents the common interest of society as a whole?

In a society composed of competing groups with different economic, occupational, and administrative interests, "common interest" is not per se a meaningful term. Even if one assumes that the general rise in the material and cultural living conditions with a maximum of individual liberty and security defines the common interest of every civilized society, it appears that in any nonhomogeneous society the realization of this interest will proceed in conflict with the interests of some of the (privileged) groups in society. The common interest would not be identical with the interest of all and each; it would remain an "ideological" concept. This antagonistic situation prevails not only in the relationship between the bureaucracy and the underlying population, but also in that between the urban and rural groups, and even between different subgroups within these groups, such as between male and female, skilled and unskilled workers. Even in a highly advanced industrial society with abundant resources, the rise in the general standard of living and of general freedom could take place only as a most unequal development, overriding the immediate interests of large parts of the population. Just as the social need is not identical with the individual needs, so is the realization of "universal" liberty and justice at one and the same time also injustice and unfreedom in individual cases (and even in the case of whole social groups). The very universality of right and law—the guarantor of freedom and justice—demands such negation and limitation by virtue of the fact that it must necessarily abstract from "particularities."

The inequality implied in the common interest would be much greater in a backward society; neither nationalization nor central planning per se would eliminate it. The common interest would retain a high degree of "abstractness" as against the immediate interest (although this abstractness may be gradually reduced as society develops). In other words, the traditional distinction between the general (common) interest and the sum-total of particular interests would hold true, and the former would have to be defined in terms of its own—as a separate entity, as the social interest over and above individual interests. Soviet Marxism defines the former in relation to the productive forces and their organization; the social interest is said to be represented by those groups and interests which promote the development of the productive forces. This relation is itself a historical factor, to be defined in terms of the political and economic situation of the respective society.

In the case of Soviet society the accelerated development of its productive forces is considered a prerequisite for the survival and competitive strength of the Soviet state in the circumstances of "coexistence." The position of the bureaucracy thus depends on the expansion of the productive apparatus, and the specific and conflicting interests within the bureaucracy are superseded, through the mechanisms of technology and force, diplomacy and power politics, by this common social interest. The Soviet bureaucracy therefore represents the social interest in a hypostatized form, in which the individual interests are separated from the individuals and arrogated by the state.

The Soviet state emerges as the institutionalized collective in which the Marxian distinction between the immediate and the real (objective historical) interest is made the rationale for the building of the political structure. The state is the manifestation of the real (the social) interest, but as such the state is "not yet" identical with the interests of the people whom it rules: their immediate interests do "not yet" coincide with the objective social interest. For example, the people want less work, more freedom, more consumer goods—but, according to the official theory, the still prevailing backwardness and scarcity necessitate the continued subordination of these interests to the social interest of armament and industrialization. This is the old discrepancy between the individual and society, represented by the state; however, in Soviet theory, it occurs at a new stage of the historical process. Formerly, the state represented not the interest of society as a whole but that of the ruling class. To be sure, in a sense, the class state too represented the collective interest [24] in so far as it organized and sustained the orderly reproduction of society as a whole and the development of the productive forces. However, the conflict between their rational development in the common interest and their private-profit utilization was, within the framework of the class state, insoluble and vitiated the identity of interests. As this conflict ripened, the class state would become of necessity ever more regressive and a fetter to the development of society. In contrast, the Soviet state is supposed to run the opposite course, capable of resolving the conflict [25] and of establishing the harmony between individual and social need on the basis of an all-out development of productivity.

[24] See below, p. 120.   [25] See above, pp. 94 f., and below, p. 167.

6. *Base and Superstructure—Reality and Ideology*

IN MARXIAN THEORY, the state belongs to the superstructure inasmuch as it is *not* simply the direct political expression of the basic relationships of production but contains elements which, as it were, "compensate" for the class relationships of production. The state, being and remaining the state of the ruling class, sustains *universal* law and order and thereby guarantees at least a modicum of equality and security for the whole of society. Only by virtue of these elements can the class state fulfill the function of "moderating" and keeping within the bounds of "order" the class conflicts generated by the production relations.[1] It is this "mediation" which gives the state the appearance of a universal interest over and above the conflicting particular interests. The universal function of the state is itself determined by the base, but contains factors transcending and even antagonistic to the base—factors which may become semi-independent forces, in turn actively affecting the base in various ways.

Engels distinguished two principal modes in which the

[1] Engels, *Origin of the Family, Private Property, and the State* (New York, International Publishers, 1942), p. 155. See also Marx and Engels, *The German Ideology* (New York, International Publishers, 1939), pp. 40–41.

state can "react" on the basic economic process, namely, either counter to or "in the same direction" as the economic development. In the latter case, the state "accelerates" the economic development.[2] The second mode of reaction presupposes conformity between the political superstructure and the development of the productive forces—a conformity which Marxian theory denies for all but the ascending phases of capitalist society (and class society in general). According to Soviet Marxism, the Bolshevik Revolution brought the political superstructure "into agreement" with the economic base, while the nationalization of the means of production rendered possible centralized control over the economic development. The economic laws continue to operate as objective forces determining the superstructure, they can neither be "created" nor "changed" by the state, but they have become susceptible to conscious use and application.[3] This, according to Soviet Marxist theory, is the decisive difference between the Soviet and the capitalist superstructure. Both forms of the state constitute a "political superstructure," that is to say, they are determined by the respective "economic structure" of society, but while this determination is blind and supreme in the capitalist state, the Soviet state can "direct" and "control" it. Thus, whereas under capitalism "it is rather the state that is controlled by the capitalist economy," the Soviet state

[2] Letter to Conrad Schmidt, October 27, 1890, in Marx and Engels, *Selected Works* (2 vols.; Moscow, Foreign Languages Publishing House, 1949–50), II, 447.

[3] Stalin, "Economic Problems of Socialism in the USSR," in *Current Soviet Policies*, ed. by Leo Gruliow (New York, F. A. Praeger, 1953), p. 18. See also articles from *Izvestiia*, January 23, 1953, in *Current Digest of the Soviet Press*, VI, No. 1 (February 14, 1953), 3–6; and below, pp. 166 f.

"becomes the directing force of the country's economic development," the "directing force" of the economy.[4]

Some analysts of Soviet developments have seen in this redefinition of the relation between base and superstructure (which is generalized and authenticated in Stalin's *Marxism and Linguistic Problems*) a revision of the fundamental Marxian conception.[5] In reality, it is only an application of Engels's proposition concerning the reciprocal action (*Wechselwirkung*) between base and superstructure. The state, if it "accelerates" the economic development, "becomes a very great active force, helping (cooperating) with its base to form and consolidate itself; it takes all measures to help the new order to destroy and liquidate the old basis and the old classes." [6] This statement from Stalin's *Marxism and Linguistic Problems* refers not only to the state but to the superstructure in general. These formulations follow logically from the assumption, indisputable for Soviet Marxism, that the Soviet society is a socialist society. Naturally, a socialist state will have an essentially different relation to the base than a capitalist state (in Soviet Marxist language, a nonantagonistic relation).

[4] G. Glezermann, "The Socialist State—Mighty Instrumentality for Building Communism," in *Current Digest of the Soviet Press*, IV, No. 41 (November 24, 1951), 7–10 (translated from *Izvestiia*, October 12, 1951). This does not preclude that "the bourgeois state influences the economic development." Stalin expands on this formulation in his "Economic Problems of Socialism," in *Current Soviet Policies*, pp. 1–20. See below, pp. 167 f.

[5] Robert Daniels, "State and Revolution: A Case Study in the Genesis and Transformation of Communist Ideology," *American Slavic and East European Review*, XII, No. 1 (February, 1953), 22–43.

[6] For the Soviet Marxist evaluation of Stalin's statement, see M. B. Mittin, *Novyi vydaiushchiisia vklad I. V. Stalina v razvitie marksistsko-leninskoi teorii* (The Distinguished New Contribution of J. V. Stalin to the Development of Marxist-Leninist Theory) (Moscow, Vsesoiuznoe obshchestvo po rasprostraneniiu politicheskikh i nauchnykh znanii, 1950), especially p. 13.

Consequently, the development from socialism toward communism can equally logically be envisaged as a non-antagonistic development in the sense that progress to the "higher stage" does not involve "destructive" alterations in the base but rather the gradual unfolding of its potentialities. The existence of a socialist base would indeed change the entire traditional function of the superstructure and establish a new relation between ideology and reality.

If we apply the traditional Marxian conception schematically to Soviet society, the base consists of the prevailing "productive forces" in the prevailing production relations.[7] The "producers" are wage earners and salaried employees of the state, and members of the collective farms. In the property relation of the producers to the basic means of production, there are no class distinctions between the groups making up Soviet society (intelligentsia, workers, peasants)—although, of course, vast distinctions exist in terms of control and living conditions. The superstructure consists of the system of administrative, legal, and cultural institutions, and of the official ideology promulgated by them and transmitted to the various fields of private and public life. As in the classical Marxian scheme, the base determines the superstructure, that is, the latter is shaped

[7] The controversy as to whether or not Stalin's definition in *Marxism and Linguistic Problems* excludes the productive forces from the base is without relevance here. In Marxian theory, the productive forces constitute per se a more fundamental level than the production relations although they operate only within specific production relations. For the whole controversy see the report on the Conference of the Communist Academy of Social Sciences, February 25 to March 1, 1952, "Nauchnaia sessiia, posviashchennaia trudam I. V. Stalina i ikh znacheniiu v razvitii obshchestvennykh nauk" (Scientific Session Devoted to the Works of J. V. Stalin and to Their Significance in the Development of the Social Sciences), *Voprosy Filosofii* (Problems of Philosophy), 1952, No. 3, pp. 240–61.

by the requirements of the productive apparatus. But the apparatus is nationalized, and these requirements are centrally planned and controlled. This introduces significant changes into the traditional scheme: the state becomes, without intermediary factors, the direct political organization of the productive apparatus, the general manager of the nationalized economy, and the hypostatized collective interest. The functional differences between base and superstructure therefore tend to be obliterated: the latter is methodically and systematically assimilated with the base by depriving the superstructure of those functions which are transcendent and antagonistic to the base. This process, which establishes new foundations for social control, alters the very substance of ideology. The tension between idea and reality, between culture and civilization, between intellectual and material culture—a tension which was one of the driving forces behind Western civilization—is not solved but methodically reduced.

For Marx and Engels, ideology is an illusion (*Schein*), but a necessary illusion, arising from a social organization of production which appears to man as a system of independent, objective laws and forces. As a "reflection" of the actual social basis, the ideology partakes of the truth, but the latter is expressed in false form. The ideas of the ruling class become the ruling ideas and claim universal validity, but the claim is founded on "false consciousness"—false because the real connection of the ideas with their economic basis and therefore their actual limitations and negations do not enter consciousness.[8] A specific historical con-

[8] Engels, Letter to Mehring, July 14, 1893, in Marx and Engels, *Selected Works*, II, 451.

tent appears as universally valid and serves to provide a prop for a specific social system. However, the function of ideology goes far beyond such service. Into the ideology has entered material which—transmitted from generation to generation—contains the perpetual hopes, aspirations, and sufferings of man, his suppressed potentialities, the images of integral justice, happiness, and freedom. They find their ideological expressions chiefly in religion, philosophy, and art, but also in the juristic and political concepts of liberty, equality, and security.

The Marxian notion of ideology here implies a dynamic which leads to a change in the function and weight of ideology relative to the base. The more the base encroaches upon the ideology, manipulating and coordinating it with the established order, the more the ideological sphere which is remotest from the reality (art, philosophy), precisely because of its remoteness, becomes the last refuge for the opposition to this order. When Marx began to elaborate his theory, he was motivated by the conviction that history had at last reached the stage where Reason and Freedom could be transubstantiated from philosophical ideas into political objectives. Philosophy (which Marx considered as the most advanced ideology) was to find its fulfillment in the action of the proletariat,[9] a fulfillment which was at the same time the end, the "loss" of philosophy. The proletariat, which provides the "material weapons" for philosophy, finds in philosophy its "conceptual weapons." Philoso-

[9] Marx, "Zur Kritik der Hegelschen Rechtsphilosophie: Einleitung," in Marx and Engels, *Historisch-Kritische Gesamtausgabe,* ed. by D. Rjazonov (Frankfurt, Marx-Engels Archiv Verlagsgesellschaft, 1927), Div. I, I, Pt. 1, pp. 620 f.

phy had elaborated the idea of the liberty and dignity of man, of his inalienable rights, his autonomy, his mastery of his life, his potentialities, and his happiness. While class society had rendered these contents ideological, the action of the proletariat, in abolishing class society, would make them reality.

However, the same development which precluded the socialist revolution in the advanced industrial countries vitiated the Marxian notion of the transition from ideology to reality, from philosophy to revolutionary practice. If the proletariat no longer acts as the revolutionary class representing the "absolute negation" of the established order, it no longer furnishes the "material weapons" for philosophy. The situation thus reverts: repelled by reality, Reason and Freedom become again the concern of philosophy. The "essence of man," his "total liberation" is again "experienced [only] in thought" (*in Gedanken erlebt*).[10] Theory —by virtue of its historical position Marxian theory is in its very substance philosophy—again not only anticipates political practice, runs ahead of it, but also upholds the objectives of liberation in the face of a failing practice. In this function, theory becomes again ideology—not as false consciousness, but as conscious distance and dissociation from, even opposition to, the repressive reality. And by the same token, it becomes a political factor of utmost significance. The struggle on the "ideological front" is, for the Soviet state, a struggle for survival.

We have seen[11] how, in this struggle, base and superstructure change their relation. According to Soviet Marx-

---

[10] *Ibid.*   [11] See above, pp. 121 f.

ism, whereas formerly progress to higher stages of social development necessitated the revolutionary alteration of the established basis, the Soviet state can achieve the transition on the already existing basis, by planful and "scientific direction." The process eliminates previously dominant ideological elements in so far as even the most blatant contradictions and illusions, even nonsense and falsehood, enter into consciousness and are consciously utilized. But this does not take care of the whole content of ideology. The conflict between the growth of productive forces and the repressive production relations to which the entire population is subjected sustains among the population the need for ideological transcendence beyond the repressive reality. According to Marxian theory, this need will disappear "as soon as it is no longer necessary to represent a particular interest as general or the 'general interest' as ruling." [12] In the Soviet system, the "general interest" is hypostatized in the state—an entity separate from the individual interests. To the extent that the latter are still unfulfilled and repelled by reality, they strive for ideological expression; and their force is the more explosive to the regime the more the new economic basis is propagandized as insuring the total liberation of man under communism. The fight against ideological transcendence thus becomes a life-and-death struggle for the regime. Within the ideological sphere, the center of gravity shifts from philosophy to literature and art. The danger zone of *philosophical* transcendence has been brought under control through the ab-

[12] Marx and Engels, *The German Ideology* (New York, International Publishers, 1939), p. 41.

sorption of philosophy into the official theory. Metaphysics, traditionally the chief refuge for the still unrealized ideas of human freedom and fulfillment, is declared to be totally superseded by dialectical materialism and by the emergence of a rational society in socialism. Ethical philosophy, transformed into a pragmatic system of rules and standards of behavior, has become an integral part of state policy.[13] What remains of these branches of philosophy is their methodical negation. The fight against Western philosophy, "bourgeois objectivism," idealism, and so forth (strikingly exemplified by the Aleksandrov controversy in 1946), aims at discrediting philosophical trends and categories which, by virtue of their transcendence, seemed to endanger the "closed" political and ideological system. (As a theoretical task, the aim seems to be self-defeating in view of the fact that the Marxian conception has cancelled but preserved [*aufgehoben*] the tabooed "bourgeois" elements. It is not surprising, therefore, that the controversy nowhere moves at the level of a substantive critique of "bourgeois philosophy.")[14] With this negation of philosophy,[15] the main ideological struggle then is directed against the transcendence in art. Soviet art must be "realistic."

[13] The second part of this study will discuss the transformation.

[14] The taboo on philosophy affects even those Marxist contributions which marked a milestone in the development of post-Marxian theory, most notably Georg Lukács's *Geschichte und Klassenbewusstsein* (Berlin, Der Malik-Verlag, 1923), while the same author's *Die Zerstörung der Vernunft* (Berlin, Aufbau-Verlag, 1954) may serve as an example of the deterioration of the Marxist critique.

[15] For the reasons indicated above, a substantive discussion of Soviet philosophy lies outside the scope of this study. The best and most comprehensive survey is in Gustav A. Wetter, *Der dialektische Materialismus; seine Geschichte und sein System in der Soviet-Union* (Freiburg, Herder, 1952).

Realism can be—and has been—a highly critical and progressive form of art; confronting reality "as it is" with its ideological and idealized representations, realism upholds the truth against concealment and falsification. In this sense realism shows the ideal of human freedom in its actual negation and betrayal and thus preserves the transcendence without which art itself is cancelled. In contrast, Soviet realism conforms to the pattern of a repressive state. The conscious and controlled implementation of state policies through the medium of literature, music, painting, and so forth, is by itself not incompatible with art (examples could be cited from Greek art to Bert Brecht). However, Soviet realism goes beyond the artistic implementation of political norms by accepting the established social reality as the final framework for the artistic content, transcending it neither in style nor in substance. Certain shortcomings, blunders, and lags in this reality are criticized, but neither the individual nor his society are referred to a sphere of fulfillment other than that prescribed by and enclosed in the prevailing system. To be sure, they are referred to the communist *future*, but the latter is presented as evolving from the present without "exploding" the existing contradictions. The future is said to be nonantagonistic to the present; repression will gradually and through obedient effort engender freedom and happiness—no catastrophe separates history from prehistory, the negation from its negation. But it is precisely the catastrophic element inherent in the conflict between man's essence and his existence that has been the center toward which art has gravitated since its secession from ritual. The artistic images have preserved the determinate negation of the established reality—ultimate freedom. When Soviet aesthetics attacks the notion of the "unsurmountable antagonism between essence and existence" as the theoretical principle of "formalism," [16] it thereby attacks the principle of art itself. In Marxian theory, this antagonism is a *historical* fact, and is to be resolved in a society which reconciles the existence of man with his essence by providing the material conditions for the free development of all humane faculties. If and when this has been achieved, the traditional basis of art would have been undermined—through the realization of the content of art. Prior to this historical event, art retains its critical cognitive function: to represent the still transcendental truth, to sustain the image of freedom against a denying reality. With the realization of freedom, art would no longer be a vessel of the truth.[17] Hegel, who saw this realization as the task of his own period, already proclaimed that art had become a thing of the past, had lost its substance. He attributed this obsolescence of art to the new scientific-philosophical spirit, which demanded a stricter formulation of the truth than that accessible to art.[18] Marxian theory retained the historical link between social progress and the obsolescence of art: the development of the productive forces renders possible the material fulfillment of the *promesse du bonheur* expressed in art; political action—the revolution—is to translate this possibility into reality.

[16] V. A. Razumnyi, "O sushchnosti realisticheskogo khudozhestvennogo obraza" (On the Essence of a Realistic Artistic Form), *Voprosy Filosofii* (Problems of Philosophy), 1952, No. 6, p. 101.

[17] Hegel, "Vorlesungen über die Aesthetik," in *Sämtliche Werke*, ed. by H. Glockner (26 vols.; Stuttgart, F. Fromman, 1927–40), XII, 215.

[18] *Ibid.*, pp. 30, 32.

Soviet Marxism claims that the Bolshevik Revolution has created the basis for this translation. What then remains as the function and content of art? Soviet aesthetics answers: Reflection of the reality in the form of artistic images.[19] "The law of our aesthetics is that the more realistic our literature is the more romantic it becomes." [20] In other words, once the reality itself embodies the ideal (though not yet in its pure form), art must necessarily reflect the reality, that is, if it is to retain its essential function, it must be "realism." The *promesse du bonheur* which, being beyond reality, constituted the "romantic" element in art, now appears as the realistic concern of the policy makers —realism and romanticism converge. But this convergence, if it were genuine, would make art superfluous. The reality of freedom would repel the ideology of freedom in its artistic transcendence. Hegel saw in the obsolescence of art a token of progress. As the development of Reason conquers transcendence ("takes it back" into reality) art turns into its own negation. Soviet aesthetics rejects this idea and insists on art, while outlawing the transcendence of art. It wants art that is not art, and it gets what it asks for.

However, the Soviet treatment of art is not simply an outburst of boundless authoritarianism; its historical significance goes beyond that of political and national requirements for regimentation. The most shocking notions of Soviet aesthetics testify to a keen awareness of the social function of art. They are chiefly derived from the strong emphasis placed on the cognitive function of art. Accord-

[19] Razumnyi, "O sushchnosti realisticheskogo khudozhestvennogo obraza" (On the Essence of a Realistic Artistic Form), *Voprosy Filosofii* (Problems of Philosophy), 1952, No. 6, p. 99.
[20] *Literaturnaia Gazeta* (Literary Gazette), November 17, 1948.

ing to Soviet aesthetics, there is no essential contradiction
and opposition between art and science; the artistic and the
logical notions are inseparable.[21] In "much the same way
as science," art expresses the "objective truth." [22] Still, art
is a specific presentation of truth—a presentation which is
incommensurate with scientific as well as common-lan-
guage communication. The reasons for this incommensura-
bility are manifold; they seem to pertain to the fact that
art reveals and at the same time consecrates the (subjectively and objectively) unmastered forces in man and his
world, the "danger zones" beneath and beyond social control. Viewed from the position of a repressive society, ultimate freedom resides in these danger zones. On its deepest
level, art is a protest against that which is. By that very
token, art is a "political" matter: if left to itself, it may
endanger law and order. Plato's treatment of art and his
system of rigid censorship which fuses aesthetic, political,
and epistemological criteria, does more justice to the nature and function of art than does its evaluation as "free"
intellectual, emotional, or educational entertainment.

But art as a political force is art only in so far as it
preserves the images of liberation; in a society which is
in its totality the negation of these images, art can preserve
them only by total refusal, that is, by not succumbing to
the standards of the unfree reality, either in style, or in
form, or in substance. The more totalitarian these stand-

[21] Razumnyi, "O sushchnosti realisticheskogo khudozhestvennogo obraza"
(On the Essence of a Realistic Artistic Form), *Voprosy Filosofii* (Problems
of Philosophy), 1952, No. 6, pp. 99 and 107.

[22] P. Trofimov and others, "Printsipy marksistsko-leninskoi estetiki" (Principles of Marxist-Leninist Aesthetics), *Kommunist* (Communist), 1954, No.
16 (November), p. 95.

ards become, the more reality controls all language and all communication, the more irrealistic and surrealistic will art tend to be, the more will it be driven from the concrete to the abstract, from harmony to dissonance, from content to form. Art is thus the refusal of everything that has been made part and parcel of reality. The works of the great "bourgeois" antirealists and "formalists" are far deeper committed to the idea of freedom than is socialist and Soviet realism. The irreality of their art expresses the irreality of freedom: art is as transcendental as its object. The Soviet state by administrative decree prohibits the transcendence of art; it thus eliminates even the ideological reflex of freedom in an unfree society. Soviet realistic art, complying with the decree, becomes an instrument of social control in the last still nonconformist dimension of the human existence. Cut off from its historical base, socialized without a socialist reality, art reverts to its ancient prehistorical function: it assumes magical character. Thus, it becomes a decisive element in the pragmatic rationality of behaviorism.

"Art teaches . . . a definite relation toward reality." [23] The relation is exemplified by the "typical" images of the Soviet hero and patriot, in his struggle against hostile and obsolete forces. Soviet art aims at creating and establishing such a relation in reality, and is to effectuate this relation *as art*, that is, through the artistic image, through the artistic illusion. But this is the principle of magic: To "enact in fantasy the fulfillment of the desired reality," "an illusory technique supplementary to the real tech-

[23] *Ibid.*, pp. 107-8.

nique." [24] The illusion, of course, cannot have a direct effect on reality, but in so far as it changes the "subjective attitude to reality," indirectly it changes reality. The regression of the cognitive function of art from the artistic to the magical comes out in the most reactionary feature of Soviet aesthetics: the rejection of "formalism" and of all "abstract" and "dissonant" structures. The progressive elements in modern "bourgeois art" were precisely in those structures which preserved the "shock" character of art,[25] that is, those expressing the catastrophic conflict. They represented the desperate attempt to break through the social standardization and falsification which had made the traditional artistic structures unusable for expressing the artistic content. The harmonious forms, in their realistic as well as classical and romantic development, had lost their transcendental, critical force; they stood no longer antagonistic to reality, but appeared as part and adornment of it—as instruments of adjustment. Communicated through the mass media, they became welcome tunes accompanying daily work and leisure, nourishment for recreation and relaxation periods. Under these circumstances, only their determinate negation could restore their content. Conversely, through the reinstatement of harmony by administrative decree, the banning of dissonance, discord, and atonality, the cognitive function of art is "brought in line," and conformity is enforced in the per se nonconformistic artistic imagination.

[24] George Thomson, *Studies in Ancient Greek Society* (New York, International Publishers, 1949), p. 440. See above, pp. 88 f.
[25] T. W. Adorno, "Die gegängelte Musik," in *Dissonanzen* (Göttingen, Vandenhoeck und Ruprecht, 1956), pp. 46 ff.

It is interesting to note that, with its denunciation of dissonant art, Soviet aesthetics reverts to Plato's dictum, which permits only beautiful, simple, and harmonious forms. Only these forms "mix" with the Good and the Truth: "And now the power of the good has returned into the region of the beautiful; for measure and symmetry are beauty and virtue all the world over" and "we said that truth was to form an element in this mixture." [26] Plato's theory of art refers to a state in which the philosopher kings guard the standards for the good, the true, and the beautiful—a state antagonistic to reality. Pressed into the service of reality, the mixture destroys its own components.

Within the general framework of the political controls over art, a wide range of policy modifications is possible. Relaxation and tightening, alteration of artistic standards and styles, depend on the internal and international constellations. Naturally, with the transition from terroristic to normal modes of societal regimentation, the claim for more artistic freedom will be heard and perhaps fulfilled. The rigidity of "Soviet realism" may well be loosened; realism and romanticism, in any case, have ceased to be opposites, and even "formalistic" and "abstract" elements may still become reconcilable with conformist enjoyment. In its societal function, art shares the growing impotence of individual autonomy and cognition.

[26] *Philebus* 64.

7. Dialectic and Its Vicissitudes

PERHAPS NOTHING is more revealing in the development of
Soviet Marxism than its treatment of dialectic. Dialectical
logic is the cornerstone of Marxian theory; it guides the
analysis of the prerevolutionary as well as of the revolutionary development, and this analysis in turn is supposed
to guide the strategy in both periods. Any fundamental
"revision" of dialectical logic that goes beyond the Marxist application of dialectic to a new historical situation
would indicate not only a "deviation" from Marxian
theory (which is only of dogmatic interest) but also a
theoretical justification for a change in the basic trend.
Interpreters of Soviet theory have therefore correctly
drawn attention to events in this sphere. They have concluded that Soviet Marxism has tuned down and arrested
the dialectic in the interest of the ideological justification
and protection of a regime which, according to dialectical
logic, must appear as subject to being surpassed by the
historical development. Chief support of this conclusion is
seen in the emasculation of the transition from quantity to
quality, the denial of explosive changes under socialism
(the notion of "nonantagonistic contradictions"), in the
reintroduction of formal logic, and in the disappearance

from the dialectical vocabulary of the "negation of the negation." [1] In point of fact, however, Soviet Marxism is nowhere more "orthodox" than in its painful elaboration of the dialectical method; we shall see that not one of the above mentioned innovations in itself runs counter to the Marxian (and even Hegelian) dialectical logic.

But while not a single of the basic dialectical concepts has been revised or rejected in Soviet Marxism, the function of dialectic itself has undergone a significant change: it has been transformed from a mode of critical thought into a universal "world outlook" and universal method with rigidly fixed rules and regulations, and this transformation destroys the dialectic more thoroughly than any revision. The change corresponds to that of Marxism itself from theory to ideology; dialectic is vested with the magical qualities of official thought and communication. As Marxian theory ceases to be the organon of revolutionary consciousness and practice and enters the superstructure of an established system of domination, the movement of dialectical thought is codified into a philosophical system. The more problematic the relation between dialectical and formal logic becomes, the more dialectic itself becomes formal logic. The difficulties of Soviet Marxism in producing an adequate "textbook" on dialectic and logic are not only of a political nature, but the very essence of dialectics rebels against such codification. This holds true for idealistic as well as materialist dialectics, for neither Hegel nor Marx developed dialectic as a general methodologi-

[1] See A. Philipov, *Logic and Dialectic in the Soviet Union* (New York, Research Program on the USSR, 1952), pp. 37 f.

cal scheme. The first step in this direction was made by
Engels in his Dialectics of Nature (which he did not pub-
lish), and his notes have provided the skeleton for the
Soviet Marxist codification.

Marx elaborated his dialectic as a conceptual tool for
comprehending an inherently antagonistic society. The
dissolution of the fixed and stable notions of philosophy,
political economy, and sociology into their contradictory
components was to "reflect" the actual structure and movement of history; dialectic was to reproduce in theory the
essence of reality. And in order to reproduce it adequately,
in order to provide an adequate theory of history, the traditional categories had to be redefined because they con-
cealed rather than revealed what happened. However, the
dialectical relation between the structure of thought and
that of reality is more than reflection and correspondence.
If Hegel consistently transgressed the clearly established
distinction between thought and its object, if he talked of
"contradictions" (a "logical" term) in reality, of the
"movement" of concepts, of quantity "turning" into quality, he indeed stipulated not only correspondence but a
specific "identity" between thought and its object—he assimilated the one with the other. But it may be assumed
that the wisdom of his critics, who note that Hegel confused
two essentially different realms, was not beyond the reaches
of his intelligence and awareness. According to Hegel, the
traditional distinction between thought and its object is
"abstract" and falsifies the real relation. Thought and its
object have a common denominator, which, itself "real,"
constitutes the substance of thought as well as of its object.

This common denominator is the inherent structure and the *telos* of all being, i.e., Reason. It is for Hegel the structure according to which all modes of being, subjective as well as objective, are modes of self-realization in an ever more conscious form—from the "blind" process of unorganic nature to the free realization of man in history. Reason is subjective as well as objective—the Logos of all being. It is dialectical in so far as the realization takes place through the development and solution of contradictions which define the various modes and conditions of being. Being is in its essence a process of "comprehending"— the process in which an object becomes what it is through constituting itself (as this particular object) in and against the various conditions and relations of its existence. By virtue of this process, existence becomes comprehending, the object becomes "subject," and comprehending, the "notion" (*Begriff*), becomes the essential "reality" of being. Self-conscious thinking is only the highest mode of an existence common to all being, and the movement of thought is only the highest and most general mode of the movement of all being. Hegel speaks of one notion turning into another, meaning that a notion, thought through, reveals contents which at first seem alien and even opposed to this notion. What happens is not that in the thought process one notion is replaced by another, by one more adequate to reality, but that the same notion unfolds its own content— a dynamic which *is* that of the reality comprehended in the notion. The reality has (or rather is) its own Logos and logic is ontology. Behind this apparent play with the equivocation of words lies the very idea which has been constitutive of Western philosophy since the Greeks—the idea of the *Logos* as the essence of being, which in turn determines the logical structure of "definition" and makes "logic" into an instrument for finding and communicating the truth. No matter how inadequate the translation of Logos as "reason" may be, it elucidates the decisive implication of this idea, namely, that the order of the cosmos (nature as well as society, physics as well as history) is at one and the same time a logical and ontological, a comprehending and comprehended (*begreifende* and *begriffene*) order. Thus the cognitive relation is constitutive of reality, is subjective *and* objective. However, the unity of the subjective and objective world is not a fact, not a given condition, but one that is to be attained in the struggle against adverse, denying conditions. Once this struggle becomes the self-conscious mode of existence, namely, in the human being, the dialectical process becomes the historical process—theory and practice in one. It comes to fruition in a "state of the world" where the conflict is resolved in the transparent harmony of subject and object, individual and universal. This is the inner logic of philosophy as well as reality. The dialectical logic may thus be called a logic of *freedom*, or rather, to be more exact, a logic of *liberation*, for the process is that of an alienated world, whose "substance" can become "subject" (as the *Phenomenology of the Spirit* formulates the thesis of Hegel's philosophy) only through shattering and surpassing the conditions which "contradict" its realization. Then, however, Hegel's dialectic surpasses the historical process itself and makes it into a part of a metaphysical system in which ultimate freedom is only the freedom of the Idea.

The Marxian "inversion" of Hegel's dialectic remains committed to history. The driving forces behind the historical process are not mere conflicts but contradictions because they constitute the very Logos of history as the history of alienation. Thus, according to Marx, (the Logos of) capitalist society speaks against itself: Its economy functions normally only through periodic crises; growing productivity of labor sustains scarcity and toil; increasing wealth perpetuates poverty; progress is dehumanization. Specifically, as Marx claims to show in *Capital*, it is the free wage contract and the just exchange of equivalents which generate exploitation and inequality; it is the capitalist realization of freedom, equality, and justice which turns them into their opposite.[2] The rationality of the system is self-contradictory: the very laws which govern it lead to its destruction. As in Hegel's conception, the process of liberation appears not as an extraneous scheme superimposed upon reality but as its objective dynamic, and the latter is the realization of the free "subject," which now finds its historical form and task—that of the proletariat. Moreover, the Marxian dialectic also is, as a political-historical process, a *cognitive* one: the true consciousness (class consciousness) of the proletariat is a constitutive factor in the objective dynamic of liberation.

These brief comments on the structure of dialectic may illustrate the fate it underwent in Soviet Marxism. The Logos of dialectic is no longer that of liberation—neither in Hegel's ontological nor in Marx's historical sense. This

[2] *Capital,* I, Chap. 4, conclusion.

is inevitable once dialectic is no longer focused on the contradictions of class society but extended beyond them. As Marxian theory is transformed into a general scientific "world outlook," dialectic becomes an abstract "theory of knowledge." Although it is to pertain to the proletariat and the Communist Party,[3] the connection is no longer transparent. Now Marxian theory may perhaps be called a "world outlook," but then its world is that of "pre-history," class society, and, specifically, capitalist society. Marxian theory analyzes and criticizes this world in all its manifestations, in its material and intellectual culture. There is no Marxian theory which may be meaningfully called a "world outlook" for postcapitalist societies—whether they be socialist or not. There is no Marxian theory of socialism because the antagonistic-dialectical laws which govern presocialist history are not applicable to the history of free mankind, and theory cannot predetermine the laws of freedom. Nor does Marxian theory "prophesy" beyond demonstrable trends in capitalist society. The essentially historical character of Marxian theory precludes unhistorical generalizations. Although Engels defined dialectic as the "science of the general laws of motion and development of nature, human society, and thought," [4] he noted that nature as well as society are "phases of historical development," and that the laws of dialectic are "abstracted" from their history.[5] In such ab-

[3] See the report on the results of the discussion of logic in *Voprosy Filosofii* (Problems of Philosophy), 1951, No. 6, pp. 143–49.
[4] "Anti-Dühring," in *A Handbook of Marxism*, ed. by E. Burns (New York, International Publishers, 1935), p. 266.
[5] *Dialectics of Nature*, trans. by Clemens Dutt (New York, International Publishers, 1940), p. 26.

straction, they can be presented as a series of general assumptions, categories, and conclusions—but the general scheme immediately cancels itself, for its categories come to life only in their historical concretion.

Consequently, in trying to present dialectic "as such," Soviet Marxists can do nothing but distill from the concrete dialectical analysis of the "classics" certain principles, illustrate them, and confront them with "undialectical" thought. The principles are those enumerated in Stalin's "Dialectical and Historical Materialism," which, in turn, are only a paraphrase of Engels's propositions in his *Dialectics of Nature*.[6] In terms of Hegel's and Marx's dialectic, they are neither true nor false—they are empty shells. Hegel could develop the principles of dialectic in the medium of universality, as a "science of logic," because to him the structure and movement of being was that of the "notion" and attained its truth in the Absolute Idea; Marxian theory, however, which rejects Hegel's interpretation of being in terms of the Idea, can no longer unfold the dialectic as logic: its Logos is the historical reality, and its universality is that of history.

The problem as to whether or not the Marxian dialectic is applicable to nature must here at least be mentioned because the emphasis on the dialectic of nature is a distinguishing feature of Soviet Marxism—in contrast to Marx and even to Lenin. If the Marxian dialectic is in its conceptual structure a dialectic of the historical reality, then it includes nature in so far as the latter is itself part of the

[6] *Ibid.* For the "omission" of the "negation of the negation" see below, pp. 153 f.

historical reality (in the interaction [*Stoffwechsel*] between man and nature, the domination and exploitation of
nature, nature as ideology, etc.). But precisely in so far
as nature is investigated in abstraction from these historical relations, as in the natural sciences, it seems to lie outside the realm of dialectic. It is no accident that in Engels's
"Dialectics of Nature" the dialectical concepts appear as
mere analogies, figurative and superimposed upon the content—strikingly empty or commonplace compared with the
exact concreteness of the dialectical concepts in the economic and socio-historical writings. And it is the *Dialectics
of Nature* which has become the constantly quoted authoritative source for the exposition of dialectic in Soviet Marxism. Inevitably so, for if "dialectic reigns everywhere," [7]
if it is the science of the "general laws of the material
world and of knowledge," [8] and therefore the only true
"scientific world outlook," then the dialectical concepts
must first and foremost be validated in the most scientific
of all sciences—that of nature. The consequence is a de-
emphasis of history.

The Soviet Marxist hypostatization of dialectic into a
universal scientific world outlook entails the division of
Marxian theory into dialectical and historical materialism,
the latter being the "extension" and "application" of the
former to the "study of society and its history." [9] The divi-

[7] K. S. Bakradze, "K voprosu o sootnoshenii logiki i dialektiki" (On the
Relationship Between Logic and Dialectic), *Voprosy Filosofii* (Problems of
Philosophy), 1950, No. 2, p. 200.

[8] V. S. Molodtsov, "Ob oshibkakh v ponimanii predmeta dialekticheskogo
materializma" (On False Conceptions of the Subject of Dialectical Materialism), *Voprosy Filosofii* (Problems of Philosophy), 1956, No. 1, p. 188.

[9] Stalin, "Dialectical and Historical Materialism," in *History of the Communist Party of the Soviet Union* (New York, International Publishers,
1939), p. 105.

sion would have been meaningless to Marx, for whom dialectical materialism was synonymous with historical materialism. In Soviet Marxism, historical materialism becomes one particular branch of the general scientific and philosophical system of Marxism which, codified into an ideology and interpreted by the officials of the Party, justifies policy and practice. History, which in Marxian theory is the determining and validating dimension of dialectic, is in Soviet Marxism a special field in which historical as well as suprahistorical laws assert themselves. The latter, arranged into a system of propositions, are presented as the ultimately determining forces in history as well as nature. The dialectical process thus interpreted is no longer in a strict sense a historical process—it is rather that history is reified into a second nature. Soviet developments thereby obtain the dignity of the objective natural laws by which they are allegedly governed and which, if correctly understood and taken into consciousness, will eventually right all wrongs and lead to final victory over the opposing forces.

But while the objective, determinist character of dialectical laws is thus strengthened, Soviet Marxism in reality appears as defying determinism and practicing voluntarism. The shift in emphasis from the former to the latter seems to be a feature of Leninism and seems to culminate in Stalinism. A straight road seems to lead from Lenin's "consciousness from without" and his notion of the centralized authoritarian party to Stalin's personal dictatorship—a road on which "scientific determinism" gives way (in practice, if not in ideology) to decisions on the ground of shifting political and even personal objectives and in-

terests. Subjective factors prevail over the objective factors and laws. However, closer analysis shows that the
abstract opposition of determinism and voluntarism is un-
tenable; their interrelation is more complex and requires
discussion to the extent that it sheds light on the socio-
historical changes reflected in Soviet Marxism.

The two elements are present from the beginning in the
Marxian doctrine; their relative weight depends on the
historical conditions under which Marxism operates.[10] In
periods of acute class struggles, when the revolution is "on
the agenda" and when a mature, class-conscious proletariat
is in political action, Marxism appears as little more than
the conscious manifestation of objective factors. In so far
as the latter tend "by themselves" toward revolution, in
so far as the capitalist structure is shaken by economic
crises and political upheavals, Marxism can interpret the
situation chiefly in terms of the harmony of the subjective
and objective factors. The function of the Marxist parties
and of their leadership and international organization then
is to comprehend and explain the objective constellation
of political forces and to direct the action of the proletariat
in accordance with it. This function is a subjective factor:
itself cognition and volition, it appeals to cognition and
volition. However, as a subjective factor, it is only the
formulation of the objective factors, which, directing the
political action, becomes an integral part and aspect of
them. In contrast, when the revolutionary potential is weakened, absorbed, or defeated, then the cognitive and voluntarist element is not embodied in the objective situation.

[10] For the following see above, pp. 17 f.

The consciousness and action of the proletariat then are largely determined by the "blind laws" of the capitalist process instead of having broken through this determinism. Consequently, the party, or rather the party leadership, appears as the historical repository of the "true" interests of the proletariat and above the proletariat, working by dictum and decree, and the proletariat becomes the object of these decisions. The subjective and objective factors are torn asunder—in reality, and this development appears in theory as the tension and antagonism between voluntarism and determinism.

It has often been noted that Marxian theory underwent a significant change after 1848. The philosophic humanism of the earlier writings, in which socialism is defined in terms of human aspirations and potentialities, gave way to a "scientific socialism governed by inexorable objective laws." [11] The transformation reflects the actual situation of the proletariat. The determinist elements in Marxian theory pertain to the structure of class society and particularly to capitalism, where men are subordinated to unmastered forces, operating "behind the back of the individuals" as inexorable laws. The abortive revolutions of 1848 and the ensuing consolidation of bourgeois society reasserted the "validity" of these laws, to which the bulk of the proletariat also succumbed. While Marxian theory reflects this extended determinism by increasing emphasis on the scientific character of the dialectic toward socialism, the "voluntarist" element comes to reside in a separate

[11] See Leonard Krieger, "Marx and Engels as Historians," *Journal of the History of Ideas*, XIV, No. 3 (June, 1953), 396 ff.

historical agency or agent, that is, in the leadership. The "true" consciousness is that which has not succumbed to the "false" determinism. But no matter how great the distance may be between the consciousness of the leadership and that of the proletariat, the former, in its theory and practice, must retain or reestablish the demonstrable connection between the "immediate" and the "real" interest of the proletariat. This relation between a highly centralized leadership and the proletariat which remains its determining base is illustrated in the period of the First International. At that time, the ideas, objectives, and attitudes of the leadership were remote from those of the proletariat and certainly not shared or even understood by the great majority of the latter. Still, the Inaugural Address, the analyses of the Paris Commune, and the communications of the leadership testify to the extent to which the factual attitude and actions of the proletariat determined the leadership's theory and strategy.

Subsequently, as ever larger strata of the industrial proletariat were installed in the capitalist system and partook of its benefits, the "natural laws" governing the system also seemed to engulf its negation. Revisionist Marxism affirmed this process. Dialectic was discarded. Eduard Bernstein's doctrine implied a determinism far more rigid than that of Marx and Engels. The subjective factor was objectified at the expense of its revolutionary content and intent: the proletariat moved—with the whole of society—under objective laws toward socialism, and the leadership operated under the same laws. We have tried to show above how Leninism attempted to restore the true relation between the subjective and objective factors by establishing the authority of the centralized revolutionary party over and above the proletariat. Again, the strengthening of the voluntarist element was accompanied by a strengthening of the determinist character of Marxian theory: Lenin's *Materialism and Empirio-criticism* replaced the dialectical notion of truth by a primitive naturalistic realism, which has become canonical in Soviet Marxism. However, in Leninism, the two factors remained closely related: during the Revolution, it became apparent to what degree Lenin had succeeded in basing his strategy on the actual class interests and aspirations of the workers and peasants. At the same time, the dialectic was reactivated and provided the conceptual tools for Lenin's guiding analyses of the historical situation. Then, from 1923 on, the decisions of the leadership have been increasingly dissociated from the class interests of the proletariat. The former no longer presuppose the proletariat as a revolutionary agent but rather are imposed upon the proletariat and the rest of the underlying population. The authoritarian voluntarism which characterized the Stalinist leadership responds to the objective determinant, the reduction of the revolutionary potential in the capitalist countries. And as the will of the leadership acts upon the proletariat from above, the theory pronounced by the leadership or endorsed by it assumes rigid determinist forms. The dialectic is petrified into a universal system in which the historical process appears as a "natural" process and in which objective laws over and above the individuals govern not only the capitalist but also the socialist society. The fate of the dialectic reveals the historical substance of Soviet society: it is not the negation of capitalism, but it partakes, in a decisive aspect, of the function of capitalism, namely, in the industrial development of the productive forces under separation of the control of production from the "immediate producers." Soviet theory here expresses what the ideology denies: that the Bolshevik Revolution did "not yet" entail a socialist revolution, that the "first phase" is not yet socialism. But while Soviet society thus partakes of the function of capitalism, it does so on an economic foundation—total nationalization—which makes for an essentially different developmental tendency beyond the present framework, in a direction which we shall subsequently try to identify. Now, we shall briefly illustrate the petrification of the dialectic and the points at which the future trend seems to become manifest.

The exposition of the dialectic in the representative textbooks is focussed on the determinist character of the dialectical process. For example, in Rozental's *Marksistskii Dialekticheskii Metod* (Marxist Dialectical Method), the capitalist development, the transition to socialism, and the subsequent development of Soviet society through its various phases is presented as the unfolding of a system of objective forces that could not have unfolded otherwise. To be sure, strong and constant emphasis is placed on the guiding role of the Communist Party and its leaders, and on the patriotic heroism of the Soviet people, but their action and its success was made possible only by their understanding of and obedience to the inexorable laws of dialectic. The subjective factor no longer appears as an integral element and stage of the objective dialectic, but rather as the mere vessel, recipient, or executor of the latter. This notion has remained obligatory during and after the Stalinist era. The Party and the Party leadership are the sole authority for the interpretation of dialectic—but this independence is qualified: the leaders themselves are subject to the objective laws which they interpret and implement.

The particular role of ideology in socialist society is determined by the nature of the development of this society, which differs essentially from the nature of the development of previous [social] formations. Under socialism, too, the laws of the social development are objective ones, *operating independently from the consciousness and will of human beings,* but under socialism, the party, the state, and society as a whole have the opportunity, unknown in past history, of comprehending these laws, consciously applying them in their activities, and, by this very token, accelerating the course of societal development.[12]

The Soviet Marxist interpretation of the relation between the subjective and objective factor transforms the dialectical process into a mechanistic one. This becomes particularly clear in the discussion of the relation between necessity and freedom. It is the key problem in the Hegelian as well as the Marxian dialectic, and we have seen that it is also a key problem in the idea of socialism itself. Soviet Marxism defines freedom as "recognized necessity." [13]

[12] M. T. Iovchuk, "Rol' sotsialisticheskoi ideologii v bor'be s perezhitkami kapitalizma" (The Role of Socialist Ideology in the Struggle with Survivals of Capitalism), *Voprosy Filosofii* (Problems of Philosophy), 1955, No. 1, p. 4 (italics added). Emphasis on the subordination of the Soviet state to the objective laws of the historical process is one of the essential points in Stalin's last article; see above, p. 121.

[13] For example, M. D. Kammari, "O novom vydaiushchemsia vklade I. V.

The formula follows Engels's restatement of Hegel's definition according to which freedom is "insight into necessity." [14] But for Hegel, freedom is not merely "insight" into necessity, but is comprehended (*begriffene*) necessity, which implies a change in the actual conditions. Mere "insight" can never change necessity into freedom; Hegel's "comprehended" necessity is "not merely the freedom of abstract negation, but rather concrete and positive freedom" —only thus is it the "truth" of necessity. The transition from necessity to freedom is that into a fundamentally different dimension of "being," and Hegel calls it the "hardest" of all dialectical transitions.[15]

Soviet Marxism minimizes this transition and assimilates freedom to necessity—in ideology as well as in reality. This assimilation is expressed in the Soviet Marxist interpretation of dialectical change, that is, of the development from one stage of class society to another. In Marxian theory, this development is (*a*) *catastrophic* (the unfolding contradictions of class society can be resolved only by explosion), and (*b*) as catastrophic development it is *progressive* (the stage initiated by the revolution is a higher stage of civilization). However, both these elements are themselves subjective as well as objective factors. The "explosion" is not automatic but presupposes the action and the consciousness of the revolutionary class; and

Stalina v marksistsko-leninskuiu filosofiiu" (On the Distinguished New Contribution by J. V. Stalin to Marxist-Leninist Philosophy), *Voprosy Filosofii* (Problems of Philosophy), 1952, No. 6, p. 32.

[14] "Anti-Dühring," in *Handbook of Marxism*, pp. 255 f.

[15] *Encyclopädie der philosophischen Wissenschaften im Grundrisse*, I, par. 158 and 159; *Science of Logic*, Book II, Sect. 3, Chap. 3, C.

"progress" denotes only the development of the productive forces and continues to involve exploitation and enslavement until the proletariat has become the historical agent.[16]

Into this conception, Soviet Marxism introduces the distinction between antagonistic and nonantagonistic contradictions ("conflicts" and "contradictions"):[17] the former irreconcilable and "soluble" only through a catastrophic explosion; the latter subject to gradual solution through political control; the former characteristic of class society, the latter characteristic of socialist society. Soviet Marxism claims that the change from the explosive to the gradual dialectical transition has been rendered possible in the USSR with the establishment of the Soviet state. In line with this conception, and following Stalin's example of 1938, the "law of the negation of the negation" disappeared from the list of the fundamental dialectical laws. Quite obviously, the Soviet Marxist conception of dialectic is most suitable to serve the ideological stabilization of the established state: it assigns to the state the historical task of solving the "nonantagonistic contradictions" and pre-

[16] See for example, Marx to Ruge, September, 1843, in "Deutsch-Französische Jahrbücher I," in Marx and Engels, *Historisch-Kritische Gesamtausgabe*, ed. by D. Rjazonov (Frankfurt, Marx-Engels Archiv Verlagsgesellschaft, 1927), Div. I, I, Pt. 1, 575; and Marx and Engels, *The German Ideology* (New York, International Publishers, 1939), p. 7.

[17] See for example M. M. Rozental, *Marksistskii dialekticheskii metod* (Marxist Dialectical Method) (Moscow, Gospolitizdat, 1951), *passim*; S. P. Dudel, "K voprosy o edinstve i bor'be protivepolonovsti: kak vnutrennem soderzhanii protsessa razvitia" (On the question of the Unity and Struggle of Opposites as the Content of the Process of Development), in *Voprosy Dialekticheskogo Materializma* (Questions of Dialectical Materialism) (Moscow, Akademia Nauk SSSR, 1951) pp. 73 ff. The Soviet Marxist doctrine of dialectical contradictions took final shape after Zhdanov's speech against G. F. Aleksandrov, June 1947, printed in *Bol'shevik* (Bolshevik), 1947, No. 16 (August 30) pp. 7–23.

cludes theoretically the necessity of another revolution on the way to communism. It should be noted, however, that the Soviet Marxist revision is theoretically consistent with the Marxian conception. According to Marx, the "catastrophic" character of the transition from quantity to quality belongs to the realm of blindly operating, uncontrolled socio-economic forces; with the establishment of socialism, these forces come under the rational control of society as a whole, which self-consciously regulates its struggle with nature and with its own contradictions. Moreover, the change in the mode of transition from one stage to another is already stipulated in Hegel's system: once the level of free and self-conscious rationality has been reached ("being-in-and-for-itself"), such rationality also governs the further transitions at this level. Similarly, Marx applied the notion of the "negation of the negation" specifically to the capitalist development. It is the "capitalist production" which, with the necessity of a "law of nature" engenders its own negation: socialism is this "negation of the negation." [18] The dialectical method does not stipulate the schematic repetition of this concept, and Hegel warns explicitly against the formalistic interpretation and application of the "triad." [19] The Soviet Marxist "revision" is "orthodox." Since Soviet Marxists maintain that Soviet society is a socialist society, they consistently invest it with the corresponding dialectical characteristics. What is involved is not so much a revision of dialectic as the claim of socialism for a nonsocialist society. Dialectic itself is used for substantiating this claim.

[18] *Capital*, I, Chap. 24.   [19] *Science of Logic*, Book III, Sect. 3, Chap. 3.

All this seems to confirm that the Soviet Marxist treatment of dialectic merely serves to protect and justify the established regime by eliminating or minimizing all those elements of dialectic which would indicate progress of the socio-historical development beyond this regime, that is, toward a qualitatively different higher stage of socialism. In other words, Soviet Marxism would represent the "arresting" of dialectic in the interest of the prevailing state of affairs—the ideology would follow the arresting of socialism in reality.

However, the situation is more complicated. We have noted at the beginning that Soviet ideology and reality are subject to a dynamic which the regime cannot arrest without undermining its own foundations. We have suggested that the international development tends to force the Soviet regime to direct its efforts toward the "second phase" of socialism—a trend which would also tend to alter the "superstructure." In line with the assimilation of ideology to reality, the trend would not only be noticeable but perhaps even anticipated in ideology. Recent developments in the Soviet Marxist treatment of dialectic seem to corroborate this assumption. Even during the last period of Stalinism, it appeared that ideological preparations were being made for rendering the regime more flexible, for "normalizing" it and for orienting Soviet society toward a long period of economic as well as political "coexistence"—a period required for the further internal growth of the Soviet system. The Soviet Marxist discussion of dialectic seems designed to adjust the ideology to the new period.

We have mentioned Stalin's reiterated emphasis on the "active" role of the superstructure in developing its base; this is not merely the ideological justification and stabilization of a prevailing form and stage of the state but also the ideological commitment of the state to introduce changes in conformity with the growth of the productive forces. As such, Stalin's statement of 1950 pointed toward his "Economic Problems of Socialism" [20] of 1952, with the stress on the contradictions between productive forces and production relations in the USSR, to be solved "gradually" under the guidance of the state. Similarly, the discussion of logic and dialectic in 1950–1951 seems not so much an ideological defence of the status quo against potential change, a protection from historical progress, as a preparation for intended changes. The discussion of the relation between formal and dialectical logic was linked throughout with Stalin's pronouncements in "Marxism and Linguistic Problems." [21] There Stalin had pointed out that it is "un-Marxist" and incorrect to talk of the "class conditioning" of language and to envisage a specifically "socialist language." He had maintained that language "differs in principle from a superstructure" in that it does not change with the base but outlives this or that base; it is created by and "serves," not certain classes, but society as a whole over the course of centuries. By the same token, Soviet Marxism declared, it is incorrect to treat formal logic as "class conditioned" and to envisage a specific

[20] In *Current Soviet Policies, ed. by Leo Gruliow* (New York, F. A. Praeger, 1953), pp. 1–20.
[21] See Stalin, *Marksizm i voprosy iazykoznaniia* (Marxism and Linguistic Problems) (Moscow, Gospolitizdat, 1950).

"Soviet logic" corresponding to the new basis of Soviet society.[22] The report on the results of the discussion on logic sums up:

The logical forms and laws of thought are no superstructure over and above the base. . . . Formal logic is the science of the elementary laws and forms of correct thinking. . . . There are not two logics: an old metaphysical, and a new, dialectical logic. . . . There is only one formal logic, which is universally valid.[23]

Dialectical logic does not deny, cancel, or contradict the validity of formal logic; the former belongs to a different dimension of knowledge and is related to the latter as higher to elementary mathematics.

We are not concerned here with the course and conclusions of the discussion.[24] Significantly, the changing trend announces itself in a return to Marxian orthodoxy after the leftist "Marrist deviations." In terms of Marxian theory, neither language nor logic as such belong to the superstructure; they belong rather to the preconditions of the basic societal relationships themselves: as instruments of communication and knowledge, they are indispensable for establishing and sustaining these relationships. Only certain manifestations of language and thought are superstructure, as for example, in art, philosophy, religion. Following the Marxian conception, the Soviet discussion dis-

[22] V. I. Cherkesov, "O logike i marksistskoi dialektike" (On Logic and Marxist Dialectic), *Voprosy Filosofii* (Problems of Philosophy), 1950, No. 2, p. 211.

[23] *Voprosy Filosofii* (Problems of Philosophy), 1951, No. 6, pp. 145, 146.

[24] They are summarized, in *ibid.*, pp. 143–49, and in Gustav Wetter, *Der Dialektische Materialismus* (Freiburg, Herder, 1952), pp. 544 ff. For the post-Stalin development see George L. Kline, "Recent Soviet Philosophy," in American Academy of Political Science, *Annals*, CCCIII (January, 1956), 126–38.

tinguished between logic itself and the *sciences* of logic. As
a specific interpretation of logic, some of the latter must
be classified as ideological.[25] Neither the Hegelian nor the
Marxian dialectic denied the validity of formal logic;
rather they preserved and validated its truth by unfolding
its content in the dialectical conception which reveals the
necessary abstractness of "common" as well as "scientific"
sense.

Compared with this tradition of dialectic, "Marrist" [26]
linguistic and logic (which stressed to the extreme the class
character of both) must indeed appear as a gross "leftist
deviation," as an "infantile disease" of communism in its
age of immaturity. It seemed to be an ideological by-
product of the first phase of the Stalinist construction of
socialism in one country. The violent struggle to overcome
the technological and industrial backwardness of the country, imposed by terror upon a largely passive and even
hostile population, found its ideological compensation in
the various doctrines of the uniqueness and superiority of
Soviet man, deriving from his "possession" of Marxism
as the only true and progressive "world outlook." But
Marxian theory is in its very substance international.
Within its framework, nationalism is progressive only as
a stage in the historical process—a stage which, according
to Marx and Engels, had already been surpassed by the
advanced Western world. Soviet Marxism has never suc-

[25] I. I. Osmakov, "O zakone myshleniia i o nauke logiki" (On the Law of
Thinking and on the Science of Logic), *Voprosy Filosofii* (Problems of
Philosophy), 1950, No. 3, pp. 318 ff.
[26] Only the Stalinist evaluation of Marr's doctrines is here discussed, not
the doctrines themselves.

ceeded in reconciling the contradiction between its own nationalism and Marxian internationalism—either in its strategy or in its ideology, as is demonstrated by the painful distinctions between "bourgeois cosmopolitanism" and genuine internationalism, between chauvinism and "Soviet patriotism." Moreover, the emphasis on a special Soviet mentality, logic, linguistic, and so forth, was bound to impair the appeal to international solidarity in the ultimate revolutionary objective as well as the appeal for peaceful coexistence, which the doctrine of socialism or communism in one country could not discard altogether. The "Marrist" theories may have fulfilled a useful function in the "magical" utilization of Marxian theory, but with the technological and industrial progress of Soviet society, with the growing political and strategic power of the Soviet state, they came into conflict with more fundamental objectives. As Soviet policy began to be oriented to the transition to the "second phase," the Marrist doctrines had to give way to more universalist, "normal," and internationalist conceptions. Far from signifying the "arrest" of dialectic in the interest of the stabilization of the attained level of development, the reiteration of the common human function and content of language and logic seems to be aimed at bringing the ideology in line with the drive toward the "next higher stage" of the development, that is, the second phase of socialism, and with the policy of "normalizing" East-West relations involved in this transition.

8. *The Transition from Socialism to Communism*

THE ENTIRE Soviet Marxist interpretation of dialectic is, as all ideological efforts since the last period of Stalinism are, focused on the transition from socialism to communism (or from the first to the second phase of communist society—the two formulations are used interchangeably). The idea of this transition has been an essential element of Soviet Marxism ever since the consolidation of the Soviet state after the first Five-Year Plan. As early as 1935, in his speech to the First All-Union Conference of Stakhanovites, Stalin hailed the Stakhanov movement as "preparing the conditions for the transition from Socialism to Communism," "the first beginnings—still feeble, it is true, but nevertheless the beginnings" of that "rise in the cultural and technical level of the workingclass of our country" which is the prerequisite for the "second phase." [1] But while the idea of this transition (without which Soviet Marxism could not even claim to be Marxism) has accompanied the construction of socialism in one country from the beginning, the transition is now presented as being in process, as the next objective of Soviet domestic policy. This is the gist of Stalin's last publication "Economic

[1] *Leninism* (New York, International Publishers, 1942), pp. 367 and 369.

Problems of Socialism in the USSR," which was then appraised by Soviet Marxism as the first authoritative Marxist theory of the concrete forms of this transition. The article retains its significance in spite of the critique to which it was subjected at the Twentieth Congress.

Implied is a "normal" development, that is, no war with the West. In accord with this presupposition, Stalin insisted on the precedence of interimperialist conflicts over the conflict between the capitalist and the socialist orbit. A whole section is devoted to the affirmation of the "inevitability" of wars among capitalist countries.[2] Apparently for the first time, Stalin cited publicly a Soviet Marxist analysis (referred to as that of "some comrades") of contemporary capitalism, which holds that the intercontinental integration of capitalism after the Second World War is not merely an extraneous political constellation, but is founded on a basis which makes wars among the capitalist countries no longer inevitable. This notion, which amounts to a denial of the Marxist-Leninist theory of imperialism, is cited only to be *rejected*. In his rejection, Stalin insisted on the reactivation of the economic conflicts between the United States on the one side, and the "subservient" capitalist countries on the other (Britain and France primarily; but also Germany and Japan). On the other hand, war between the imperialist and the Soviet camp is *not* inevitable.

The modification of the thesis on the "inevitability of war" is highly ambiguous. First of all, in traditional Marxist usage, it refers primarily to wars among *capitalist*

[2] "Economic Problems of Socialism in the USSR," in *Current Soviet Policies*, ed. by Leo Gruliow (New York, F. A. Praeger, 1953), pp. 7 f. For the following discussion see above, pp. 66 ff.

countries. As such, the thesis is in the center of the doctrine of imperialism. Conversely, the "correction" of the
thesis refers primarily to wars between the imperialist
and the Soviet camps: the war that is no longer inevitable
is this East-West war. Once this ambiguity is cleared up,
there appears to be a strange consistency in the Stalinist
and post-Stalinist conception. The statements on the sharpening of the intracapitalist contradictions made at the
Twentieth Congress [3] are substantively (and sometimes
even literally) in line with the Stalinist formulas! The consistency is explained by the main point at which post-
Stalinist policy continues and strengthens late Stalinist
policy, namely, by the reliance on "normal" capitalist development, stabilization of East-West relations, internal
growth of Soviet society, and economic-political competition. The war whose evitability is now so strongly emphasized is first of all the war between capitalist and socialist
countries. It can be prevented by virtue of the increased
power of the socialist camp and the latter's impact upon
the "peace-loving" populations in the capitalist countries.
However, these very same factors in turn would tend to
counteract war in general—therefore, even war between
capitalist countries would seem no longer "inevitable."

The shift in the Soviet Marxist position on the inevitability of war thus seems thoroughly consistent. As compared with the period when Lenin asserted the inevitability

[3] See the statements by Mikoyan and Khrushchev at the Twentieth Party
Congress, in *XX S"ezd Kommunisticheskoi Partii Sovetskogo Soiuza; Stenograficheskii otchet* (The Twentieth Congress of the Communist Party of the
Soviet Union; Stenographic Account) (2 vols.; Moscow, Gospolitizdat,
1956), I, 14–20. 319–21.

of imperialist wars, the internal and international situations have changed fundamentally, and a "balance of power" has been established (i.e., the strength of the Soviet camp), which serves as a deterrent against an East-West war. But this same deterring force has also reduced the possibility of military conflicts within the imperialist camp (from which the Soviet camp would emerge as beneficiary), while aggravating the economic and political difficulties in the capitalist world.

We have seen that this thesis on the aggravating capitalist contradictions belongs to the hard core of Soviet Marxism. However, the context in which Stalin repeated it in his last article gave it a special significance. The proposition introduces the discussion of the transition from socialism to communism as the next phase in the development of Soviet society. In this context, the proposition serves to reiterate the priority of domestic over foreign policy. In the first representative article on Soviet foreign policy after Stalin's death, *Kommunist* recalled that, according to Marxism-Leninism, "the foreign policy of any state is a continuation of its domestic policy and is governed by it." [4] For the USSR, this "normal" Marxist-Leninist constellation was interrupted by the Second World War, the subsequent strategic adjustments, and the period of restoration. The Nineteenth Party Congress seems to herald the return to the normal supremacy of domestic policy and to initiate its new phase. We have stressed that the discussion of Stalin's article in *Voprosy Ekonomiki* (Problems of

[4] 1953, No. 7, translated in *Current Digest of the Soviet Press*, V, No. 20 (June 27, 1953), 3.

Economics) explicitly states that "in actuality," the inter-imperialist conflicts supersede the conflict between the imperialist and the Soviet camp.[5] This portion of Stalin's article has remained mandatory for the party line: the conflicts among the imperialist powers and within the imperialist countries make for a "peaceful" internal reduction of capitalist strength.

The aggressive foreign policy of the USA sharpens the contradictions in the very camp of imperialism. . . . Soviet foreign policy . . . cannot refuse to take into account both the presence of considerable contradictions between individual capitalist countries and the presence of contradictions within these countries and even within individual parties adhering to capitalist classes and groups. It is our task to utilize these contradictions for the sake of preserving and solidifying peace and weakening the aggressive, anti-democratic forces.[6]

The imperialist policy of strength is now opposed—so the argument runs—not only by the broad masses of the people but also by a part of the "well-to-do classes."[7] While one should not underestimate the danger that a small "handful of exploiters" may unleash war out of sheer desperation, "it would be a still greater mistake to over-estimate imperialism's forces."[8]

While the reevaluation of the interimperialist situation suggests a new trend in foreign policy, the discussion of

[5] See above, p. 65.
[6] "Za uprochenie mira mezhdu narodami" (For the Consolidation of Peace Between Peoples), *Kommunist* (Communist), 1955, No. 4 (March), p. 12.
[7] "Sud'by mira i tsivilizatsii reshaiut narody" (The Peoples Decide the Fates of Peace and of Civilization), *Kommunist* (Communist), 1955, No. 4 (March), p. 12.
[8] *Ibid.*, p. 18.

the economic problems of socialism indicates the internal basis (and perhaps also the reason) for this trend. The re-orientation in foreign policy seems to have been necessitated by a domestic reorientation. The attainment of the international objectives—chiefly the weakening of Western society from within—ultimately depends on the attainment of a higher level of Soviet society (in Marxist language, the second stage of socialism).[9] Stalin's political testament reformulated Lenin's in terms of this transition: it stipulated the need for a new prolonged "respite" as the prerequisite for the further development of Soviet society.

In the "Economic Problems of Socialism," Stalin's proposition on the inevitability of interimperialist conflicts is followed by his definition of the "basic economic law of present-day capitalism," that is, the "need to obtain maximum profit." Stalin contrasts this "law" with the "law of the average profit norm" that was valid for the preceding stages of the capitalist development. Marxist interpreters of this passage have been troubled by the question of orthodoxy involved here: in Marxian terms, the need for maximum profit is inherent in the capitalist mode of production itself and cannot be contrasted with the "law of the average profit norm" because either it is subject to the latter law or it remains an exception—pertaining only to "privileged" groups of enterprises. Soviet commentators have disregarded this difficulty and taken Stalin's formulation as a cue for redefining the situation of present-day capitalism.

The notion of the "second phase" of the general crisis

[9] See above, pp. 76 f.

of capitalism,[10] as formulated by this redefinition, serves
as the contrasting background for the transition to the "second phase" of socialism. The crisis provides the favorable international environment for concentrating domestic
Soviet policy on this transition. In its discussion, there is
a striking emphasis on the need for changes within the Soviet system—changes which are to transform the system
itself into the "higher" second phase. A large part of Stalin's article is devoted to the refutation of the statements of
those who maintain that under socialism (that is to say,
in the present Soviet system) the correspondence between
productive forces and production relations is such as to
exclude contradictions. Against this view, Stalin maintains
that there is no "full conformity" between the elements of
the economic basis. The productive forces "run ahead" of
the production relations also under socialism—this, according to Stalin, is the matrix of progress—and the production relations are bound to turn into a fetter of social
development. However, while under conditions of private
appropriation and control these contradictions must lead
to a conflict which can be resolved only through an "explosion," under socialism, society is able to bring the lagging production relations into conformity with the character of the productive forces in good time and without
"exploding" the social order. At a certain stage of the development, the growth of productivity will render possible
a "distribution of labor among the branches of production
. . . regulated not by the law of value . . . but by the
growth of society's need for goods." [11] This is the basic fea-

[10] See above, pp. 58 f.
[11] "Economic Problems of Socialism," in *Current Soviet Policies*, p. 5. The
contradictions existing in socialist society are again emphasized in Khrush-

ture of the "second phase of socialism" ("communism").
Stalin refers to Engels: "Socially planned regulation of production in accordance with the needs both of society as a
whole *and of each individual.*" [12] The underscored words
in the Engels quotation (which did not occur in Stalin's
own formulation above) are decisive: they preclude the
authoritarian identification of *society*'s need for goods with
the needs of all its *individual members.* According to Marx
and Engels, communism prevails only if and when society's
needs are really the individual needs, and when their development and satisfaction determines the social division
of labor. But nothing in Stalin's own characterization of the
second phase suggests the abandonment of the administrative authoritarian identification of society's needs with
those of its members. According to his conception, since the
growth of the productive forces is no longer counteracted
by antagonistic private interests, the adjustment of production relations to this growth can be undertaken by the "directing agencies" of the Soviet state.[13] The transition from
socialism to communism is *their* work; "communism" will
be introduced as an administrative measure.

As to the timing in terms of years, Soviet theoreticians
still take as the basis the figure of three five-year plans,
given by Stalin in his speech of February 9, 1946. Con-
sidering the adjustments that were made recently, this
would locate the transition to the second phase between
1960 and 1965 at the latest.[14] More important is the timing

chev's speech of November 6, 1957 (as broadcast by Moscow Home Service,
p. A-23).

[12] "Anti-Dühring," in *A Handbook of Maxrism*, ed. by E. Burns (New
York, International Publishers, 1935), p. 294. Italics added.

[13] "Economic Problems of Socialism," in *Current Soviet Policies*, p. 15.

[14] Ts. A. Stepanian, "Usloviia i puti perekhoda ot sotsializma k kommu-

in terms of objective conditions. Stalin listed three "basic preliminary conditions": (1) Constant growth of all social production, with preponderant growth of the means of production," (2) the "raising of collective farm property to the level of property of the public as a whole," (3) "a cultural development of society as would ensure to all its members comprehensive development of their physical and mental abilities." [15] Stalin emphasized as the first necessary step for the attainment of the last condition the reduction of the working day "at least to six and then to five hours." As basic measures of economic policy during this period he considered the raising of real wages by at least 100 percent (through both an increase in money wages and a systematic reduction in prices of the goods of mass consumption),[16] and a gradual extension of the system of "product exchange" at the expense of the sphere of "commodity turnover" (especially by including the surplus collective-farm production in the sphere of product exchange).[17]

This outline of the transition to the second phase reiterates the traditional Marxist conception, derived chiefly from Engels's remarks in the third part of *Anti-Dühring*. But within the context of Stalin's statement, the standard propositions obtained the weight of a policy directive and were as such accepted by Stalin's anti-Stalinist successors.

The first fact to be noted is that the present post-Stalinist

nizmu" (The Conditions and the Paths of the Transition from Socialism to Communism), in *O sovetskom sotsialisticheskom obshchestve* (On Soviet Socialist Society), ed. by F. Konstantinov (Moscow, Gospolitizdat, 1948), pp. 540–42.

[15] Stalin, "Economic Problems of Socialism," in *Current Soviet Policies*, pp. 14 f.

[16] *Ibid.*, p. 14.   [17] *Ibid.*, p. 19.

and anti-Stalinist trend continues the main line of late Stalinist policy with respect to the problems of "transition."
We have tried to show this in the case of the evaluation of
capitalist development.[18] The same holds true with regard
to the principal objectives of Soviet policy. The resolution
adopted by the Twentieth Congress reasserts "the main
economic task," namely, "to catch up with and to outstrip
the most developed capitalist countries in production per
capita." For the attainment of the goals, the Resolution reasserts the priority of heavy industry, together with a need
for "rapid development" in the production of consumer
goods. Like Stalin, Khrushchev rejected "utopian views" of
the transition. Following Stalin's statement of the "basic
preliminary conditions" for progress, the Resolution provides for the reduction of the working day in the course of
the Sixth Five-Year Plan to seven hours for all workers and
to six hours for those in the coal- and ore-mining industries.
The same consistency prevails in the emphasis on technological education, the training of "specialists," and the
"ties of the country's scientific establishments with production." [19]

The continuity between Stalinism and post-Stalinism
might still be that of basic propaganda requirements, were
it not for the possibility that it may reflect a dynamic inherent in the Soviet social system itself.

We have proposed that the Soviet construction of socialism, while progressing, develops a dialectic of its own. On
the one hand, the totalitarian administration strengthens

[18] See above, pp. 65 ff.
[19] *XX S"ezd Kommunisticheskoi Partii Sovetskogo Soiuza* (The Twentieth
Congress of the Communist Party of the Soviet Union), II, 434, 475, 480.

itself *and* the very forces against which it acts (thereby creating a stronger consolidation of Western society); in doing so, it perpetuates the repressive economic and political features of the Soviet system. On the other hand, the administration depends, for the attainment of its main objective ("to catch up with and outstrip") on the all-out development of the productive forces at its disposal. This development—under the impact of an international competition which Soviet Marxism regards as a struggle for survival—drives the growing productivity, with the most streamlined weapons of modern technology and science, toward a level at which it will tend to "overflow" into production for individual needs. Given conditions under which the growing production can be sustained at full capacity, and under which this capacity is not to an increasing degree utilized for wasteful and destructive purposes, production is likely to generate the material and cultural wealth that would permit the stipulated features of the second phase. (They are modest enough.) This seems to be the case even if in their development the productive forces also sustain a large and greatly privileged bureaucracy. Productivity may be expected to run ahead of privileges and effectuate a gradual but qualitative change in the circumstances of the underprivileged population and, correspondingly, in the political institutions—as it did at preceding stages of an expanding civilization.

The totalitarian administration has, of course, sufficient power to counteract this trend, and it must be expected to do so if the administration operates under an interest antagonistic to the growth of productivity and its use for the satisfaction of individual needs, or if it considers counter-action necessary for the existence of the Soviet state. We have tried to show [20] that the first condition does not prevail. The "class interest" of the bureaucracy (that is, the common denominator of the special interests of the various branches of the bureaucracy) is linked to the intensified development of the productive forces, and administrative progress into a "higher stage of socialism" would most effectively secure the cohesion of Soviet society. On the other hand, the Soviet state has consistently diverted a very large sector of the productive forces (human and material) to the business of external and internal militarization. Does this policy forestall the transition to the "second phase"? The compatibility of an armament economy with a rising standard of living is more than a technical economic problem. The maintenance of a vast military establishment (armed forces and secret police) with its educational, political and psychological controls perpetuates authoritarian institutions, attitudes, and behavior patterns which counteract a qualitative change in the repressive production relations. Inasmuch as the bureaucracy is a separate class with special privileges and powers, it has an interest in self-perpetuation and, consequently, in perpetuating repressive production (and political) relations. However, the question is whether the repressive economic and political relations on which this bureaucracy was founded are not increasingly contradicting the more fundamental and general interests and objectives in the development of the Soviet state.

[20] Pages 116 ff. above.

If our analysis of Soviet Marxism is correct, the answer must be affirmative. The fundamental Soviet objective in the present period is the breaking of the consolidation of the Western world which neutralizes the "interimperialist conflicts" on whose effectiveness the final victory of socialism depends. The same forces which make for and preserve this consolidation also endanger and delay the attainment of the goal "to catch up with and surpass" the capabilities of advanced capitalism. In the Soviet Marxist analysis, Western consolidation is based on a "permanent war economy," which, taking advantage of the head start of capitalism, sustains the rapid development of productivity in the capitalist countries and the integration of the majority of organized labor within the capitalist system. Thus it continues to delay the revolution in the capitalist world which even Stalin considered as ultimately indispensable for the triumph of socialism.[21] The capitalist war economy is in turn sustained by the "hard" Soviet policy, which also stands in the way of Soviet progress to the second phase where it can effectively compete with capitalist capabilities. Consequently, the first step must be the relaxation of the "hard" policy. This, however, is a matter of internal as well as foreign reorientation, of shifting the emphasis from military and political to more effective economic competition, and of liberalizing the Stalinist bureaucracy. The shift presupposes a high level of industrialization. Soviet success in the utilization of atomic energy may have been one of the significant events which has convinced the Soviet

---

[21] Soviet Marxism considers the socioeconomic rather than the military potentialities of the international constellation: the internal strength of Western society, most conspicuously expressed in the higher standard of living and in "class collaboration" is, in Marxian terms, a greater long-range threat to the "final victory of socialism" than is Western military power.

leadership that the adequate competitive level of industrialization has been reached.

We believe that these factors are behind recent Soviet
developments. If this is the case, the shift is part of a long-
range trend, originating in an objective historical situation
and pertaining to the very structure of Soviet society. The
objective historical situation (i.e., the interrelation between Stalinist power politics and capitalist consolidation)
drove the Soviet state to a reconsideration of its basic strategy, a "relaxation" which, if successful, tends toward an
increasing use of the growing productivity for consumers'
needs. The basic economic trend would generate a corresponding political trend, that is, liberalization of the repressive totalitarian regime.

In Soviet policy toward the Western world, evidence for
the new trend had been cumulative from the end of the
Korean war to the upheavals in Eastern Europe in 1956.
Corresponding developments had also taken place in inter-
communist relations: the Soviet-Yugoslav *rapprochement;*
the commitment of the Indian and the Japanese parties to
a "legal-democratic" program; continuation (and even
intensification) of the "soft" strategy of the Western Communist parties, especially of the united front policy—de-
Stalinization. It was this de-Stalinization which stimulated
the events in Poland and Hungary. The Soviet leadership
reacted in accordance with the underlying policy conception. Soviet Marxism has never acknowledged a genuine
third alternative to socialism or capitalism, and the former
is defined, for the period of coexistence, in terms of a firm
alliance with the Soviet Union. A break in the "protective
belt" of Eastern European states is, in the Soviet interpre-

tation, therefore tantamount to an ascent of capitalist influence and to a change of the international balance of power at a vital point in favor of the capitalist world. Moreover, while the liberalization in the Soviet Union rested on a firm basis of industrialization and collectivization, this was not the case in the Eastern European countries. Industrialization was still at a very backward stage, and the peasantry was not yet effectively coordinated with the nationalized economy and its political institutions. The movement toward "national communism" was therefore considered as objectively premature and antisocialist regardless of the sincere subjective intentions of the national leadership and their followers among the working classes and the intelligentsia.

The Eastern European events were likely to slow down and perhaps even reverse de-Stalinization in some fields; particularly in international strategy, a considerable "hardening" has become apparent. However, if our analysis is correct, the fundamental trend will continue and reassert itself throughout such reversals. With respect to internal Soviet developments, this means at present continuation of "collective leadership," decline in the power of the secret police, decentralization, legal reforms, relaxation in censorship, liberalization in cultural life. The relation of this policy to the long-range socio-economic trend may be illustrated by the continued preferential development of heavy industry as against the development of consumers' goods industries. The "Malenkov line" interpreted Stalin's statement on the prevailing conflict between productive forces and production relations as necessitating a change in the relation between the two main divisions of production in favor of the second division, namely, that of consumers' goods industries [22]—in spite of Stalin's injunction that the "predominant growth" of the first division must remain the basis of socialist planning. Although the theory of shifting the priority to the second division was not officially rejected until January, 1955, opposition to it was already outspoken in 1954 under the Malenkov regime:

There must be no place in Soviet science for discussion with vulgarizers and falsifiers of Marxism. Some economists : . . attempted to revise one of the fundamental principles of economic teaching of Marxism, i.e., the thesis that enlarged reproduction, especially under socialism, requires preferential development of Subdivision I (production of means of production) as against Subdivision II (production of means of consumption).[23]

Distorting the substance of the action carried out by the party and the Soviet government steeply to raise agriculture and increase production of products for popular consumption, some economists started asserting that under socialism enlarged reproduction to become effective does not necessarily require a more rapid development of the production of the means of production as compared to production of consumers' goods.[24]

Priority for the development of heavy industry is considered essential for the transition to communism not only

[22] See for example A. N. Maslin, "Printsip material'noi zainteresovannosti pri sotsializme" (The Principle of Material Interest under Socialism), *Voprosy Filosofii* (Problems of Philosophy), 1954, No. 4, pp. 3–14; 1955, No. 1, p. 15.

[23] M. T. Iovchuk, "Rol' sotsialisticheskoi ideologii v bor'be s perezhitkami kapitalizma" (The Role of Socialist Ideology in the Struggle with Survivals of Capitalism), *Voprosy Filosofii* (Problems of Philosophy), 1955, No. 1, p. 15.

[24] I. Doroshev and A. Rumiantsev, "Protiv izvrashcheniia marksistskoi teorii vosproizvodstva" (Against the Distortion of the Marxist Theory of Reproduction), *Kommunist* (Communist), 1955, No. 2 (January), p. 14.

in terms of the internal growth of the social product but
also in terms of the international implications—in other
words, the military as well as economic position of the
USSR must be strengthened:

Having fulfilled the industrialization program devised by the party
in the prewar Five-Year Plans, the Soviet people established a solid
economic basis for an active defense of the country. A mightly
heavy industry proved the foundation of the USSR's indestructible
defensive power.[25]

Under the conditions of coexistence with the capitalist
world, the party and the government are thus committed to
maintain the policy of preferential development of heavy
industry for the communist as well as socialist construction
of Soviet society.

To be sure, behind the doctrinal controversy probably
lies a struggle between the top bureaucracies for their
share in power. Unquestionably, a decisive shift in production priority would involve a corresponding shift in political weight: the influence of the managerial strata in heavy
industry would be bound to decline. However, the political
struggle has a more basic content; Soviet society seems to
have reached another turning point in its development. The
Soviet leadership itself has defined this turning point: a
level of growth has been reached where progress no longer
requires the alternative of either increasing heavy industry
or the standard of living, but where the latter can be
achieved as a result of the former. Reduced to its funda-

[25] E. Frolov, "Tiazhelaia industriia—osnova ekonomicheskogo mogush-
chestva SSSR" (Heavy Industry—The Basis of the Economic Might of the
USSR), *Kommunist* (Communist), 1955, No. 3 (February), pp. 29 f. See
also the second editorial in the same number, p. 22.

mental contention, the idea now is: not competitive preparedness for war *or* competitive satisfaction of popular needs,
but *both*. The alternative was that of the Stalinist era; it is
now held surpassed by the success of this era.

On this Malenkov and his opponents seem to have
been in agreement. When Molotov was called upon in
October, 1955, to retract his "erroneous" statement (of
February, 1955) that merely the "foundations" of a socialist society had been laid, and instead to confirm that a
socialist society itself had been built, he was called upon
to acknowledge the completion of a whole period (with
which he himself has been identified) and the beginning
of a new one. But it was Khrushchev who stated most suc-
cinctly the socio-economic reasons for the superseding of
the Stalinist alternative. In his report on the agricultural
program, delivered in September, 1953, he said:

The Communist Party has steadily maintained a course of overall
development in heavy industry as essential to the successful development of all branches of the national economy, and it has achieved
great success on this road. Chief attention was turned to solving
this immediate national economic problem, and basic forces and
means were diverted to it. Our best cadres were occupied with
the work of industrializing the country. We did not have the means
for high-speed, simultaneous development of heavy industry, agriculture, and light industry. For this it was necessary to provide
needed prerequisites. *Now these prerequisites exist.* We have a
mighty industrial base, strengthened collective farms and cadres
trained in all branches of economic construction.[26]

This is the internal reason for the new trend: the Leninist
program of "civilization" [27] has been fulfilled in the first

[26] *Current Digest of the Soviet Press*, V, No. 39 (November 7, 1953), 11 f.
[27] See pp. 46 f. above.

phase; through the Stalinist construction, an industrial base has been created sufficiently strong to meet international "emergencies" and to raise the consumption level in the USSR. What could not have been done "simultaneously" before can now be undertaken: the "forced development" of heavy industry can continue while allowing an increasing proportion of the social product to flow into the satisfaction of individual consumers' needs.

But if the decision to accelerate and enlarge the production of consumer goods while continuing the preferential development of heavy industry indicates the measure of progress beyond the Stalinist period, it also indicates that progress will be kept within the framework of "nonantagonistic" contradictions and administrative adjustments. In other words, any expectation of a qualitative change which would amount to an explosive "negation" of the past stage is rigidly opposed. Improvement and liberalization will be conditional upon the relentless struggle for higher productivity of labor, upon socialist competition, and upon total mobilization of the people for work and for training. Again, such continuity in the "spirit" of socialism cannot simply be explained by the "power drive" of the Soviet leadership—it is rather rooted in the objective conditions under which the Soviet state operates, in the "anomaly" of capitalist and socialist coexistence which Lenin's political testament epitomized. The notion of socialism in a "capitalist environment" precludes abandonment of the total mobilization of the people; it also precludes a fundamental change in the value system which subordinates socialist freedom to toil and discipline. It is the Soviet government and the party which will raise the level of popular consumption. This constantly repeated formula expresses the basic policy that progress and liberalization, the effect of the "basic law of socialism," will not be the result of freedom and initiative "from below" but rather of the utilization of an expanding economy, regulated by the state in accordance with the political requirements (national and international). The resolution to maintain this policy is demonstrated by the manner in which political and cultural liberalization remains fused with improvement in a repressive morality, private and public, in work and in leisure.

We shall analyze the social function of Soviet morality in the second part of this study. Here, the question arises whether the "spirit" of socialist construction as institutionalized during the Stalinist period will also be fundamentally affected by the new trend. Even a most tentative answer would have to discuss two chief factors: the attained stage of the economic-political development, and the inner dynamic of the established behavior pattern and value system, which, though planned and controlled, have their own exigencies and aims. Only a tentative answer with respect to the economic-political factor can be sketched at this point.

We have seen that, in the Stalinist conception, the disappearance of the state as repressive machinery is made conditional on the strengthening of the socialist state, and that the latter is to continue into the second phase. There are no indications that this conception has been altered since Stalin's death. Although Stalin's "erroneous formula" on the aggravating class struggle during the progress of socialism is rejected,[28] although a considerable "democratization" of the state, decentralization, and self-government is proclaimed and even implemented, the continued strengthening of the state and of the party agencies remains on the agenda.[29] Nor—and this is far more important—are there any objective factors or tendencies which would allow such alteration. The reorientation in international strategy, and the corresponding domestic reorientation, especially in the field of agriculture, confront the regime with problems of such a magnitude that intense regimentation from above seems to be required for the very success of the new efforts. Relaxation no less than hardening of the system necessitates planned control. The gulf, in terms of privileges and of power, between the bureaucracy and the underlying population is still great enough to make for the self-perpetuation of the former. Moreover, education and training of the people are geared to a well-functioning mass of competitive subjects of administration. According to the doctrine itself, the very nature of the state as an independent power over and above the individuals must sustain the separation of the "immediate producers" from control over the means of production: social unfreedom reproduces political unfreedom. The trend we have suggested is toward alleviating the

[28] Resolution of the Central Committee of the Communist Party of the Soviet Union, June 30, 1956, in *The Anti-Stalin Campaign and International Communism*, ed. by Russian Institute, Columbia University (New York, Columbia University Press, 1956), p. 290.

[29] Khrushchev at the Twentieth Congress of the Communist Party of the Soviet Union, *XX S"ezd Kommunisticheskoi Partii Sovetskogo Soiuza* (The Twentieth Congress of the Communist Party of the Soviet Union), I, 91 ff.

latter; but only if it affects the former, or, in Stalin's terminology, only if the contradictions between the growing
productive forces and the production relations have really
been solved, would the entire structure change. This solution is reserved for the "final victory of socialism," and
the "final" victory of socialism is still linked to the international revolution. In this respect, the initiative in the
turn toward the "withering away" of the state is not with
the Soviet leadership—the turn depends on the break in
the "capitalist environment" and its effects on Soviet society.

The sustained power of the state sustains the controls
over the ideological sphere. The relaxation might be considerable; individual liberties are likely to increase with
increasing economic benefits—but quantity will not turn
into quality unless the economic benefits have themselves
become political ones, that is to say, have led to the control
of production by the "immediate producers," or, according
to the progress of automation, by the "immediate consumers." As long as this is not the case, the post-Stalinist welfare state will remain the direct heir of the Stalinist state.
And for just as long, the basic "spirit" of socialism will remain the same. Soviet society in this case pays tribute to
the dialectic of ideology and reality, consciousness and
societal relations. According to this dialectic, a genuinely
socialist base is reflected in an ideology which is *free* in a
strict sense. The mental development in all its manifestations is freed from the blind determination by the "realm
of necessity" and tends toward a free play of humane individual faculties. Materialism is canceled through its reali-

zation; as the economy is brought under the control of the associated individuals whose material needs are fulfilled, their mental development is released from control. The rational regulation of the necessities, of the struggle for existence and the struggle with nature, enables society to dispense with the regulation of the instinctual and intellectual life of its members. Reason appears as individual freedom. In Soviet society, however, the progressing control of the base continues to be accompanied by a progressing control of the ideology, and by the regulation of the realm of freedom gained by conquest of the necessity. In the very passage where Stalin calls for the reduction of the working day "at least to six and then to five hours" (a measure in which Marx saw the basic prerequisite for freedom), he states that this reduction is necessary "in order that members of society may receive the leisure time necessary for a thorough education." Thus the time saved will not be *free* time—it will have to be spent in education.

To be sure, education is the prerequisite for liberation: only the freedom to learn and to know the whole truth, to grasp the arrested, violated, and destroyed potentialities of man and nature can guide the building of a free society. What kind of education did Stalin envisage? He demanded the introduction of "universal, compulsory, polytechnical education, so that a member of society may be able to make a free choice of occupation and not be shackled for life to any one occupation." [30] Following up this program, the Twentieth Congress again places all emphasis on "training"—the training of "specialists on the basis of a close

[30] "Economic Problems of Socialism," in *Current Soviet Policies*, p. 14.

cooperation between studies and production" and calls for "strengthening the ties of the country's scientific establishments with production, with the concrete demands of the national economy." [31] The exchangeability of functions, the elimination of the institutionalized division of labor,[32] is indeed in Marxian theory the characteristic of a socialist society—as a precondition for the all-sided development of the genuinely human faculties *outside* the process of material production. But in Stalin's context the Marxian idea appears as that of a society in which all men are technicians and engineers. For Marx and Engels, the goal of communism was the "abolition of labor," [33] in the Soviet Marxist conception, all will be laborers of the one communist society.[34] With the free time transformed into education time for polytechnical training, with the work morale anchored in the instinctual structure of man, administrative control is secured, and the past is safely transferred into the future. Stalin could thus quote without danger Engels's statement that labor will change from a burden into enjoyment. The enjoyment, however, will not be qualitatively different from that permitted under repression.

The ideological perspective parallels the political per-

---

[31] Resolution as broadcast by Tass, February 25, 1956; *XX S"ezd Kommunisticheskoi Partii Sovetskogo Soiuza* (The Twentieth Congress of the Communist Party of the Soviet Union), II, 480.

[32] *Not* the division of labor as such—only that mode of division which chains the laborer for life to one specialized performance and function.

[33] Marx and Engels, *The German Ideology* (New York, International Publishers, 1939), pp. 49, 69.

[34] Stepanian, "Usloviia i puti perekhoda ot sotsializma k kommunizmu" (The Conditions and the Paths of the Transition from Socialism to Communism), in *O sovetskom sotsialisticheskom obshchestve* (On Soviet Socialist Society), pp. 486 f.

spective. The state will continue into the period of communism—as will the "capitalist environment." For the state is the "collective subject" of the national economy which organizes the whole of society, and this organization has become the objectified representative of society over and above the individuals. Since societal production is systematically directed by the state and since the basic decisions are imposed upon the society by the state, progress itself, that is to say, the use of the growing productivity for the needs and aspirations of the individuals, must pass through the agencies of the state. The continuity of the administration thus bridges the gap between necessity and freedom, and assimilates the first and the second phase, socialism and communism. And the administration, as we have tried to show, depends on the ever more effective growth and utilization of the productivity of labor: it tends to drive society to a higher stage. Industrialization and rationalization, carried through according to standards of competitive efficiency at the national and international level, and developing human beings as ever better functioning instruments of material and intellectual labor, are likely to bear economic as well as political fruits—overruling the diverging interests and intentions of particular groups and individuals.

The reward will not be the end of domination of man by man; administration of things is not likely to replace the administration of men in any foreseeable future. Marx stressed the essentially "neutral" character of technology: although the windmill may give you a feudal society, and the steammill an industrial capitalist society, the latter may just as well give you another form of industrial society. Modern machinery is susceptible to capitalist as well as socialist utilization. This amounts to saying that mature capitalism and socialism have the same *technical* base, and that the historical decision as to how this base is to be used is a *political* decision. During the period of coexistence, the economic factors are political factors; it is the period of political economy with respect not only to the state's role in the economy, but also to the political implications of the development of consciousness. The consciousness of the underlying population, permeated with the power of ever growing productivity, with the efficiency of an ever better mechanized and coordinated apparatus, and with the rewards of an ever more indispensable compliance, does not attain any other political level than that of the apparatus itself. Thus it is barred from developing the political consciousness which may serve as a guide to political change.

The two antagonistic social systems here join in the general trend of technical progress. It has been noted (and we shall attempt to demonstrate this notion by the example of Soviet ethical philosophy in the second part of this study) how much the present "communist spirit" resembles the "capitalist spirit" which Max Weber attributed to the rising capitalist civilization. The Soviet state seems to foster the disciplining, self-propelling, competitive-productive elements of this spirit in a streamlined and politically controlled form. "Businesslike management," directorial initiative and responsibility, and scientific rationalization of the human and material resources have remained the consistently imposed demands throughout both the Stalinist and post-Stalinist period,[35] in times of both "hard" and "soft" policy, of both personal and collective leadership. And "businesslike management" has also been applied to grand international strategy, to the conduct of foreign affairs. The change in the type of leader, from the professional revolutionary to the manager (a change which began as early as 1922, with the development of the New Economic Policy), now seems to be consummated. In 1922 Lenin proclaimed preference for the merchant, the trader, the administrator over the loyal revolutionary communist who did not know how to trade, how to sell, how to do business. He went further than that: "We are not afraid to say that the character of our work has changed. Our worst internal enemy is the Communist who occupies a responsible (or not responsible) Soviet post and enjoys universal respect as a conscientious man."[36]

However, the spirit of businesslike politics and competitive efficiency in the twentieth century is no longer that described by Max Weber. Developed industrial society requires a different organization and a different behavior. Soviet society, in the position of a "latecomer" telescoping entire phases of growth, meets its antagonist in a common situation. At the "atomic" stage of the mastery of man and

[35] See for example Bulganin's report to the Central Committee of the Communist Party, July, 1955, in *Current Digest of the Soviet Press,* VII, No. 28 (August 24, 1955), 3–20, and Zverev's speech at the session of the Supreme Soviet, February 1955, in *ibid.,* VII, No. 6 (March 23, 1955), 19–20, and No. 7 (March 30, 1955), 8.

[36] "Report at the All-Russian Congress of the Metal Workers' Union," in *Selected Works* (12 vols.; New York, International Publishers, 1937–38), IX, 318, see also p. 326.

nature, societal productivity surpasses the traditional forms of control and utilization. The cohesion of society is no longer left to the free play of economic forces and their individual evaluation and calculation; they have to be supplemented by more powerful regulation. The fusion between economic, cultural, and political controls is an international phenomenon, cutting across differences in economic, cultural, and political institutions. In the Soviet Union, this fusion is an avowed ideological as well as economic goal: at the very time when Soviet industry is again to be revamped in accordance with the standards of business efficiency, the government emphasized that this program is to be implemented by strengthening the "industrial leadership" of the Communist Party! [37]

There is no prospect that this fusion of economic and political controls in a self-perpetuating state will dissolve; it is doubly grounded, in the nationalized but not socialized Soviet economy, and in the international situation of large-scale industry. This framework of the state leaves room for many changes within the administration: the top rule may pass from one group to the other, from party to army predominance, from "committee rule" back to personal rule, and so forth. However, these changes would not fundamentally alter the basis of Soviet society, nor the basic direction in which this society is moving. Unless another world war or similar catastrophe occurs which would change the situation, the direction is toward a growing welfare state. Rising standards of living up to a prac-

[37] See Bulganin's report to the Central Committee of the Communist Party, July, 1955, in *Current Digest of the Soviet Press*, VII, No. 28 (August 24, 1955), 18 ff.

tically free distribution of basic goods and services, steadily extending mechanization of labor, exchangeability of technical functions, expanding popular culture—these developments constitute the probable trend. It is likely to lead to the gradual assimilation of urban and agricultural, intellectual and physical labor—brought under the common denominator of technology. Technical progress will overtake the repressive restrictions imposed at earlier stages—they will become technically obsolete. This will lead to further changes in the political structure: it will make for a spread of the bureaucracy and its privileges, for a reduction of the gap between the top strata and the underlying population, for the transformation of political into technological controls. Personal rule will increasingly be replaced by collective administration, even if a new dictator should concentrate the leadership at the top. Social mobility within the system will grow. But these changes themselves will take place within the framework of universal control, universal administration. Whether or not the growth of the welfare state will ultimately bring the administration under direct popular control, that is to say, whether or not the Soviet state will develop into a socialist or communist democracy, is a question for which the prevailing facts and tendencies do not provide a workable hypothesis. Negatively, it seems that nothing in the structure of Soviet society would exclude such a long-range development, and that it would depend neither on a "decision" of the Soviet leadership nor on the internal situation of the Soviet orbit alone. From our analysis, it follows that the emergence of a socialist democracy in the USSR would be conditional upon two main prerequisites, which in turn are interrelated: (1) a level of social wealth which would make possible the organization of production according to individual needs and thus cancel the prerogatives of privileged powers; and (2) an international situation in which the conflict between the two social systems would no longer define their economy and their policy.

We have suggested that such qualitative change is no longer an economic but a political problem: [38] the technical-economic basis for the change is there. It is not the still terrifying scarcity and poverty which prevents "socialist democracy," that is, the control of production and distribution "from below." In Marxist terms, distribution of scarcity and the concerted struggle for its abolition pertain to the content of socialism from the very beginning—even during the first phase.[39] On the basis of the nationalized economy, establishment of this control remains a political act. As such, it involves the abolition of the repressive state and its repressive machinery—which does not necessarily mean violent overthrow in civil war. However, the political act itself seems to be dependent on the second prerequisite. The rising welfare state may render life more comfortable and more secure, but as long as the East-West conflict remains a determining economic and political factor, it precludes the decisive transformation, for it serves to justify—subjectively and objectively—repressive competition and competitive mobilization on a totalitarian scale. The history of Soviet society seems to be fatefully linked to that of its antagonist. Over and above the con-

[38] Page 185 above.   [39] Page 20 above.

struction of socialism or communism in one country and in one orbit, the essentially international element of socialism seems to prevail.

But in this constellation, the prospective development of the Soviet state stands under the dialectical law which it invokes. The qualitative change can never be envisaged as an automatic one. No matter how high the level of technical progress and material culture, of labor productivity and efficiency, the change from socialist necessity to socialist freedom can only be the result of conscious effort and decision. The maintenance of repressive production relations enables the Soviet state, with the instrumentalities of universal control, to regiment the consciousness of the underlying population. We have suggested that the bureaucracy may not have a vested interest in perpetuating the repressive state machinery.[40] However, this does not dispose of the question as to whether or not the "spirit" of Soviet socialist construction, the specific "rationality" of the system, tends to perpetuate repression by and in the underlying population itself—in other words, whether repression from above does not meet repression from below. The Soviet system would then repeat and reproduce that determinism which Marx attributed to the basic processes of capitalist society. There, Marxian theory and practice themselves were to be the lever which would break this determinism and free the subjective factor, that is, the class consciousness of the proletariat. We have tried to show that, in Soviet society, Marxism no longer has this function. Left without a conceptual level for the "deter-

[40] See pp. 109 ff. above.

minate negation" of the established system, for comprehending and realizing its arrested potentialities, the ruled
tend not only to submit to the rulers but also to reproduce
in themselves their subordination. Again, this process is not
specific to Soviet society. The means and rewards of highly
advanced industrial society, the work and leisure attitudes
called forth by its organization of production and distribution, establish a human existence which makes for a change
in basic values—for a transformation of freedom into security. Such a transformation in turn would counteract the
development of a "negative" political consciousness and
thus counteract qualitative political change. The basic
value system, the prevalent "spirit" of the society, would
then assume the role of an active factor determining the
direction of the societal development. As a partial contribution to the analysis of this factor, the second part of this
study will examine the main structure of Soviet ethical
philosophy.

PART II: ETHICAL TENETS

9. *Western and Soviet Ethics:*
Their Historical Relation

IN THE FIRST part of this study we have analyzed certain basic trends of Soviet Marxism in their relation to the development of Soviet society. The analysis led to the conclusion that the specific conditions and objectives of industrialization, carried out in antagonistic competition with the Western world, determined even the most theoretical features of Soviet Marxism. At the same time, it appeared that in some significant aspects the two antagonistic systems showed a parallel tendency: total industrialization seemed to exact patterns of attitude and organization which cut across the essential political and ideological differences. Efficient, "businesslike management," highly rationalized and centralized, and working on equally rationalized and coordinated human and technical material, tends to promote political and cultural centralization and coordination. In the West, this trend has led to a corrosion of the humanistic liberal ethics which was centered on the idea of the autonomous individual and his inalienable rights. But the system of values derived from an earlier stage has by and large been maintained (after the liquidation of the Fascist and Nazi states which subverted it)—though in increasingly overt contradiction to the prevailing practice.

In the Soviet state, total industrialization occurred under conditions incompatible with liberal ethics; therefore, the revolutionary and postrevolutionary state created its own system of values and indoctrinated the population accordingly. However, contemporary total industrialization with contemporary technics and methods of work provide a common denominator which makes the abstract contrast between Western and Soviet ethics questionable.

Neither centralization nor coordination militate by themselves against progress in freedom and humanity (they have more than once been effective weapons in the struggle against oppression and reaction). Nor is there anything in the technics and economics of total industrialization that would necessarily encroach upon human freedom. On the contrary, if there is anything common to the Marxian and anti-Marxian evaluation of industrial society in nineteenth-century philosophy, it is the insistence that increasing industrialization is the prerequisite for progress in the ethical as well as the material sense. The protest against the "alienation" of man, which materialist and idealist philosophy express, is in both cases directed against the *political organization* [1] of industry—not against industry as such. In Marxian (but certainly not in Soviet-Marxist) terms it would be easy to identify the common element in the political organization of industry which militates against prog-

---

[1] "Political" as distinguished from "social" refers to an organization and utilization of industry which is not determined by the faculties and needs of the individuals but by particular interests conflicting with the free development of individual faculties and needs. Under this condition too, production fulfills a "social need," but the latter is superimposed upon the individual needs and shapes them in accordance with the predominant specific interests.

ress in freedom, namely, the enslavement of man by the means of his labor, his subordination to his own "objectified" (*vergegenständlichte*) labor. Still, in history, such subordination had very different functions: it may initiate a new stage in the development of the productive forces or prolong an old one; it may promote or arrest the development. The political organization of industry can by itself not explain the specific content of Soviet ethics and its relation to Western ethics.

We propose to approach the problem through a brief comparison between the representative ideas of Western and Soviet ethics. Such a comparison asumes that there is on both sides an identifiable body of ethical theory sufficiently homogeneous to be treated as a whole. The assumption seems plausible in the case of Soviet ethics: throughout all changes to which Soviet ethical theories have been subjected since the Bolshevik Revolution, they have been governed by one unifying principle, namely, the formulation and evaluation of ethical standards in accordance with the objectives of the Soviet state. And in so far as these objectives themselves have been determined by the long-range policy of socialism under conditions of coexistence,[2] a striking continuity and consistency have been preserved notwithstanding all adaptations to the changing situation. But can a similar case be made for the contrasting homogeneity of Western ethics? The case seems to be legitimate *a contrario*. If we look at the ethical standards and ideas on which the Soviet discussion of Western ethics is centered and which are criticized and reinterpreted, we discover

[2] See Chapter 4 of this study.

certain general features which appear as characteristic of
Western ethics. They are as follows:

1. The notion of freedom obtains; according to this the
essential condition of man is that he be sufficiently *free
from* external determination to become *free for* self-
responsible action and behavior.

2. This essential freedom validates the proposition of
universally binding ethical norms, to be observed regardless of the individual's accidental situation and objectives.

3. The ethically legitimate aims of the individual are
those which involve the best possible development and satisfaction of his faculties, but individual self-realization is
subordinated to (*a*) the universally valid norms of Christian ethics and their humanistic secularization; (*b*) the
more specific norms of the social and political community
in which the individual lives.

4. The two sets of norms are sanctioned (*a*) by God
and/or "the nature of man"; and (*b*) by the requirements
of sustaining and improving the social and national community.

5. But regardless of the ultimate sanction of morality,
the supposition is that there is no *fundamental* conflict [3]
between individual morality on the one hand, and com-
munal (social and political) morality on the other; that is
to say, in the countries of Western (industrial) civilization,
the basic social and political relations are held to be organized in such a way that the objectives of the individual
(Point 3 above) and his "essence" (Points 1–2 above) can

---

[3] Although there certainly is (and ought to be) factual tension and difference.

be attained or at least reasonably aspired to *within* the institutions of the established society. These institutions can and must be improved, and their improvement may even imply large-scale changes; however, such changes are generally envisaged, not as the negation of the established society but as its expansion and growth.

The last proposition states the hidden *historical* denominator of Western ethics: it presupposes that civilization has finally established the institutions and relationships within whose framework man can realize his "nature," that is to say, unfold his potentialities and fulfill his needs. This presupposition is common to both idealistic and pragmatist-positivistic ethics, to the theories expounded by the French rationalists, the English utilitarians, the German idealists, and by Saint-Simon and his followers. But the political and industrial revolutions of the eighteenth and nineteenth centuries are not its only source. Its moral substance is deeply rooted in the Christian tradition. Ever since Christian ethics ceased to be an "oppositional" ethics, since its adoption by the state, the representative ethical philosophies have condemned as heresy a morality which maintained that the established civilization was in *irreconcilable* conflict with the potentialities of man. To be sure, man's salvation and redemption are not of this world; but this world does not only not preclude his salvation, his moral behavior in it is also a necessary precondition for his salvation.[4] All philosophy which does not accept this presupposition is, from the point of view of representative Western

---

[4] Calvinist doctrine is no exception. "Good works" and merits are not identical with moral behavior in the Christian sense.

ethics, in a strict sense not only *heretic* but also *amoral* if not *immoral*. For such nonacceptance implies rejection of the fundamental assumption on which the universal validity of the moral principles rests, namely, the possibility of their realization.

However, the "heretic" philosophies have survived in many forms—from the Gnostic schools of the first Christian centuries, the Cathari and other radical spiritual sects, to the revolutionary social philosophies of the modern era. Common to all of them is their commitment to a qualitatively new history—a history which must shatter the established institutions so that the real destiny of man may be fulfilled. Common to all of them is their attraction among the underprivileged and "marginal" strata of the population (and their acceptance by various political and intellectual "elites"). Their morality has a different historical denominator and therefore appears as the negation of the prevailing morality. But at the same time, the heretics claim to preserve and even fulfill the principles and promises maintained by their orthodox adversaries: the medieval Cathari claimed to be the true Christians; the radical sects of the Reformation represented themselves as the true Protestants. During the modern period, the opposition, increasingly secular, continues within the humanist tradition. The great materialists and skeptics of the sixteenth century, the extreme left wing of the Enlightenment and its socialist-communist heirs justify their "subversive" philosophy in terms of the humanist ideal. Marxism is an integral part of the same tradition. It was more than a manner of speaking when Marx and Engels considered themselves as heirs of the Enlightenment, the French Revolution, and German idealistic philosophy. Liberty, Equality, and Justice are key terms in Marx's *Capital,* and its economic theory is in a more than chronological sense preceded by and completes the humanist philosophy of the German Ideology (1846) and the Economic-Philosophical Manuscripts (1844).[5]

This outline, though oversimplified, may help to clarify the historical relation between Western and Soviet ethics. The main impact of Soviet ethical philosophy is not that of an external force operating from outside and against Western civilization. Nor does the challenge come from the specific content of Soviet ethics—from the ideals of "communist morality." Soviet ethics bases its claim to represent a "higher" morality on the historical mission of Marxian theory, and Marxian theory has no independent ethics but claims to demonstrate the *realization* of humanistic ethics. According to Marx, the capitalist economy is the fate and the denial of this code of ethics, and its abolition the prerequisite for the development of ethics. The historical roots of Soviet philosophy are not alien to the West (no matter how closely they have been fused with the Eastern tradition and adapted to the national and international interests of the Soviet Union). Nor are they primarily defined by the requirements of power and propaganda. They derive

[5] No complete English translation of the latter is available. The full text was first published in Division 1, Vol. III of the *Marx-Engels Gesamtausgabe* (Berlin, Marx-Engels Verlag, 1932). Also not available in English is Marx's *Grundrisse der Kritik der Politischen Oekonomie,* written 1857–58 (Berlin, Dietz, 1953). This is the most important of Marx's manuscripts, which shows to what extent the humanist philosophy is fulfilled and formulated in the economic theory of *Capital.*

(1) from the revolutionary formulation of the humanist ideal in the theory of "scientific socialism," and (2) from its use for establishing a new society opposed to and competing with capitalist society. No matter how much the former contradicts the latter (the first part of this study tries to show how much it does), the connection is close enough to render possible the employment of the ideal in defense of the reality. The forces and circumstances which led to the abuse and violation of the ideal appear as more objective than those of mere power politics—objective to such an extent that they may easily be presented as the working of Historical Reason. Within this framework, Soviet ethical philosophy is an internally consistent, rational system of values, sufficiently separable from political expediencies to attract the self-interest of large populations outside the Soviet dominion.

This attraction seems to rest to a great extent on an argument which implies that Marxism has rescued humanistic ethics from capitalist distortion. It may be summarized as follows:

The people in the Western world have been educated in the spirit of Christian-humanistic ethics. Their societal relations are supposed to conform essentially to this spirit and to render possible its ever more adequate and universal realization—especially the liberty and equality of man, and the development of his human potentialities. Western civilization at its industrial stage has indeed assembled all the material and cultural resources necessary for implementing this idea. However, the existing societal institutions prevent its implementation because they sustain injustice, exploitation, and repression. Consequently, they must be destroyed in order to fulfill the promises of Western civilization.

This argument, which has been publicized in very popular formulations and on various levels of sophistication, persuasion, and evidence, has had a lasting influence. The mainsprings of this influence may be defined as follows: The argument (1) derives the pervasive discontent in civilization from one tangible and easily identifiable cause, namely, the capitalist organization of society; (2) it criticizes this society, not by any extraneous and transcendental standards, but by those promulgated and accepted by Western society (i.e., the "humanistic values"); (3) it thus explains and justifies discontent and protest not only on material but also on ethical grounds; (4) it offers an alternative which, again, is presented, not as an extraneous abstract possibility, but as the fulfillment of the very promises and capabilities of the existing society.

The last point indicates what seems to be the main force of the appeal—the combination of ethical maxims with scientific objectivity. Working with Marxist theory, Soviet ethics claims to unite, on a scientific basis, values and facts, ideal and reality, the particular interest of the individual and the general interest of society, even of mankind, as a whole. Moreover, Soviet ethical philosophy claims to be capable of demonstrating the attitude, behavior, and practice which alone will bring about freedom and a humane existence for all. And this practice is individual as well as social, that is to say, it is to unite the individual with a social group on the ground of a common cause by virtue of

which the specific concerns of the individual are taken over
by the entire group.

Soviet ethics thus claims to weld together ideas and
spheres of life that appear as torn asunder in Western
ethics. According to the latter, man was to come into his
own in a natural and social environment which was com-
patible with a free and moral existence—at least it did
not preclude the attainment of this end. In reality, however, the conditions of life turned out to be rather limiting
and hostile, and the environment was experienced, rather,
as adverse to the development of an ethical personality.
The experience therefore, had to be devaluated and reinterpreted: the "inner man" was separated from his external existence, and the ethical personality was defined
in such a way that it included—and even necessitated—
renunciation, suffering, and repression. The tension which
motivates Western ethics expresses—and at the same time
justifies—the experienced contrast between the ever-grow-
ing material and intellectual resources and their avail-
ability for individual needs, between the demand for self-
determination and the limits imposed upon it in reality,
between essential equality and the still prevailing inhu-
manity of man against man, between the ideal of justice
and unjust practices. These factual restrictions of the
morally sanctioned and professed ideal seem to whittle
down the central notions of Western ethics; moreover, they
seem to confront human existence with a welter of conflicting loyalties and values (divine versus human, or natural
versus positive, law; individual versus commonwealth;
private versus public values; family versus social stand-

ards). In contrast, Soviet ethics seems to represent the effective solution of these contradictions—an integration of moral with practical values which Western ethics cannot accomplish and does not want to accomplish because it considers the tension between the two spheres as a precondition of moral behavior. The contrast between Western and Soviet ethics may now be illustrated by the different weight given to the values of freedom and security.

The Western idea of freedom is realized through economic and political institutions which are to enable the individual to be the self-responsible architect of his fate. His existence is to be the result of his own activity, that is, his own performance in free competition with other individuals who are about equally equipped. In accordance with this philosophy, the institutionalized safeguards of freedom (the rule of law; civil rights; property guarantees) necessarily leave the individual to his own devices in large areas of his existence. These areas tend to become areas of *insecurity* as the economic process becomes complex and incalculable, beyond the control of the average individual, and dependent on a whole array of supraindividual forces and processes. Freedom in the economic sphere then is canceled by the factual "closing" of whole categories of employment, by the rigidity of prescribed behavior patterns, by the standardization of required work performances, or it involves a risk which the majority of the people cannot afford to take (risk of unemployment, of "falling behind," of becoming an outsider, and so forth). The encroachments on freedom appear as rational and technical processes—nobody's fault and doing, but the by-product (or perhaps even the condition) of the division of labor in late industrial society and, as such, tokens of efficiency and progress. The value itself of freedom seems to become questionable. In reality (though not necessarily in ideology) freedom is being *redefined*. It no longer means being the self-responsible architect of one's life, of one's own potentialities and their realization. Instead, freedom becomes that which the representative political philosophy of ascending individualistic society has always meant it to be, namely, the surrender of the "natural" liberty of the individual to the civil liberty of being able to do what is not prohibited by law or not accessible to law, or, the recognition of legitimate unfreedom. But this is *security*. The standards of freedom are shifted from the autonomous individual to the laws governing the society which governs the individual. They merge with the laws governing the economy, the commonwealth, the nation, the alliance of nations. However, while the individual is supposed to be made secure within this overwhelming political and economic cosmos, his "true" freedom is still to derive from and even to consist of the "inner" being (freedom of conscience, thought, religion, and so forth). Thus, while in the factual existence the striving for security prevails upon the value of freedom and is desired even at the expense of freedom, freedom and security come into conflict with each other—a conflict which can be minimized only by reducing the elements of independence and autonomy, that is to say, by sacrificing them to the value of security. However, the entire ideological tradition of Western ethics, with its image of man as free master and lawgiver, militates against this trend; and where the latter asserts itself against all tradition, under the impact of economic necessity, it only throws in sharper relief the difference between ideology and reality. The ideology is still strong enough to block the sanctioning of the surrender of individual freedom and to counteract total coordination; the conflict between freedom and security still remains an avowed condition of existence, and the mastery of the conflict an ethical task. But the task becomes ever more unrealistic.

Soviet ethics promises to solve the conflict by supporting the Soviet state in its elimination of the "negative" aspects of freedom, namely, those areas in which the individual was still left to his own devices, although his devices were grossly inadequate for the great majority of the people. The choice of education, training, and occupation; the liberty to provide for one's own care and old age; the right to read and write and listen to different and conflicting opinions were reduced or abolished, and Soviet ethics justified this policy. The traditional liberties in these areas succumbed to the regimentation of employment, control of movement, health insurance, censorship, and so forth. The realm of legitimate unfreedom was vastly extended, and the surrender of the "natural" liberty of the individual was openly and methodically enforced in spheres of the human existence which remained sacrosanct in the West. But within the context of Soviet ideology and Soviet objectives, the suppression of traditional liberties assumes a "positive" function which Soviet ethical philosophy interprets as the preparation of true freedom. The traditional liberties can be safely devaluated in Soviet ethics, for, from the Soviet point of view, they are merely ideological or even illusory for the great majority of the population until and unless they are substantiated in economic security, that is, freedom from want.

This independence from want will, according to Marx, only prevail if and when man is no longer enslaved by his labor—in other words, political and intellectual freedom presuppose freedom from the daily struggle for the necessities of life, which in turn presupposes the existence of a classless society. The Marxian conception implies that man ceases to be an economic subject precisely to the degree to which the economy ceases to be his "fate," that is to say, is no longer a determining factor but is itself determined, namely, brought under rational control exercised by the associated individuals. In so far as economic freedom is free competition in the incessant struggle for "earning one's life" (i.e., making a living), it is, to Marx, the negation of true freedom because it compels man to spend practically all his time and energy in procuring the necessities of life—in "alienated labor." And in so far as the notion of the free individual involves the free economic subject, it is itself the notion of unfreedom. For the "economy," that is, the entire realm of necessity in which the competitive struggle for existence takes place, cannot be the realm of individual freedom as long as it is the realm of alienated labor. To the degree to which this realm comes under the rational, collective control of the associated individuals, the "economic subject" ceases to be essential to the free individual, as do those liberties which are instruments and supplements of economic freedom. A large and decisive segment of what belonged, previously, to the rights of the private individual then becomes the concern of society. And if the realm of necessity is brought under the rational control, not of the associated individuals but of the state superimposed upon the individuals, the rights of the individual in this sphere become the concern of the state.

As the individual changes his social function, so does the idea of freedom itself. Where the "free economy" no longer exists, the Western individual is no longer a reality or even ideology—he is reshaped and redefined together with his freedom. It is then incumbent upon society to organize and direct the production and distribution of the necessities which are the prerequisites for freedom. And as long as these necessities are not available to all, and all are free, the state, as an independent power, is likely to arrogate to itself this organization and direction, and with it legislation over the private as well as public existence of the individual. For no matter how protected it is, the private remains the "negative" of the public existence, and the individual part of the universal. The state which, as an independent power, controls the realm of necessity, also controls the personal aspirations, objectives, and values of the individual. The systematic reduction of the antagonism between the internal and external, between private and public existence (an antagonism which has become the life element of Western ethics) has been one of the basic functions of Soviet society as well as Soviet ethical philosophy. The inner and private values are externalized, that is to say, man is to be in *all* his manifestations a social and political being.

10. *Soviet Ethics—The Externalization of Values*

THE EXTERNALIZATION of values is a universal feature of Soviet ethics. It is the concomitant and corollary of nationalization and shares its function and content. Although the abolition of private property is confined to ownership of the means of production, it also affects private property as an existential category.[1] If private property is no longer

---

[1] The ideology according to which private property is essential to the realization of the "free person" is epitomized in Hegel's *Philosophy of Right,* paragraphs 41 ff., especially paragraph 46. However, the extent to which otherwise most fundamentally different thinkers agree on the *essential* connection between the human person and private property is truly remarkable. We may be permitted to recall just a few of the best known statements to this effect:

Thomas Aquinas (*Summa Theologica,* II.II.qu.66a.1,2) : It is not only "lawful" but "necessary" that man should possess property. As regards the use of things, "man has a natural dominion over external things, because by means of his reason and will he can make use of them for his own purpose, as though they were made for him" (trans. Dominican Fathers of the English Province).

John Locke (*Of Civil Government,* Second Treatise, Chap. III, par. 26) : Every "man has a 'property' in his own 'person'. . . . The 'labour' of his body and the 'work' of his hands, we may say, are properly his. Whatsoever, then, he removes out of the state that Nature hath provided and left it in, he has mixed his labour with, and joined to it something that is his own, and thereby makes it his property."

Hegel (*Philosophy of Right,* par. 41) : "In order that a person be a fully developed and independent organism, it is necessary that he find or make some external sphere for his freedom. . . . The rationality of property does not lie in its satisfaction of wants, but in its abrogation of the mere subjectivity of personality. It is in property that person primarily exists as reason" (trans. J. M. Sterrett and Carl J. Friedrich).

regarded as the instrument through which the individual asserts himself, as the expression and embodiment of his self against other selves, then the whole area of individual privacy, which has traditionally been permeated with the values of private property, becomes externalized—it becomes the legitimate concern of society. To Western ethics, the effects of this externalization are particularly abhorrent in those two spheres which are regarded as the sanctuary and reservoir of the individual per se, namely, the privacy of thought and conscience, and the privacy of the family. In these two spheres perhaps more than in any other, freedom, according to the Western conception, is a function of *privacy,* and privacy is linked to property—as the institution through which the person is legally constituted as having a realm of his own. Freedom of thought and conscience requires freedom from interference with matters which belong to the individual and not to the state and society. The thoughts and feelings of the individual and their expression are to be "his own"; [2] he is to utilize and direct them according to "his own" faculties and conscience; he is not merely to obey the universal standards but rather to "appropriate" them and make them his own (moral) legislation.

Here again, the historical denominator of the Western conception comes to the fore. The free *privacy* of thought has assumed the dignity of an unconditional right during that period of modern society when the ideas held to be true for the human existence have appeared as *antagonistic*

[2] A "natural person" is one "whose words or actions are considered as his owne." (Hobbes, *Leviathan,* Chap. XVI.)

to the truths promulgated or represented by the *public* authorities, especially by the state, by whom those ideas were *not* held valid and self-evident. It is sufficient to recall the fact that "freedom of thought" emerged as a moral and political right in the struggle against feudal and clerical despotism. Even today, where this right has been firmly institutionalized in the Western democracies, its value is activated only in emergency situations in which authoritarian groups and policies encroach upon privacy. Conversely, where there is no real conflict between private thought and public ideology or between private conscience and public morals, freedom of thought and conscience does not seem to be experienced as an essential value on which the individual existence depends—nor does it seem to have an essential content. In the most extreme case, the conflict between private and public values is "resolved" in complete coordination: the individual thinks and feels and values privately what is thought and felt and valued in "public opinion" and expressed in public policies and pronouncements (not necessarily by the government, but by leaders of public opinion, "heroes" and models of aspirations, in general education, and by the predominant forms of entertainment). Such coordination can be established by terror, by the standardizing trends of "mass culture," or by a combination of both. The costs for the individual and for society are incomparably greater if it is accomplished by terror, and the difference may well be that between life and death. However, at the end of the coordinating process, if and when conformity has been successfully established, the effect on the hierarchy of values tends to be the same: individual freedom of thought and conscience appears to be losing its independent and unconditional value and to be submerging in the unification of private and public existence. In the course of a few generations, if the effectiveness of the regime is sustained, repressiveness may be reduced by spreading over the whole of society, extending to all parts of the material and intellectual culture. When privacy and inner freedom no longer have a definable experiential content, their abolition no longer has the quality of oppression which is still attached to it in the Western hierarchy of values.

With the "socialization" of privacy, the locus of freedom is shifted from the individual as a private person to the individual as a member of society. Society as a whole,[3] represented by the Soviet state, defines not only the value of freedom, but also its scope, in other words, freedom becomes an instrument for political objectives.

The instrumentalization of Soviet ethics does not exclude the consideration of motives and does not cancel the moral concept of "character." On the contrary, we shall see that motives and character themselves become subject to objective societal evaluation: the concrete historical situation of Soviet society and the goals which it is to attain "call for" and define specific motives and a specific character as *moral*. The same shift occurs with respect to all other ethical values: they are all referred to a new general denominator, and it is this new common denomi-

[3] In Part I of this study, we have emphasized that, in Soviet Marxism, "society" is made into an independent or at least separate power over and above its individual members. In speaking here of "society" as the new denominator for all ethical values, we refer to this "reification" of society, which makes it practically coextensive with "the state."

nator which gives Soviet ethics rational inner consistency and coherence. The individual acts and thinks "morally" in so far as he promotes, in his actions and thoughts, the objectives and values set by society. Ethical value is in this sense "external" to any specific individual action or thought, the latter being instruments for attaining an ethical goal which is that of society. However, while Soviet ethics is essentially instrumentalistic, it is grounded in a new historical position which defines the specific function of communist morality as surpassing instrumentalism.

The function of communist morality was authoritatively defined in Lenin's address to the Third All-Russian Congress of the Communist Youth in 1920,[4] as (1) the negation of the traditional (bourgeois and prebourgeois) morality, that is, the rejection of all ethical values and principles based on transcendental (religious) sanction and/or "idealistic" propositions (Lenin makes no substantive distinction between these two ethics); and (2) the affirmation of a new "communist" morality, which is in its entirety subordinated to the interests of the proletarian class struggle. The principles of this morality are to be derived from the requirements and objectives of this struggle. It must be noted that this exposition of communist morality does not preclude the "taking over" of "bourgeois" ethical values if and when they coincide with the needs of the respective stage of the class struggle. It must also be noted that the avowedly "instrumentalist" character of communist morality (to serve the interests of the proletariat in the

[4] *Sochineniia* (Works) (3d ed., 30 vols.; Moscow, Institut Lenina, 1928–37), XXX, 403–17.

class struggle) is, according to Lenin, directed toward a goal which would surpass the pragmatist level: the purpose of morality is "to raise human society to a higher stage and to liberate it from exploitation."

As to the specific content of communist morality: "For the communist, the entire morality consists in the firm solidarity and discipline [of the class struggle] and in the conscious struggle of the masses against the exploiters." [5] Lenin's definition points up the absence of all specifically ethical values apart from and outside the class struggle (a necessary result of the historical position of communist morality), and, at the same time, indicates the direction in which these values will subsequently be concretized. "Solidarity and discipline" focus communist ethics on the rigid work morale of the Stalinist period, while the emphasis on the *conscious* struggle (reiterated throughout Lenin's address) reveals the strongly "intellectualist" character of Soviet ethics—learning, training, the systematic and methodical appropriation of the technical and cultural knowledge accumulated in civilization is made one of the foremost prerequisites for the building of communism. In this respect, too, Soviet ethical philosophy claims to be the heir of the Western rationalist tradition: the attainment of freedom, in other words, the realization of man, is to be based on knowledge and reason.

Lenin's primitive and brutal definition of communist morality presupposes a complex historical dialectic which is to raise these ethics from the realm of relative to that of absolute validity. The "higher stage of human society"

[5] *Ibid.*, XXX, 413.

(the stage of total and universal liberation) would cancel the specific character of communist morality and make the instrument an end in itself.

The instrumentalistic character of Soviet ethics has been made the main target of Western criticism, and this criticism has been focused on the principle that "the end justifies the means"—a principle which is considered as unethical in itself. However, Soviet ethics aims beyond instrumentalism, and the critique in terms of the means-end relation misses the target. The suprapragmatic tendencies of Soviet ethics derive from the specific features of Soviet instrumentalism.

The society which provides the general denominator for Soviet ethics is, according to Soviet philosophy, defined by two essential characteristics (they were more fully discussed in Part I): (1) It is supposed to be organized in such a way that it has established the *preconditions* for the free development and fulfillment of all humane faculties for all its members (by the abolition of private control over the means of production and, thereby, of exploitation and class justice). (2) Owing to the particular circumstances of "backwardness" and "capitalist environment," these conditions for freedom have not yet been fully utilized for the immediate benefit of the individuals. Repression, scarcity, and unproductive use of the productive forces (production of armaments) still prevail (marks of the lower stage of socialism as distinguished from the higher stage of communism). The conditions of freedom are thus still preconditions; their realization depends on the continued exertion of the still unfree individuals.

The interrelation of these two conceptions of society gives Soviet instrumentalism its specific dynamic. The first (affirmative) conception furnishes a set of objective ethical standards, that is to say, those pertaining to a fully developed classless society ("communism"). These standards recapture the traditional ideal of Western civilization —freedom, justice, and the all-round development of the individual—condensed in the formula: "From each according to his abilities; to each according to his needs." The formula reestablishes the individual as the ultimate point of reference for ethical norms: what furthers the free development of the individual is good. The extreme relativism inherent in this norm is supposedly freed from harmful connotations by the socialist institutions: the general will is to coincide with the will of all individuals; the inequality of needs and faculties becomes an absolute value if and when it no longer involves the development of one individual at the expense of others. The prospective end result of socialist morality thus bestows upon Soviet ethics the dignity of universally valid and objective norms, culminating in the principle of solidarity and cooperation. Instrumentalism terminates in ethical absolutism; partisanship and class morality are proclaimed as mere vehicles (although the *only* historical vehicles) for the realization of *humanitas*. These standards of the future are then related to the actual situation of Soviet society, but they retain their "transcendental" connotation,

that is, the image of a future which will compensate the individuals for their present sufferings and frustrations. Soviet ethics here contains a "safety valve": the image of
the future seems to perform a function corresponding to
that of the transcendental elements of Western ethics—in
this image we seem to have a real Soviet substitute for religion. However, there is an essential difference from
which Soviet ethics derives much of its appeal. The transcendental goal in Soviet ethics is a historical one, and the
road to its attainment a historical process—the result of a
concrete social and political development. Final human
fulfillment and gratification are not oriented on the "inner
self" or the hereafter, but on the "next stage" of the actual
development of society. And the truth of this conception
is to be, not a matter of faith, but a matter of scientific
analysis and reason—of necessity.[6]

Unquestionably, this official argument for Soviet ethics
serves well to justify a repressive regime which may use it
only as an ideological veil for the perpetuation of the
present state. However, what holds true for the Soviet
use of Marxism in general [7] may also be applied to its

[6] To be sure, the ideology of *progress*, which rationalizes the present
deprivation, suffering, and repression as preconditions of their eventual
disappearance, is also inherent in the Western bourgeois tradition—as a
matter of fact, it is even "taken over" from this tradition. However, two
facts constitute the decisive difference: (1) The religion of technical-
scientific progress has never been sanctioned as the avowed goal and expression of humanist development. The schools of thought which came
closest to this philosophy (for example, that of Saint-Simon) were always
considered as suspect and "heretic". (2) By the same token, Western ethics
refused to accept the straight correspondence between (technical) progress
and ethics. Here too, the tension (and even conflict) between these two
remained itself a mainspring of morality.

[7] See Part I of this study.

ethical philosophy: once it has become an essential part of the psychical and behavioral structure of the individuals, once it has become a factor of social cohesion and integration, it assumes a momentum of its own and moves under its own weight. Only as such a factor, not as an objective of the Soviet leadership, is Soviet ethics considered in the context of this study. The claim that it is founded on objective historical necessity gives Soviet ethics an extreme rigidity but also a greatly increased scope and intensity. Precisely because it is relative to an absolute end, in this sense "outside" any specific individual action and position, Soviet ethics regards as *immoral* all actions and positions which run counter to or retard the alleged historical necessity. Many areas of human existence, which, in the Western tradition, are morally "neutral," thus become subject to moral evaluation, for example, the area of scientific and artistic pursuits. A scientific theory, though it may be scientifically corroborated, may be condemned if it is deemed to be detrimental to communist morality. The epistemological notion of truth (theoretical reason) and the moral notion of good (practical reason) tend to converge—just as, in the sphere of art and literature, aesthetic truth tends to converge with epistemological truth.[8] They converge in the medium of politics which coordinates the traditionally separated spheres of human existence as well as the values reflecting this separation. Moreover, the new historical basis of Soviet ethics also necessitates the application of moral judgments to "neutral" areas in the private sphere—again through the medium of politics. A

[8] See pp. 132 f. above.

love relationship with a "class enemy" is morally con-
demnable because it is politically "wrong"—particularly
if it is a true love relationship. For then it engages the entire existence of the individual and not only the "private"
part of his existence, and thus it affects his relationship to
others, to work, and to the state. Consequently, in so far as
ethical standards apply to it at all, the same standards as
the political ones apply—there is no dual morality. Soviet
ethics is political instrumentalism—but so that the political sphere is not one among others, but rather that it is
the sphere of human realization.

Politicalization of ethics stands at the beginning and at
the end of Western philosophy. In both, Plato and Hegel,
the autonomy of ethics succumbs to (or rather is transformed into) the autonomy of the *res publica,* the state.
And in both, not relativistic pragmatism but absolutism is
the result. If the "idea of the good" demands the Polis for
its realization or approximation, then the good is attainable
only in the *bios politicos;* and the Polis embodies the
absolute ethical standards. It embodies them—which
means that it is not the ultimate good itself. However, for
the realization of human existence, the moral good presupposes the political good; and the latter is defined in
terms of the resources, institutions, and relationships
which allow the best possible realization of man (of his
essence as a "rational being"). According to this conception, the ethical conflict is, not between the (moral) individual and the (amoral) Polis, not between two antagonistic moralities, but between moral and immoral behavior
in the Polis. Socrates represents, not the right of the indi-

vidual against that of the Polis, but the right against the
wrong Polis. It is not private freedom of thought and conscience that is at stake, but political thought and conscience, that is, the Polis, which is accepted by both Socrates and his judges. Ethical and political philosophy, ethics
and politics, have a common epistemological basis: truth
in ethics and politics derives from knowledge of the objectively true order in nature and society. Ethical truth is
thus political truth, and political truth is *absolute* truth.
Essentially the same conception survives in Marxian theory, especially in the treatment of ideology. We have noted
that Soviet statements on intellectual culture recall, even
in their formulation, Plato's *Republic* and *Laws*.[9]

In order to understand the full implications of the Soviet conception, it is advisable to identify its deep roots in
the very civilization which it challenges. The usage of the
word "totalitarianism" as a catchall for the Platonic, Hegelian, Fascist, and Marxian philosophies readily serves to
cover up the historical link between totalitarianism and its
opposite, and the historical reasons which caused classical
humanism to turn into its negation.

As long as the humanistic values, and particularly freedom, are not translated into reality, their very content remains subject to the conditions under which they can be
translated into reality. This translation is a political one
because it involves society as a whole and not only the
private individual. The realization of freedom is thus an
objective process in a twofold sense: (1) it implies the
transformation of an established society, and (2) this

[9] See p. 132 above.

transformation depends on the respective historical conditions. On both grounds, the realization of freedom presupposes thought and action (theory and practice) in accordance with the historical truth, that is, with objective reason.
Then this theory and practice, and not the preservation of
isolated individual freedom, appears as the primary ethical task and ethical value. The verification of the "right"
theory and practice, the validation of objective reason,
may be sought in idealistic ontology or in dialectical materialism—the two systems are on opposite philosophical
poles, but they both imply the *transitional absorption of
freedom into historical and political necessity,* that is, into
objective reason.

The common ground is laid in Hegel's philosophy. We
have pointed out that the Soviet Marxist notion of freedom restates Engels's paraphrase of Hegel's conception:
freedom is "recognition of necessity" and action in accordance with recognized necessity.[10] It is more than questionable whether this paraphrase gives the real meaning
of Hegel's notion; still, it is true that, in Hegel's system,
the private sphere of freedom is dissolved into the public
sphere of State and Law, and subjective rights are dissolved into objective truths. It has often been remarked
that there is no special discipline of "ethics" in the otherwise all-embracing Hegelian system. The power which
makes for this "disappearance" of independent ethical
philosophy and for the dissolution of private ethical values
is *History.*

This is the point where the politicalization of ethics,

[10] See p. 152 above.

which grew out of the Western tradition, consolidated into
a new system of thought claiming to be the heir as well as
the adversary, the fulfillment as well as the negation, of
this tradition. The progress of Western civilization itself
placed on the agenda the translation of internal values
into external conditions, of subjective ideas into objective
reality, and of ethics into politics. If Hegel interpreted
Reason in terms of history, he anticipated, in an idealistic
formulation, the Marxian transition from theory to practice. The historical process has created the preconditions,
both material and intellectual, for the realization of Reason (Hegel) in the organization of society (Marx), for
the convergence of freedom and necessity. However, freedom which converges with (or is even absorbed by) necessity is not the final form of freedom. At this ultimate point,
Hegel and Marx again agree. The realm of true freedom
is beyond the realm of necessity. Freedom as well as necessity are redefined. For Hegel, ultimate freedom resides in
the realm of the Absolute Spirit. For Marx, the realm of
necessity is to be mastered by a society whose reproduction
has been subjected to the control of the individuals, and
freedom is the free play of individual faculties outside the
realm of necessary labor. Freedom is "confined" to free
time—but free time is, quantitatively and qualitatively,
the very content of life. Moreover, according to Marx, the
historical process, governed by objective laws, generates
socialism as the rational organization of the conditions
for freedom through the political activity of the proletariat. Historical necessity thus turns ethics into politics,
and insight into historical necessity anchors politics on

"scientific" grounds and gives politics an objective character. On such ground, Soviet ethical philosophy presents
itself as the very opposite of "bourgeois" opportunism,
pragmatism, and irrationalism—as the protagonist of Reason against the destroyers of Reason. The attack on bourgeois ethical philosophy is waged on behalf of the "betrayed" rationalistic tradition.

The struggle against bourgeois ethics becomes the more
vital for Soviet social philosophy the more the two seem
to have certain features in common. The progressive, critical trends in bourgeois philosophy become the chief target
of the attack, and the chief indictment leveled against them
is that of the defamation of Reason. Nietzsche and Freud,
Schopenhauer and Dewey, pragmatism, existentialism, and
logical positivism are branded as irrationalistic, antiintel-
lectualistic—and by this token "reactionary," "immoral,"
and "imperialistic." According to Soviet interpretation,
they are necessarily so—in their objective historical function—no matter what the personal intentions and convic-
tions of the respective philosophers may have been. For
any compromise with the historically surpassed values
of bourgeois society, any attempt to deny the objective
validity of the historically defined direction of progress
and of man's capacity to grasp it, appears to this conception as justification of an obsolescent social system.

It is not necessary here to follow the course of this criticism: we shall merely attempt to show the method which
it applies. (It is largely the same that prevails in the Marxist critique of capitalism and that gives this critique its
rational appeal). One of the main elements of this method

is to assume the validity of the adversary's ideas and objectives, to accept them, as it were, and then to show that
they are unrealizable within the theoretical and societal
framework in which the adversary operates. Consequently,
they are being betrayed, vitiated, or made illusory by
bourgeois philosophy and its society. In the case of ethical
philosophy, the two chief targets of Soviet criticism are:
(*a*) the effort of contemporary Western ethics to come to
grips with the concrete existential situation of the individual and to derive from this situation the conceptual and
practical tools for progress in freedom and reason; and
(*b*) the attempt to give ethics a scientific (logical or ex-
perimental) basis. These objectives, according to the Soviet critique, not only cannot be attained by bourgeois
ethical theorists, but, in the effort to attain them they are
being turned into their opposite. In so far as progressive
bourgeois ethics works with the institutions and ideologies
of capitalist society, it sustains the very forces which prevent progress. Thus denying the higher historical stage of
reason and freedom which implies the elimination of capitalism, this philosophy is irrational and abstract where it
claims to be rational and concrete: it retains an obsolete
definition of reason, and it disregards (abstracts from)
the concrete historical conditions of freedom. By virtue
of this position, progressive bourgeois ethics is regressive
even where it is critical of the established society. Moreover, Soviet theory rejects Western philosophy the more
violently the more the latter is critical, because, in the
Soviet view, the bourgeois critique of present-day society,
while pointing up its repressive features, at the same time

diverts the struggle against the causes of repression. The scientific devices and paraphernalia of this philosophy are alleged to be spurious and to fulfill the function of obscuring and withdrawing attention from the real issues, that is, the stagnation and the destructiveness of the capitalist system. We shall illustrate this interpretation by the Soviet treatment of Dewey's pragmatism.

There seems to be a close affinity between Marx's and Dewey's reorientation of theory on practice. However, the Soviet critique emphasizes that Marxism and pragmatism are not only essentially different but opposed to each other. As formulated by Shariia, according to the Marxist thesis, "not that which is useful is true, but that which is true is useful." [11] The formulation refers to Lenin's *Materialism and Empiriocriticism*. There, Lenin had stated that to the Marxist, practice is the criterion of truth only in so far as it is itself derived from true knowledge and cognition,[12] and in so far as it is the practice of that social group which is alone capable of recognizing and fulfilling the truth, namely, the class-conscious proletariat. The Marxian unity of theory and practice presupposes the existence of an objective, even "absolute" truth, to be demonstrated by dialectical materialism (for example, the truth about the potentialities and prospects of a society, and thus the truth about the potentialities and prospects of freedom and "growth"). The content of this truth is historical, and so is its accessibility and its realization, but these relative ele-

[11] P. Shariia, *O nekotorykh voprosakh kommunisticheskoi morali* (On Several Problems of Communist Morality) (Moscow, Gospolitizdat, 1951), p. 220.

[12] *Sochineniia* (Works), XIII, 112–17.

ments are the characteristics of the objective reality and of the objective truth about this reality. According to Lenin, dialectics "includes" relativism, but does not "reduce itself" to relativism; relative are only the historical conditions for the "approach" to and for the realization of the objective truth.[13] Applied to morality, this position permits not only the rejection of certain supposedly unconditional moral principles as ideological distortions of the objective truth, but also the acceptance of certain "elementary principles" of human morality *independent of class content.*[14] Since the rejection of the moral libertinism of the early twenties, Soviet ethical philosophy places increasing emphasis on the fact that the Marxian thesis, according to which the societal existence of man determines his consciousness, does not vitiate the validity of general ethical norms. For no matter how different the historical modes of societal existence are, certain basic relationships and behavior patterns are common to all forms of civilized society, and they are expressed in certain general "rules of ethical conduct" which are valid for all men, regardless of class. The Soviet Marxist insistence on the general validity of ethical principles closely parallels the Soviet Marxist position on language and logic; it was this same argument that was applied in the defense of formal logic against the attempts to dissolve the latter into dialectical logic,[15] and also against the class doctrine of language.

These ideological trends express the development by

[13] *Ibid.*, XIII, 107–12.

[14] Shariia, *O nekotorykh voprosakh kommunisticheskoi morali,* chap. VIII. See also pp. 63 f.

[15] In the logic discussion of 1950–51; see Part I of this study, pp. 148 f. above.

virtue of which the Soviet state loses its unique revolutionary position and partakes of the organizational and behavioral pattern characteristic of contemporary industrial civilization. At this stage, long-range rationalization, efficiency, and calculability become primary economic and political requirements. The stress on objective truths in ethics belongs to the recent efforts to bring the ideology in line with the new stage of Soviet society. But the latter also requires insistence on the claim that the Soviet society alone is on the right historical road toward the realization of these truths. The objective principles of Soviet ethics are thus of a twofold character: they claim (1) to refer to the moral principles valid for any form of civilized society, and (2) to pertain to the socialist society which alone can realize genuine freedom and justice. From the first position Soviet moral philosophy assails all bourgeois ethics labeled prefascist or fascist which deny universal moral principles in favor of such amoral forces as Life, Will to Power, Eros, and so forth. The second position is the center of the attack against Dewey.

The assault against "bourgeois irrationalism" is particularly illuminating because it reveals the traits common to the Soviet and Western rationality, namely, the prevalence of technological elements over humanistic ones. Schopenhauer and Nietzsche, the various schools of "vitalism" (*Lebensphilosophie*), existentialism, and depth psychology differ and even conflict in most essential aspects; however, they are akin in that they explode the technological rationality of modern civilization. They do so by pointing up the psychical and biological forces beneath this rationality and the unredeemable sacrifices which it exacts from man. The result is a transvaluation of values which shatters the ideology of progress—not by romanticist and sentimental regression, but by breaking into tabooed dimensions of bouregois society itself. This transvaluation acts upon precisely those values which Soviet society must protect at all cost: the ethical value of competitive performance, socially necessary labor, self-perpetuating work discipline, postponed and repressed happiness. Thus, Soviet Marxism, in its fight against "bourgeois values," cannot recognize and accept the most destructive critique of these values in the "bourgeois camp" itself; instead, it has to deny these critics by isolating and ridiculing the (obviously) regressive aspects of their philosophy.

The attack against Dewey takes a different direction. Since his pragmatism does not recognize any objective evaluation which condemns bourgeois society as historically obsolescent, his effort to overcome the ideological limits of bourgeois ethics must necessarily end in conformistic relativism. Dewey opposes to the unscientific absolutism of the ethical idealists the infinite plurality of existential situations, experiences, and aspirations, each with its own potentialities of "growth" and therefore with its own values. However, such a plurality, according to Soviet criticism, is not per se a ground for positive ethical evaluation. It can provide such a ground only where the society which integrates the plurality of situations and goals affords the real possibility of free "growth." Now Marxism maintains that precisely such a possibility cannot exist in the "declining" bourgeois society—except in

marginal cases and at the expense of others. The refusal
to transcend beyond this society into its "objective" historical future therefore vitiates Dewey's efforts to overcome a conformistic ethical relativism. To be sure, Dewey's
pragmatism does not exclude social change and reform:
they are to be promoted by education for true and full
knowledge, and this knowledge in turn is to guide gradual
reform. However, this program is self-contradictory, according to the Soviet critics; society cannot grant the educational facilities and rights to a knowledge which would
make for the destruction of this society. This situation
compels Dewey's philosophy to accept implicitly (and perhaps even against the intentions of Dewey himself) the
standards and goals prevalent in the established society.
Moreover, it also condemns Dewey's attempt to found ethics on a scientific basis. The frame of reference within
which Dewey's propositions are to be verified is the institutional and ideological system of bourgeois society, which is
itself in need of "verification." Short of such transcending
verification (which would show that the framework is
faulty), Dewey's "science of conduct" amounts simply to a
description (and even justification) of socially prevalent
conduct. The refusal to extend the scientific method into the
historical future, which is accessible to science through the
analysis of the fundamental trends in the present society,
confines pragmatism to a mere description of what is.[16]

[16] Shariia, *O nekotorykh voprosakh kommunisticheskoi morali* (On Several
Problems of Communist Morality), pp. 24, 85 f., 223.

11. *The Principles of Communist Morality*

ACCORDING TO the Soviet interpretation of its ethical position, we should expect two levels of moral philosophy: one defining the "elementary principles of human morality independent of class content," and another showing the expression of these principles, and their specific realization in "communist morality." However, we are confronted with the problem that there seems to be no systematic exposition of the former which could adequately provide representative material for analysis. The lack of any systematic derivation of the "elementary principles of human morality" is, of course, inherent in the politicalization of ethics: the more the moral values become political values and the more moral behavior becomes right political behavior, the less room there is for *independent* ethical principles, or rather for the derivation of their objective validity. Still, Soviet ethics claims objective validity in so far as the specific goals of Soviet society are to coincide with the universal interest of mankind, namely, the interest in the realization of freedom for all. But this is also the claim of "bourgeois ethics." *Formally*, the "elementary principles of human morality" assumed by Soviet moral philosophy will thus coincide with those assumed by its antagonist.

By the same token, the universally valid principles tend to merge with the specific principles of communist morality. Within the context of Soviet ethics, the former receive their real significance from the latter, which in turn are defined in accord with the development of Soviet society. Therefore, presently, we shall discuss these principles in terms of their social and political function. And from the first step on, we are confronted with the fact that, to a striking degree, the specific principles of communist morality as well as the universal "principles of human morality" resemble those of bourgeois ethics. Just as the Soviet constitution, in the proclamation of the "Fundamental Rights and Duties of Citizens" seems to copy the "bourgeois-democratic" ideology and practice, so do the Soviet statements of ethical principles. It is needless to emphasize the difference between ideology and reality—the fact of imitation or assimilation remains. The world-historical coexistence of the two competing systems, which defines their political dynamic, also defines the social *function* of their ethics.

In going through the enumerations of the highest moral values given in Soviet ethical philosophy, it is difficult to find a single moral idea or syndrome of moral ideas that is not common to Western ethics. Care, responsibility, love, patriotism, diligence, honesty, industriousness, the injunctions against transgressing the happiness of one's fellow men, consideration for the common interest—there is nothing in this catalogue of values that could not be included in the ethics of the Western tradition. The similarity continues to prevail if we look at the specific principles of communist morality.[1] The hierarchy of values stated by Lenin in 1920 is almost literally repeated; the moral norms added to it are hardly more than a reformulation with respect to the situation of a fully and firmly established Soviet state. Soviet patriotism; national pride in the Soviet state; international, national, and individual solidarity; respect for socialist property; love for socialist labor; love, loyalty, and responsibility for the socialist family and for the Party —in order to be able to evaluate the actual function of these commonplace notions, we have to place them in the concrete context in which they are illustrated in Soviet ethics. This context is provided by the discussion of work relations, marriage and family matters, leisure activities, and education, and by their presentation in literature and in the entertainment industry. The moral values converge on the subordination of pleasure to duty—the duty to put everything one has into service for the State, the Party, and society. Translated into private morality, this means strict monogamic relations, directed toward the production and raising of children; discipline and competitive performance in the established division of functions; and leisure activities as relaxation from work and re-creation of energy for work rather than as an end in itself. It is in every respect a *competitive work morality*, proclaimed with a rigidity surpassing that of bourgeois morality—softened or hardened according to the specific interests of the Soviet state (for example, softened as in the treatment of illegitimate children, or if rigidity comes into conflict with the

[1] See also N. I. Boldyrev, *V. I. Lenin i I. V. Stalin o vospitanii kommunisticheskoi morali* (V. I. Lenin and J. V. Stalin on the Training of a Communist Morality) (Moscow, Pravda, 1951).

requirements of political loyalty, work efficiency, party discipline, and so forth; hardened as in the punishment for theft or "sabotage" of state property).

One of the most representative exhortations designed to "strengthen Communist morale" [2] is entirely centered on work morale. The "highest principles" governing this morale are said to be Soviet patriotism and love for the motherland, which are joined with "proletarian internationalism." They serve as justification for the complete endorsement of work as the very content of the individual's whole life. Not only is work itself honor and glory, and "socialist competition" an unconditional duty, *all* work, under socialism, has a creative character, and any degradation of manual labor impairs Communist education. In Soviet society, "love for one's work" is per se one of the highest principles of Communist morality, and work per se is declared to be one of the most important factors in the building of moral qualities. In view of the moral value of work in a socialist society, the differences between intellectual and manual labor, between elevated and lowly work, become irrelevant.

This moral equalization of the various modes and spheres of work is of the greatest significance for defining the actual function of Soviet ethics. Marxian theory made an essential distinction between work as the realization of human potentialities and work as "alienated labor"; the entire sphere of material production, of mechanized and standardized performances, is considered as one of alienation. By virtue of this distinction, the realization of free-

---

[2] "Neustanno vospityvat' sovetskikh liudei v dukhe kommunisticheskoi morali" (Unceasingly Educate Soviet People in the Spirit of Communist Morality), *Kommunist* (Communist), 1954, No. 13 (September), pp. 3–12.

dom is attributed to a social organization of labor fundamentally different from the prevailing one, to a society where work as the free play of human faculties has become a "necessity," a "vital need" for society, while work for procuring the necessities of life no longer constitutes the working day and the occupation of the individual. It is in the last analysis the abolition of alienation which, for Marx, defines and justifies socialism as the "higher stage" of civilization. And socialism in turn defines a new human existence: its content and value are to be determined by free time rather than labor time, that is to say, man comes into his own only outside and "beyond" the entire realm of material production for the mere necessities of life. Socialization of production is to reduce the time and energy spent in this realm to a minimum, and to maximize time and energy for the development and satisfaction of individual needs in the realm of freedom.

In contrast with this conception, Soviet work morale does not recognize any difference in the value of alienated and nonalienated labor: the individual is supposed to invest all his energy and all his aspirations in whatever function he finds himself or is put by the authorities. It is this obliteration of the decisive difference between alienated and nonalienated labor which enables Soviet Marxism to proclaim for the Soviet system the full development of the all-round individual as against the mutilated individual of Western society.[3] But application of Marx's and Engels's notion of a communist society to the Soviet-socialist con-

[3] Igor' Semenovich Kon, *Razvitie lichnosti pri sotsializme* (The Development of Personality under Socialism) (Leningrad, Vsesoiuznoe obshchestve po rasprostraneniiu politicheskikh i nauchnykh znanii, 1954), pp. 3 ff.

struction of communism only points up the contrast between the Marxian and the Soviet notion: in the latter, the
full development of the individual is that of the all-round
laborer, investing his individuality in his labor. It is
claimed that the "very character of labor under socialism
has changed"; consequently, "every person" is "required
to work according to his capabilities for the good of the
people and for himself." There is nothing socialist or communist in this formula—as long as the work according to
his capabilities is still work within "the realm of necessity," that is, as long as it is not yet the free play of human
faculties.

The considerable relaxation which has recently been proclaimed and implemented has not eliminated the merging
of technical and moral standards, of labor productivity and
ethics, efficiency and happiness. Under the old slogan of the
fight against the remnants of capitalist influence in the
mentality of the people, a systematic struggle is still being
fought against all libertarian tendencies which might endanger the objectives of the regime.

Soviet Marxism links the survival of capitalist elements
to the continuation of the "capitalist environment." The
Western powers are accused of trying to reactivate those
remnants of the past which still have a foothold inside the
Soviet state. But the struggle against capitalist ideologies
and attitudes has significance primarily for domestic policy: it is to counteract the danger of relaxation involved
in growing productivity. Moreover, and perhaps even more
important, it is to improve and augment a well-trained,
skilled, and disciplined labor force. The fight against the

heritage of the past thus greatly resembles early capitalism's own fight against precapitalist values and attitudes.[4]

The ideological reeducation is still centered on the "socialist" attitude toward work, instead of the negative attitude said to be characteristic of and appropriate to the worker in an exploitative society. The demand for positive identification of the worker with his work, the pressure for relentless "socialist emulation," continues in all fields. According to Soviet statements, the pressure seems to be successful:

In the development of the new attitude toward work, socialist competition played a major role. From the first "Communist Saturdays" (unpaid work) born in the years of civil war, to the storm brigades of the period of the country's large-scale industrialization, to the mass movements of pioneers in industrial innovation— such are the main stages in the development of socialist competition. If participants in Communist Saturdays were only advanced groups of workers, socialist competition and the storm-brigade movement in the late 1920s and early 1930s already encompassed the greater part of the workers who participate in socialist competition, and the number of innovation pioneers among them increases incessantly.[5]

[4] M. M. Rozental, *Marksistskii dialekticheskii metod* (Marxist Dialectical Method) (Moscow, Gospolitizdat, 1951), p. 303.

[5] G. Glezerman, "Tvorcheskaia rol' narodnykh mass v razvitii sotsialisticheskogo obshchestva" (The Creative Role of the National Masses in the Development of Socialist Society), *Kommunist* (Communist), 1955, No. 3 (February), p. 48. In an article on "Recent Trends in Soviet Labor Policy" (*Monthly Labor Review*, July, 1956) Jerzy G. Glicksman draws attention to the fact that "Stakhanovism underwent modifications." As a result of the rapid technological progress after the Second World War, emphasis shifted from "physical effort, individual pacemaking, and record breaking to the search for new working processes leading to technical progress and that mastering and widespread application of these processes" (p. 6). However important this modification may be, it does not change the function of Stakhanovism as streamlining of alienated labor.

Stakhanovism is presented as creating the preconditions for the "all-round development of the personality." [6] Just as the withering away of the state is to be preceded by the strengthening of the state, so the abolition of toil is to be preceded by the intensification of toil.

By definition, there is no alienated labor in Soviet society because production is nationalized. But nationalization does not preclude alienation. The latter prevails as long as (socially necessary) labor time is the measure of social wealth.

For true wealth is the developed productivity of all individuals. Then, no longer labor time but free time (disposable time) is the measure of wealth. Using labor time as the measure of wealth places wealth itself on the foundation of poverty . . . and makes the entire time of the individual into labor time, thereby degrading him to a mere laborer, subsuming him under his labor. The most highly developed machinery therefore forces the laborer now to work longer than the savage did, or longer than he himself did with the most primitive, the simplest tools. [7]

The denial of alienation in Soviet ethics may at first appear as a mere subtlety of abstract theoretizing; however, upon closer analysis, it reveals the concrete substance of Soviet ethical philosophy. In canceling the notion of alienation as applicable to Soviet society, Soviet ethics removes the moral ground from under the protest against a

[6] Ts. A. Stepanian, "Usloviia i puti perekhoda ot sotsializma k kommunizmu" (The Conditions and the Paths of the Transition from Socialism to Communism), in *O sovetskom sotsialisticheskom obshchestve* (On Soviet Socialist Society), ed. by F. Konstantinov (Moscow, Gospolitizdat, 1948), p. 502.

[7] Marx, *Grundrisse der Kritik der Politischen Oekonomie* (Berlin, Dietz, 1953), p. 596.

repressive social organization of labor and adjusts the moral structure and the character of the individual to this organization. Laboring in the service of the Soviet state is per se ethical—the true vocation of Soviet man. The individual needs and aspirations are disciplined; renumeration and toil is the road to salvation. The theory and practice which were to lead to a new life in freedom are turned into instruments of training men for a more productive, more intense, and more rational mode of labor. What the Calvinist work morale achieved though strengthening irrational anxiety about forever-hidden divine decisions, is here accomplished through more rational means: a more satisfying human existence is to be the reward for the growing productivity of labor. And in both cases, far more telling economic and physical force guarantee their effectiveness. The resemblance is more than incidental: the two ethics meet on the common ground of historical "contemporaneousness"—they reflect the need for the incorporation of large masses of "backward" people into a new social system, the need for the creation of a well-trained, disciplined labor force, capable of vesting the perpetual routine of the working day with ethical sanction, producing ever more rationally ever increasing amounts of goods, while the rational use of these goods for the individual needs is ever more delayed by the "circumstances." In this sense, Soviet ethics testifies to the *similarity* between Soviet society and capitalist society. The basis for the similarity was established in the Stalinist period.

In the development of Soviet society, the Stalinist period

is that of industrialization, or rather "industrial civilization" in the sense outlined by Lenin in his last writings,[8]
with the far-reaching principal objective of "catching up"
with and surpassing the level of productivity prevailing in
the advanced Western countries. Given the starting point for
industrialization in the backward state of Bolshevik Russia,
this period would correspond to the early stages of capitalist industrialization, after the "primary accumulation" had
been completed.

However, the advantageous position of the "late-comer,"
nationalization of the means of production, central planning, and totalitarian control makes it possible for the Soviet state to telescope several stages of industrialization, to
utilize the most rationalized technology and machinery,
advanced science, and the most intensive working methods
without being seriously hampered by conflicting private interests. Soviet ethical philosophy formulates the basic values of primary industrialization, but it also expresses,
simultaneously, the different (and even conflicting) requirements of the later stages. Soviet ethics must combine the
need for "primary" disciplining of the laboring classes
with the need for individual initiative and responsibility—
the standardized compliance of the human tool with the
intelligent imagination of the engineer. It must foster a
morale conducive to a long working day as well as to a
high productivity of labor, to quantitative as well as qualitative performance. The conditions of backwardness which
defined Soviet industrialization have met with those of advanced technology (eighteenth-century with twentieth-

[8] See pp. 48 f. in Part I of this study.

century industrialism)—in the political institutions as well
as in the ethics of Soviet society. Administrative absolutism
faces the effective constitutionalism of the democratic
West, a privileged authoritatian bureaucracy must be re-
fined and renewed and kept open to ascent from below. This
is required not only by the need to increase the scope and
efficiency of the productive apparatus, but also by the obvious competition with the capabilities and realities of the
Western world. Increasing cultural and material compen-
sations for the underlying population are indispensable—
not only for political reasons, but also on economic
grounds; they belong to the "development of the productive
forces" which constitutes the backbone of long-range Soviet
policy.[9]

Soviet ethics tries to integrate this diversity of economic
and political needs and to translate it into a coherent system of moral values. Thus one finds side by side the exhortation to individual initiative and spontaneity and to
authoritarian discipline, to Stakhanovist competition and
to socialist equality; the glorification of work and the glorification of leisure, of toil and of freedom, of totalitarian
and of democratic values. Soviet social philosophy reflects
throughout the objective historical contradiction inherent
in Soviet society—a contradiction generated by the fact
that the principles of socialist economy were made into an
instrument of domination, to be applied to a backward
country confronted with a far more advanced capitalist
world. The need for "catching up" with capitalism called
for enforced and accelerated industrialization as the only

[9] See pp. 114, 187 f. above.

available road to socialism. While the humanist values attached to the *end* of the road became ritualized into ideology, the values attached to the *means,* i.e., the values of total industrialization, became the really governing values. (In Part I of this study,[10] we have speculated on the possibility that in some not too unforeseeable future the present communist parties outside the Soviet orbit—and perhaps even within it—may become heirs to the traditional Social Democratic parties. Here we seem to hit upon a striking parallel in the ideological field. The end recedes, the means becomes everything; and the sum total of means is "the movement" itself. It absorbs and adorns itself with the values of the goal, whose realization "the movement" itself delays. Was not this the implicit and explicit philosophy of German Social Democracy since Eduard Bernstein?) Socialist morality thus succumbs to industrial morality, while the various historical stages of the latter are condensed into one comprehensive unit, combining elements from the ethics of Calvinism and Puritanism, enlightened absolutism and liberalism, nationalism, chauvinism, and internationalism, capitalist and socialist values. This is the strange syndrome presented by Soviet ethics.

Within this syndrome, the repressive elements are predominant. Many of the rules of conduct in school and home, at work and leisure, in private and in public, resemble so much their traditional Western counterparts at earlier stages that they have the sound of secular sermons documenting the "spirit of Protestant-capitalist ethics." They are not too far from Puritan exhortations to good business.

[10] See pp. 73 f.

The praise of the monogamic family and of the joy and duty of conjugal love recalls classical "petty-bourgeois ideology," while the dissolution of the sphere of privacy reflects twentieth-century reality. The struggle against prostitution, adultery, and divorce evokes the same ethical norms as in the West, while the requirements of the birth rate and the sustained investment of energy in competitive work performances are praised as manifestations of Eros. To be sure, the public exhortations to combine erotic relations with meritorious occupational performance should not be taken too seriously: there is evidence of official and semiofficial ridicule and protest, and of widespread private transgression. What is decisive is the general trend, and the extent to which the individual's own evaluation of his personal relationships agrees with the politically desired evaluation.

Relaxation recently has been widespread, but without changing the underlying morality. The trend seems to be toward normalization rather than abolition of repression. In line with tendencies prevalent in late industrial civilization, repression is to be "spontaneously" reproduced by the repressed individuals; this allows a relaxation of external, compulsory repression. The popular and official protests against the subordination of love to work morale may provide an illustration. They are rigidly antilibertarian; they emphasize that love, responsibility, family morale, and even happiness are duties to the state:

Underestimation of the theme of love has brought many of our film men to the point where they overlook a number of problems of immense, primary social importance. A lag is most possible precisely in questions of love, the family, and everyday existence, where people are not directly part of a larger group. It often happens that, at his work, a man seems to be advanced—he is both a Stakhanovite and an active person in the community—but in his family he demands a rigid domestic regime, he is egotistic and coarse or has a thoughtless, irresponsible attitude. We must always remember that, sooner or later, this will affect all his working and public life and every moral aspect of the man. The sphere of private life must not be forgotten. It is essential to mobilize all resources of the cinema, including such genres as comedy and satire, which scourge with humor and sear with fire the bourgeois survivals not only in the people's public, but in their private life.[11]

The protests thus fall in line with the requirements for Soviet discipline in the service of the Soviet state. The new principles of sexual morality, which are to reaffirm the *autonomy* of the erotic relationships as against their subordination to the work relationships and values of the "larger community," actually proclaim the need for a more harmonious accommodation of the former to the latter. Love is to become a necessity rather than the reflex of freedom in the realm of necessity. The law of value, which, according to Marx, regulates the exchange relations between commodities, is admitted to govern also the relations between the individuals. This is most brutally expressed by a woman whose talk at the Second Collective Farms Congress was quoted by Stalin: [12]

[11] M. Shmarova, "On Those Who Do Not Love to Talk About Love," in *Current Digest of the Soviet Press*, V, No. 18 (June 13, 1953), 27 (translated from *Sovetskoe Iskusstvo* [Soviet Art], May 6, 1953). See also *Current Digest of the Soviet Press*, V, No. 25 (August 1, 1953), 17 f.

[12] According to S. Wolfson, in *Changing Attitudes in Soviet Russia: The Family in the U.S.S.R.*, ed. by Rudolf Schlesinger (London, Routledge & Kegan Paul, 1949), p. 292 (quoted from Wolfson's *Socialism and the Family*).

Two years ago there was no bridegroom for me—no dowry! Now I have 500 labor days, and the result is: I cannot rid myself of would-be suitors who say they want to marry me. But now I shall look around and make my choice.

The fusion of economic and moral values is certainly not a distinguishing feature of Soviet ethics. It makes apparently little difference whether the "dowry" is counted in labor days or in stocks, securities, real estate, but, according to Western standards, such fusion is considered as amoral and is covered up by ideological commitments. In Soviet ethics, the "ideological veil" is much thinner, is almost nonexistent; love and work efficiency are made to go together quite well. The societal conditions of love are brought into the light of consciousness and of political regulation. This is shocking to Western ethics, and the loss is really great: it affects the most cherished images and ideals of Western culture. As Wolfson puts it:

In the conditions of socialism, [the theme of Romeo and Juliet] has outlived itself. Socialist society offers no scope for the tragic collisions which are produced by capitalism where social conditions prevent the union of lovers, their association in marriage and the family.[13]

The statement reveals more than what its crudity suggests. The story of Romeo and Juliet certainly depends on the "social conditions which prevent the union of the lovers"—as do the stories of Tristan and Isolde, Don Juan, Madame Bovary, Anna Karenina. But these social conditions define not only the unhappiness but also the happiness of their love because they create the dimension

[13] *Ibid.*, p. 300.

in which love has become what it is: a relation between individuals which is antagonistic to the *res publica* and which
draws all its joy and all its pain from this antagonism. If
Tristan and Isolde, Romeo and Juliet, and their like are
unimaginable as healthily married couples engaged in
productive work, it is because their (socially conditioned)
"unproductiveness" is the essential quality of what they
stand for and die for—values that can be realized only in
an existence outside and against the repressive social group
and its rules. The more this love obeys its own laws, the
more it threatens to violate the laws of the social community. Western civilization has recognized this conflict and
made it an essential element of its ethics. Law stands
against law, value against value—there is no moral decision as to which law shall prevail. Two value systems, two
ethics, exist side by side, each in its own right—and each
is to assert its own right. The dual morality pertains not
only to the erotic loyalty which Western ethics celebrates,
but also to other loyalties when group conflicts with group,
cause with cause, tradition with tradition. Antigone is right
against Creon as Creon is right against Antigone; the revolution is right against the status quo as the status quo is
right against the revolution. By sustaining each of the conflicting parties in its own right, the dual morality has justified individual and group aspirations which transgress the
restrictive social order; the end of the dual morality would
mean the end of an entire period of civilization.

With the conquest of the erotic danger zone by the state,
the public control of individual needs would be completed.
Effective barriers would have been erected in the very in-
stincts of man against his liberation. If and when the sec-

ond phase is reached with the distribution of the social product according to individual needs, these needs themselves will be such that they perpetuate "spontaneously" their political administration. As long as the *res publica* is not the *res* of the individuals who are its members and citizens, the harmonization of private sexual morality with political morality, with the *res publica* must be repressive. The best it can achieve is probably a higher degree of rationality in ethics, for example, by reduction or avoidance of conflicts, of neurosis, of private, personal unhappiness. This may be a goal worth striving for, provided happiness does not mean a state of mental and phychical impoverishment. If the harmonization succeeds within the framework of authoritarian administration, it would only add one decisive dimension—that of erotic needs—to the administered social needs. The development of harmonious love relations would become part of the "science of consumption" which looms on the horizon. A very frank statement to this effect was made by S. G. Strumilin at the conference of the Economics Institute in June, 1950:

Before speaking about distribution according to needs, the needs being referred to must be clearly defined. The needs of the members of the communist society are the needs of educated, cultured people who do not abuse their opportunities of obtaining consumers' goods. A science of consumption is already being created now. An Institute of Nutrition, which studies rational norms of nourishment, exists in the USSR. People's requirements under communism will be extremely diverse and individual, but on an average there must be a gravitation toward fixed norms which would completely satisfy the needs of socially developed people.[14]

[14] *Voprosy Ekonomiki* (Problems of Economics), 1950, No. 10, as translated in *Current Digest of the Soviet Press*, III, No. 2 (February 24, 1951), 7.

12. *Ethics and Productivity*

IT IS NOTEWORTHY that some of the most significant features of Soviet ethical philosophy long predate the Stalinist period. The repressive and rigid morality of this period is usually sharply contrasted with the licentious twenties, when sexual morality was factually and legally free to a degree unknown in previous history. The contrast is partly justified: the "heroic period" of the Russian Revolution had quite different ethical as well as political values. However, as the two periods share certain long-range objectives of socialism in one country and orbit, so they do certain political elements of morality. Kollontai, who is considered as the representative spokesman of revolutionary sexual morality, sees in childbearing and child raising a mode of "productive labor," and brands the prostitute as a "deserter from the ranks of productive labor." [1] The antagonism between private and public morality, which Kollontai regards as characteristic of bourgeois ethics, is in her ethical philosophy to be reconciled by "social feelings" which could not be generated by the individualist morale of bourgeois society. In socialist society, the "col-

[1] *Prostitutsiia i mery bor'by s nei* (Prostitution and the Measures of the Struggle Against It) (Moscow, Gosudarstvennoe Izd., 1921), pp. 22–23.

lective" has become a reality which "excludes any possibility of the existence of isolated, self-enclosed family cells." [2] But already at that time, the new morale was that of a work collective rather than of a community of free individuals. Productivity, "development of the productive forces," is then and now the ethical value which is to govern the personal as well as the societal relationships.

The ethical connotation of the term "productivity," or "productive," refers, since the formation of the "capitalist spirit," to the output of material as well as cultural goods with a market value—goods which satisfy a social need. Marx, who maintained that there was a necessary correlation between growing productivity and impoverishment under capitalism, expressed the repressive character of this notion of productivity by reserving the term "productive" only for labor creating surplus value, and designating all other modes of labor, including independent creative intellectual work, as "unproductive." The discrepancy between social and individual needs, social and individual productivity, must, according to Marxian theory, prevail as long as social production is not collectively controlled by the individuals whose labor produces the social wealth. Short of this revolution in the mode of production, the discrepancy will remain: what is good for society and for the state, is not necessarily good for the individual. And by the same token, as long as the state remains a superimposed independent power, personal relationships cannot be dissolved into a *res publica* without remodeling them according to the repressive needs of the latter. Under such

[2] *Ibid.*, p. 22.

conditions, the output of children is indeed productive in the same sense as is that of machine tools, and a loving husband and father is "good" in the same sense as is an efficient factory worker.

The subordination of individual morality to the development of the productive forces was greatly strengthened by the changes in Soviet ethics during the Stalinist period, i.e., by the restoration of a rigid, disciplinatory, authoritarian morality in the early thirties. The facts are well known and may just be recalled: tightening of the marriage and divorce laws; reemphasis on the family and its responsibility; praise of "productive" sexual relations; reintroduction of authoritarian education, and so forth. However, it is not the philosophical content of Soviet ethics that has changed, but rather its social content, namely, the level and scope of industrialization and the international framework within which industrialization takes place. With the first Five-Year Plan, the Soviet Union entered the long-range economic, political, and strategic competition with the advanced countries of the West, while the "end of capitalist stabilization" failed to produce a "rise in the revolutionary tide": isolation and conflict rather than an international spread of socialism seemed to be the prospect.[3] The reestablishment of authoritarianism in ethics was clearly part of the general tightening of controls —part of the mental and physical preparation for war, toil, and discipline.

But if the elimination of libertarian ethics belongs to the requirements of primary industrialization, why does

[3] See Part I, pp. 50 ff.

the struggle against these ethics continue *after* the creation of the industrial base, with growing productivity and social wealth? Surely the Stalinist policy of totalitarianism has paid off: the use of formerly denounced methods of "capitalist industrialization" (rigidly enforced labor discipline, long working day, "scientific management," directorial authority, piece wage and bonus system, competitive profitability) have enabled the Soviet economy to "telescope" several stages of industrial development into two decades. However, the Soviet system, like its counterpart, is self-propelling in the sense that continuous growth of labor-productivity and continuous rationalization become the inherent mechanisms which keep the system going. At the same time, the continued existence of the "capitalist environment" and the maintenance of the preparedness economy also make the centralized control of individual needs self-propelling—even though the rate of progress allows relaxation. Soviet ethics testifies to the conflict between increasing productivity and wealth on the one hand and the social need for toil and renunciation on the other. The greater the possibility of using the former for satisfying individual wants and enhancing individual liberty, the greater the need for minimizing the contradiction without weakening the driving power which propels the system. As industrialization progresses and economic competition with the West becomes more imperative, terror becomes unprofitable and unproductive. It is no durable substitute for the productive and rational coordination which a highly developed industrial society requires; these requirements must be injected into the individuals and become their own moral values. What could be left free from institutionalized control and to the pressure of external forces and circumstances during the "heroic period" of the Revolution, what was implemented by terror during the Stalinist period, must now be normalized and made a calculable resource in the moral and emotional household of the individuals. Morality, in the form of an efficient organization of values guiding individual behavior inside and outside the plant or farm or office assumes decisive significance as an integral part of progressing rationalization. Thus it is only an apparent paradox that Soviet ethical philosophy continues to taboo—although in a very different form—the libertarian ideas of the revolutionary period at a stage when their realization seems more logical than at the stage of extreme scarcity and weakness.

But with growing productivity and spreading industrialization, international competition is intensified. Within the Soviet state, shortage continues and demands intensive mobilization. While sexual morality has to be sustained and the sexual emancipation of women has to be restricted, female *labor power* must be emancipated beyond the traditional restrictions. According to Soviet ethics, one of the highest values which elevates communist morality over bourgeois morality is the abolition of patriarchal domination and the establishment of equality between the sexes. Soviet spokesmen do not conceal the economic rationale for the new ethics of equality. In a representative justification of Soviet policies in connection with the antiabortion legislation of 1936, Wolfson discussed the emancipation of women in the Soviet Union chiefly from the point of view of the emancipation of female labor productivity. "Socialist society has created conditions in which the work of rearing and educating children leaves woman a chance of combining her maternal functions and duties with active, productive and social work." [4] He pointed out that "the composition of skilled labor in the U.S.S.R. has been sharply modified towards an equalization of female with male labor," and he regards as the "most interesting point" the fact that "Soviet women have gained and continue to gain in those branches of industry which are closed to women in capitalist society." As an example he mentioned the high rate of female labor in the mining and metal industries.[5] The equality of women is not confined to the field of manual labor. "Many women occupy an honored place in the ranks of innovators of industry, transport, and agriculture, and of scientific and cultural figures"; they "participate actively in the management of the Soviet state." [6] Here, Soviet society has probably surpassed the older industrial countries—but until the growing productivity is controlled by the individuals themselves, the economic and cultural emancipation of women gives them only an equal share in the system of alienated labor.

It thus appears that the methodical increase in human productivity is mainly an increase in "abstract" labor power, whose value is measured in terms of the calculated

[4] Quoted from *Socialism and the Family*, in *Changing Attitudes in Soviet Russia: The Family in the U.S.S.R.*, ed. by Rudolf Schlesinger (London, Routledge & Kegan Paul, 1949), p. 283.

[5] *Ibid.*, p. 287.

[6] I. S. Kon, *Razvitie lichnosti pri sotsializme* (The Development of Personality under Socialism) (Leningrad, Vsesoiuznoe obshchestvo po rasprostraneniiu politicheskikh i nauchnykh znanii, 1954), p. 16.

social need. The distinctions adhering to the concrete work
of the individuals are reduced to this common denominator
(which allows for a whole system of quantifiable differences, expressed in the large wage differentials). For the
individuals, this means training for *technical* productivity:
the social need is chiefly expressed in scientifically organized and rationalized labor time. In Part I of this study,
we have stressed the policy of using whatever working time
may be saved for universal vocational education.[7] Such
education tends to develop the individual as an all-round
technical instrument (with a highly developed technical
intelligence). To be sure, vocational training is to be supplemented by an ever better education for "higher culture"
—the technical and political individual is to be the cultured
individual. But the same historical trend which establishes
the predominance of technological rationality within a repressive political system also vitiates the efforts to rescue
the ethics of higher culture. The latter was the product of a
civilization in which the ruling groups were genuine leisure
classes; their "unproductive" existence (in terms of socially necessary labor) provided the cultural climate. In
other words, "higher culture" depended on the institutionalized and ethically sanctioned separation of intellectual
from manual labor. The values of the "personality" were
not supposed to be and could not be practiced "on the side":
they were meant to shape the entire individual existence. In
contrast, industrial civilization has progressively reduced
the distinction between manual and intellectual labor by
subjecting the latter to the values of commodity exchange,

[7] See especially pp. 181 ff. above.

and has progressively denied the ethical value of an "unproductive" leisure class. Deprived of its social basis for resistance, culture has become a cog in the machine—part of the administered private and public existence.

The ethics of productivity expresses the fusion of technological and political rationality which is characteristic of Soviet society at its present stage. At this stage, the fusion is clearly repressive of its own potentialities with respect to individual liberty and happiness. Freed from politics which must prevent the collective individual control of technics and its use for individual gratification, technological rationality may be a powerful vehicle of liberation. But then, the question arises whether the ethics of productivity does not contain tendencies pushing beyond the restrictive political framework. The question clearly parallels the one asked in Part I of this study: there,[8] we suggested that, under the condition of international "normalization," the development of the productive forces in the Soviet system may tend to "overflow" its repressive regimentation and vitiate possible political countermeasures designed to perpetuate regimentation. Now the question arises whether there is any corresponding trend in the development of individual productivity. The latter is, of course, part of the former, but as such it is a subjective factor whose laws of motion remain its own even if they are "given" from outside (by the state or by the society). Does the development of individual productivity as technical productivity perhaps tend to overflow its political direction— and limitation? Any attempt even at a preliminary answer

[8] See especially pp. 185 ff.

would involve a sociological and psychological discussion far beyond the framework of this study. However, because of the importance of the question for the evaluation of prospective Soviet developments we venture to offer some suggestions.

One fact seems to be of foremost significance: in Soviet society, there seem to be no *inherent* forces which resist accelerated and extensive automation—either on the part of management or on the part of labor. The transfer of socially necessary and unpleasant work from the human organism to the machine is therefore bound to progress rather rapidly —the more so since it is one of the most effective weapons in the competitive struggle with the Western world. Naturally, the saving of human energy thus achieved is largely cancelled in its liberating effect by the repressive usage of technology: length of the working day, speed-up methods, production of waste, and so forth. It is this usage of technology which makes for its dehumanizing and destructive features: a restrictive social need determines technical progress. Any reorganization of the technical apparatus with a view to the best possible satisfaction of individual needs presupposes a "redefinition" of the social need which determines technology. In other words, the truly liberating effects of technology are not implied in technological progress per se; they presuppose social change, involving the basic economic institutions and relationships.

Would the nationalization of the economy perhaps enable Soviet society to skip, as it were, this stage of *social* change and require only *political* change, i.e., transfer of control from above to below while retaining the same social base (nationalization)?[9] The prospects for such a development are linked to the international balance of power. It is precisely the international situation (of "co-existence") which enforces accelerated and extensive automation in Soviet society. As long as this international situation prevails, technological rationality tends to militate against the restrictive political rationality and to drive the latter toward liberalization on the established base.

The technological rationality also contains an element of playfulness which is constrained and distorted by the repressive usage of technology: playing with (the possibilities of) things, with their combination, order, form, and so forth. If no longer under the pressure of necessity, this activity would have no other aim than growth in the consciousness and enjoyment of freedom. Indeed, technical productivity might then be the very opposite of specialization and pertain to the emergence of that "all-round individual" who looms so large in Marxian theory—a theory which, in its inner logic, is based on the idea of the completed rationalization of necessary labor, on the truly technical administration of things.

Needless to say, the present reality is so far removed from this possibility that the latter appears as idle speculation. However, the forces inherent in a systematically progressing industrialization are such that they deserve consideration even if the strongest political forces seem to arrest or suppress them.

[9] The distinction between social and political change is, of course, very precarious, but here it might serve to underline the difference between a devlopment involving a change in the economic structure of society (for example, from private enterprise to nationalization or socialization) and changes within an established economic structure.

13. *The Trend of Communist Morality*

WE HAVE SUGGESTED that the common requirements of industrialization make for a high degree of similarity between the featured values of "bourgeois" and Soviet ethics; such similarity appears in the work morality as well as in the sexual morality. Soviet ethical philosophy itself takes cognizance of this relation between the two antagonistic systems by claiming that the ethical values which were vitiated by bourgeois society are being realized in Soviet society—that what had to remain an ideology in the former could become a reality in the latter. The claim of Soviet ethics that, in the Soviet Union, ethical principles govern reality rather than ideology may be just as easily disputed as similar claims in the West. But in spite of all similarity, the question would still be open whether, from the social function of Soviet ethics, a different prospect of development may be inferred. The technical-economic base of Soviet ethics per se does not "prescribe" any such prospects: it makes for the affinity as well as for the fundamental difference between the systems. The common requirements of industrialization may define the affinity; the essentially different mode of industrialization may generate the essential difference behind the apparently identical values.

When we now try to identify the prospective direction
of Soviet ethics, we take again the illuminating statement
on Romeo and Juliet as a starting point. The statement
proclaims the passing of the bourgeois individual by his
fulfillment in the *res publica* and thereby the passing of
the autonomous "subject" which, as *ego cogitans* and
agens, was to be the beginning and the end of Western
culture. In the telescoped Soviet scheme, the dissolution
of the autonomous "bourgeois" individual would correspond to the latest stage of the prevalent industrial civilization, where mass production and mass manipulation
lead to the shrinking of the ego and to the administrative
regulation of his material and intellectual needs. The coordination between private and public existence, which,
at the postliberal stage of Western society, takes place
largely unconsciously and behind the backs of the individuals, occurs, in the Soviet Union, in the light of a well-
trained consciousness and as a publicized program. It is
part of the total mobilization of the individuals for the
requirements of competitive total industrialization. Here,
and only here, are the remnants and relics of preindustrial
culture conquered: the romantic elements of the individual, especially in erotic relations, which were almost identical with "unproductive," socially unuseful relations, are
made congruous with and conducive to political, socially
useful work relations. If this indoctrination is effective, it
would mean, to the individual, the loss of the entire sphere
in which his existence was still free from the needs of the
res publica; to the state, it would mean control over one
of the danger zones in which explosive demands and as-

pirations could be kept alive. With the passing of the individual, the ethical values lose their autonomous character, and this loss is not compensated by transcendental
sanctions and promises. Ethics as a philosophical and
existential discipline in its own right disappears.

But the validity of ethics does not necessarily depend
on autonomy or on transcendental sanction. If it did, civilized society would long since have exploded, for the autonomous personality and the efficacy of transcendence
have become increasingly corroded by the growth of technological controls. Sanction may indeed come from the
res publica instead of being vested in a transcendental
agency or in the moral autonomy of the individual conscience. However, such sanction would be ethically binding for the individual (i.e., would be more than external
or internalized compulsion) only if the *res publica*, in its
institutions, were to protect and promote a truly human existence for all individuals. Ethics may indeed be political in
substance. Nor is it obvious that an effective system of
overtly political ethics must necessarily result in a totalitarian state of robots. The pattern of behavior which Soviet
ethics envisages would presuppose that human existence as
well as society is rebuilt: the "bourgeois individual," whose
substance is to a great extent apart from the *res publica*
and whose needs are apart from the social need, would
give way to an individual who is an integral part of the
res publica because *his* needs are at the same time social
needs. Theoretically and historically, such a development
is not impossible: political philosophy has described it as
"community" (*Gemeinschaft*) against "society" (*Gesell-*

schaft), as the ideal "Polis," or, in Hegelian terms, as the harmony of the universal and the particular; its interpretation in Soviet ethics makes use of the Marxian idea of classless society as the association of "all-round individuals." In all these theories, the realization of such a harmony between the ethical and the political values presupposes a free and rational organization of social labor, that is, the disappearance of the state as an independent power over and above and against the individuals; whereas Soviet ethics fuses ethical and political values in and for a state which wields independent power over the individuals. As long as this situation prevails, the new ethics will continue to function as a subservient instrument for the primary social objective of the state, that is, in the present period, the objective of total industrialization.

However, even at this stage, where Soviet ethics merely seems to recapture and "catch up" with the initial function of "bourgeois ethics," the different social basis of the former does not preclude a different trend of development. Once firmly established, the basic societal institutions enforce and perpetuate the morality which their effective functioning demands. In the Soviet case, this process is not left to the slow but almost automatic impact of the institutions on individual behavior and values—rather, it is systematically directed by the political agencies. But this does not arrest the dynamic according to which the people thus conditioned must in turn influence the development of the conditioning system. No matter how thoroughly they are controlled and how deeply they are conditioned, they perform the necessary labor which reproduces the controlled society. Thus, no matter how "abstract" and "general" this labor may be, they remain the ultimate "productive force." We have suggested that the reemphasis on the "bourgeois values" in the construction of socialism recaptures that stage of ethics where the state relies on the "introjection" of the socially required values rather than on their extraneous imposition, on "spontaneous" reproduction of ethical behavior rather than on terroristic enforcement. But here the "human material" with which Soviet ethics works militates against a mere repetition of the process of "bourgeois ethics."

In the Western tradition, the introjection of ethical values took place in and with the "individual": his emancipation from older traditional economic, political, and ideological bonds was the precondition for the efficacy of the process. Man's *separation* from the state, from the community, from custom and tradition, his *antagonistic* relation to them as well as to the new powers and institutions was to be prerequisite to his moral autonomy, to the spontaneous, internal elaboration and reproduction of ethical values. Only on such ground could introjection become genuine internalization, that is, demands of the individual's own conscience and faith. Their validity is thereby greatly strengthened. They do not appear as imposed upon the individual from outside but rather as flowing from the individual's own ideal nature, sanctioned not by force but by universally valid ethical laws, and obedience to them tends to become instinctual and almost automatic. Duty, work, and discipline then serve as ends in themselves, no longer dependent on rational justification in terms of their actual necessity. Renunciation becomes an integral part of the individual's mental household (part of his constitution, as it were), transmitted from generation to generation through education and the social climate; it does not have to be enforced continually by specific political and economic measures. However, in Soviet society, this process from the beginning is counteracted by the politicalization of ethics, by the absorption of the individual into the *res publica*. The externalization of ethical values allows only for a very low degree of internalization. With the dissolution of the traditional substance of the individual, the basis of internalization is undermined. All ethical values are systematically referred to the requirements of Soviet society: the specific situation of this society, and the objectives and needs of the Soviet state are to validate moral norms. This reference, and this mode of validation is made explicit and perpetually brought to consciousness.

We have tried to show that the political externalization of ethics is ultimately guided by an absolute, i.e., communism, and thus distinguished from pragmatistic relativism. But the absolute standard pertains ultimately to the goal toward which society is to move—not to the moral (and technical) instrumentalities for attaining the goal. No matter how close the latter are identified with the former, the moral norms are not ends in themselves; they aim at the future, and they obtain their sanction only from the societal norms formulated for the future by the state and its organs. Thus, toil as such is not a value, but only toil *for socialism and communism;* not all competitive behavior but only *socialist* competition; not property but only *socialist* property; not patriotism but only *Soviet* patriotism, and so forth. To the individual, this makes no difference as long as he has no choice and as long as the state defines what socialism and communism are and enforces the definition. However, the weakness of internalization impairs the social cohesion and the depth of morality.

Soviet ethics is rationalistic to an extent which may endanger its stabilization at the desired level. In the first part of this study,[1] we have stressed the magical and ritual elements in Soviet Marxism. In this connection, we have suggested that even these apparently irrational elements operate in the service of the overriding rationality of the system. Its rationalism is inherent in the methodical orientation of moral norms on the "absolute" communist goal, which is in turn rationally defined in verifiable terms. Whether the working day is reduced to five hours and less or not, whether the individual's free time is really his or not, whether he must "earn his living" by procuring the necessities of life or not, whether he can freely choose his occupation or not—all these can be verified by the individuals themselves. No matter how regimented and manipulated the latter may be, they will know whether communism thus defined is a fact or not. Here lies the decisive difference between Soviet social philosophy on the one hand, and fascist and nazi on the other. The latter center around essentially a-rational, pseudonatural entities such as race, blood, charismatic leadership. No matter how rational the actual organization of the fascist and nazi state may have been (the total mobilization and the

[1] See Chap. 3, especially pp. 87 ff.

total war economy in Germany belong to the most efficient performances of modern industrial civilization), this state itself was irrational in its historical function; that is to say, it arrested the development of the material and cultural resources for human needs and organized them in the interest of destructive domination. Its inherent goal constituted the historical limit of the fascist state. In contrast, Soviet rationalism does not stop at the instrumentalities but extends to the direction and goal of social organization. Marxian doctrine provides the conceptual link. The definition of communism in terms of a production and distribution of social wealth according to freely developing individual needs, in terms of a quantitative and qualitative reduction of work for the necessities, of the free choice of functions—these notions certainly appear to be unrealistic in the light of the present state of affairs. But in themselves they are rational; moreover, technical progress and the growing productivity of labor make evolution toward this future a rational possibility.

The question whether or not the structure of the Soviet regime precludes the future realization of the possibility has been discussed in the first part of this study.[2] There we have suggested that the continued promulgation and indoctrination in Marxism may still turn out to be a dangerous weapon for the Soviet rulers. Thus far, the regime has tried to reconcile ideology and reality by justifying its basic policy in Marxian terms. The repressive morality canonized during the Stalinist period is said to express the objective requirements of the first phase, that is, the con-

[2] See Part I, Chap. 6.

struction of an adequate socialist base. The ethics of work
and leisure discipline, of competitive patriotism in love
and toil—the entire morality of political Puritanism—is
supposed to conform to the stage of socialism which was
compelled by scarcity to evaluate individual behavior according to its socially useful performance. The ethical rationale is identified with the sociological rationale.

If this identification, which is essential to the Soviet
ideology, is to be maintained, long-range changes in the
development of society must be accompanied by changes
in the ideology: the repressive morality must be reduced
with the progressive reduction of scarcity. In the first part
of this study, we have proposed that continued growth in
productivity under circumstances of long-range "peaceful
coexistence" would tend to such reduction. If the Soviet
regime cannot or does not wish to relax correspondingly
the repressive morality, it would become increasingly *irrational* according to its own standards. This irrationality
in turn would tend to weaken the moral fiber of Soviet society. The whole indoctrination was focused on the rationality of the objectives in the individual as well as general interest; faith in this rationality seems to have been
a decisive element in the popular strength of the regime.
Here the limits of internalization, which seem to be inherent in the prevailing structure of Soviet ethics, may
prove to be decisive. Its values are not autonomous since
they are in the last analysis validated by an "external"
political goal. Only thoroughly internalized ethics can in
the long run operate with *autonomous* values, and only a
high degree of ethical *autonomy* can in the long run sustain

calculable and durable ethical behavior reasonably independent of the vicissitudes of individual existence. Only
on such ground can the individual be made morally shock-
proof against socially required sacrifices, injustices, and
inequalities which appear as irrational. The political rationality of Soviet ethics militates against such moral
shockproofing of the individual and sustains the idea that
the potentialities for human development should grow in
accord with the growing social productivity of Soviet society. Ideological pressure thus seems to tend in the same
direction as technical-economic pressure, namely, toward
the relaxation of repression. To be sure, ideological pressure and even the weakening of the established morality
are not per se a serious threat to a regime which has at
its disposal all the instruments for enforcing its objectives.
However, substantially linked with the economic and political dynamic on an international scale, these forces, though
unformed and unorganized, may well determine, to a considerable extent, the course of Soviet developments.

Index